INSIGHT GUIDES

SAN FRANCISCO

smart guide

Contents

Areas

A–Z

Below: all aboard at the Cable Car turnaround.

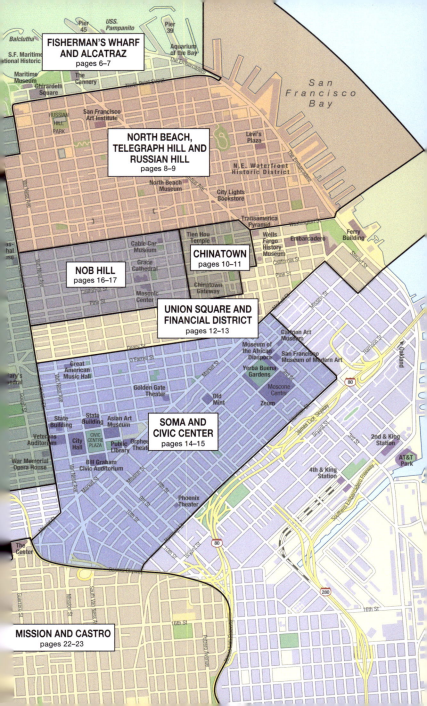

FISHERMAN'S WHARF AND ALCATRAZ
pages 6–7

Pier 45

USS. Pampanito

Pier 39

Balclutha

Aquarium of the Bay

S.F. Maritime National Historic

The Embarcadero

Maritime Museum

The Cannery

Ghirardelli Square

San Francisco Bay

RUSSIAN HILL PARK

San Francisco Art Institute

NORTH BEACH, TELEGRAPH HILL AND RUSSIAN HILL
pages 8–9

Levi's Plaza

North Beach Museum

N. E. Waterfront Historic District

City Lights Bookstore

The Embarcadero

Transamerica Pyramid

Tien Hou Temple

Washington St

Wells Fargo History Museum

Ferry Building

Cable Car Museum

CHINATOWN
pages 10–11

Embarcadero

Grace Cathedral

California St

NOB HILL
pages 16–17

California St

Pine St

Masonic Center

Pine St

Chinatown Gateway

UNION SQUARE AND FINANCIAL DISTRICT
pages 12–13

Cartoon Art Museum

Museum of the African Diaspora

San Francisco Museum of Modern Art

Great American Music Hall

O'Farrell St

Yerba Buena Gardens

Golden Gate Theater

Moscone Center

Old Mint

Zeum

State Building

State Building

Asian Art Museum

SOMA AND CIVIC CENTER
pages 14–15

Veterans Auditorium

CIVIC CENTRE PLAZA

City Hall

Orpheum Theatre

2nd & King Station

War Memorial Opera House

Public Library

AT&T Park

Bill Graham Civic Auditorium

4th & King Station

Phoenix Theater

James Lick Skyway

Southern Embarcadero Freeway

The Center

MISSION AND CASTRO
pages 22–23

16th St

16th St

Potrero Avenue

Left: the Golden Gate Bridge, wreathed in the famous fog.

The Presidio to
    the Fillmore 132
Fisherman's Wharf to the
    Financial District........134
The Richmond to
    Castro 136
The Western Addition
    to SoMa....................138

*Inside Front Cover:
    City Locator
Inside Back Cover:
    The Bay Area*

*Street Index: 140
General Index: 142–4*

Below: a sunbathing sea lion at Fisherman's Wharf.

San Francisco

Locals are proud of their City by the Bay, and who can blame them? Built on fog-capped, sloping hills and surrounded by sparkling waters, San Francisco is often called the most beautiful American city. It is also idiosyncratic: many are drawn west by the allure of the city's open-minded character, fertile ground for idealists and entrepeneurial gold-prospectors alike.

San Francisco Facts and Figures

Population of city: **845,599 (7.4 million in Bay area)**
Area: **47.3 miles**
Major ethnic groups: **White (44.7 percent); Asian (31.2 percent); Hispanic (13.5 percent); African American (7.1 percent)**
Annual visitors: **16.4 million**
Number of restaurants: **3,489**
Tallest building: **Transamerica Pyramid (853ft/250m)**
Cable car riders per year: **7.4 million**
Miles of shoreline: **29½ miles (47.5km)**
Number of hills: **43**
Steepest street: **Filbert (between Leavenworth and Hyde) and 22nd (between Church and Vicksburg), both with 31.5 percent gradient**
Official ballad: *I Left My Heart in San Francisco*

The City by the Bay

San Francisco has been enticing dreamers for the last century and a half. Gold in the 19th century and technology in the 20th made this city an economic boomtown, while conversely, its non-conformist ethos has put it at the center of important countercultural movements. This combination is tantalizing; today, space in this compact city is at a premium and the cost of property is the second highest in the US, close behind New York City.

The threat of earthquakes and the reality of frequent fog do nothing to deter the many who fall in love with San Francisco; the city offers enough diversity of culture to ensure most will find something to suit them. Foodies, politicos, film buffs, aspiring poets, jazz-fiends, and 1960s nostalgists can find plenty to get their teeth into. All this nestles in the San Francisco peninsula, alongside the natural splendors of the Pacific Ocean, and there's no denying that the city's looks are beguiling; many even argue that the fog is romantic.

The San Franciscans

Perhaps more importantly, however, the local people are welcoming, taking an immense pride in their home, and promoting a stronger sense of a community than is found in most other cities of a similar stature. The term 'multicultural' certainly applies here: San Francisco is home to truly diverse demographics, representing all ethnicities, sexual persuasions, and proclivities. The Chinatown area is famous, but San Francisco also has a vibrant Hispanic-origin population, and large communities of people of Italian, Japanese and Russian descent. The city's gay and lesbian population is 15.4 percent, the highest among the country's major cities.

Many are attracted to the city by its liberal spirit. Mutal tolerance towards all is part of the city's ethos, not to mention public policy. This is perhaps all the more impressive as San Francisco is a small city, only seven square miles of overlapping and interrelating yet highly distinctive neighborhoods. For instance, the Mission, traditionally the

Below: park festivals are still a part of the summertime in San Francisco.

nexus of the city's Chicano culture, is increasingly popular with lesbian couples and bar-prowling hipsters, while the adjoining Castro is the epicenter of the city's significant gay community.

Today, there are rich pickings for nightlife, culture, and particularly food, as San Francisco boasts a world-class restaurant scene. While the average earnings enable enough eating out to sustain the city's eating establishments, and the general standard of living is high, at the other end of the spectrum, there is a big homelessness problem. Recent initiatives are making a difference, but visitors will undoubtedly notice the many down and

outs, particularly in the Tenderloin and Civic Center neighborhoods.

Tales of the City

Throughout its dramatic history, San Francisco has often taken center stage culturally and politically: the Gold Rush, the Beatniks, the summer of love, the gay rights movement, the dot-com boom, then bust. Yet no matter what dramas befall this beautiful city, its charms just seem to grow. Some come to absorb the city's legacy, others to shop and eat, or to investigate Alcatraz; most want to ride up steep hills in an iconic cable car and admire the views. Whichever side of San Francisco intrigues, most find it's hard not to leave your heart here.

Highlights

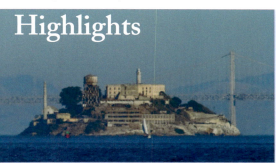

▲ **Alcatraz** 'The Rock' is the world's most legendary penitentiary, once used to incarcerate the likes of Al Capone.

▶ **Mission Dolores** San Francisco was founded on the site of this adobe chapel.

▲ **Chinatown** A fascinating city within a city, full of tiny temples, markets, and dim sum eateries.

▶ **Golden Gate Bridge** The enduring, defining symbol of San Francisco.

▶ **M.H. de Young Memorial Museum** Striking architecture and culture amid the green of Golden Gate Park.

▲ **Ferry Building Market** This mouth-watering gourmet emporium is a foodie's paradise, housed in an historic building.

Fisherman's Wharf

Fisherman's Wharf is filled with knick-knack stores, carnival-esque attractions, and scores of tourists, making it easy to forget that it represents the maritime past that is so integral to San Francisco's character. In the maritime present, it is still the place to pick up a ferry to Alcatraz or Angel Island, as well as across the bay. Back on dry land, if crowds and trinkets hold no appeal, visit the waterfront in the evening when the stores have closed and everyone has gone home. Then, accompanied only by barking sea lions and the city's lights on the bay, it is much easier to enjoy the saltiness of this once bustling harbor.

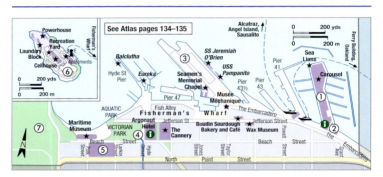

Jefferson Street and Pier 39

Jefferson Street is the main drag of Fisherman's Wharf, and home to multiple street vendors hawking boiled shellfish and clam chowder in an edible sourdough bowl, alongside several more expensive

Below: you can't miss Pier 39.

seafood restaurants. Vintage streetcars on the F-Line provide a direct route downtown.

Pier 39 ①, built from old wharves and anchoring the 45-acre Fisherman's Wharf, is at the heart of the action. The Wharf has traditionally accommodated some of the city's most famed inhabitants – sea lions camping out on pontoons in the water. Most of the creatures mysteriously disappeared in late 2009 (some think to Oregon), but they may return in the future.

To get even closer to the bay's sealife, you can descend into the nearby **Aquarium of the Bay** ② and view local sharks, other fish and crustaceans from an underwater, glass tunnel.
SEE ALSO CHILDREN, P.40

Pier 45

Today, **Pier 45** ③ and Fish Alley form the working center of Fisherman's Wharf. From here, fishermen depart in the pre-dawn hours and return mid-morning. Their catch is packed and sold in the tin-roofed sheds on Fish Alley. Often these fishermen guide or captain the many bay tours that launch from here in the afternoon. Pier 45 is also home to the submarine USS *Pampanito* and the **Liberty Ship SS *Jeremiah O'Brien***, which participated in the Normandy Invasion of D-Day.

Also on Pier 45, at the end of Taylor Street, the **Musée Méchanique** is an exercise in nostalgia, an arcade packed with vintage games, antique slot machines and dubious fortune-tellers. Nearby stands

Left: sea lions soak up sun and attention at Pier 39.

hotel, the **Cannery**, once the largest fruit and vegetable cannery in the world, is now a shopping center. **Ghirardelli Square** ⑤ sits just west and is another shopping complex. It is named for the original Ghirardelli Chocolate Factory, which opened just 13 days before the legendary gold was struck at Sutter's Mill.

Fisherman's Wharf is the place to catch a ferry across the bay to destinations including Sausalito, Oakland, and Angel Island, not to mention **Alcatraz** ⑥; ferries depart for 'The Rock' from Pier 41. This infamous, former maximum-security prison remains one of the biggest tourist draws in the city.

SEE ALSO ALCATRAZ, P.32; FOOD AND DRINK, P.55; HOTELS, P.68; MUSEUMS AND GALLERIES, P.82; SHOPPING, P.112

Aquatic Park and Fort Mason

Perched above **Aquatic Park**, one block west of the Hyde Street Pier, is the historic Aquatic Park Bathhouse, home to the **San Francisco National Maritime Museum**. Built in the 1930's with the rest of Aquatic Park, it resembles a beached ocean liner in the Art Deco style of its day. The romantic Aquatic Park promenade leads to the Municipal Pier and on to **Fort Mason** ⑦, one of the city's earliest military installations, dating back to the 1850s. Fort Mason offers stunning views of the Golden Gate Bridge, while its rugged shore below is the last original bay coastline in the city.

SEE ALSO MUSEUMS AND GALLERIES, P.82

Tucked away amid a network of piers and boats, the tiny Fishermen's and Seamen's Memorial Chapel is dedicated to those lost at sea in North California. Once a year – traditionally the first Sunday in October – there is ceremony blessing San Francisco's fishing fleet.

---

the flagship **Boudin Sourdough Bakery and Café**. You can watch bread being made in the two-story, glassed-in bakery, and buy it for a picnic or dine in the café.

SEE ALSO CHILDREN, P.40; FOOD AND DRINK, P.55

Ships, Ferries, and Cable Cars

Hyde Street Pier is the original Ferry terminal for Sausalito and Berkeley, and has an impressive array of 19th-century sailing vessels, including one of the original trans-bay ferries, the *Eureka*, and the steel-hulled

Balclutha, a Scottish square-rigged sailing ship. The pier is part of the **National Maritime Park**. Its Visitor Center is located across the street in the **Argonaut Hotel**.

Victorian Park is frequently filled with lines for the **Powell-Hyde Cable Car**, whose terminus ④ is here; be warned, the crowds mean that the wait to board a cable car from here can be a long one. On the other side of the

Below: the USS *Pampanito*.

North Beach, Telegraph Hill, and Russian Hill

Named 'Little City' by its earliest settlers, North Beach is a colorful, compact, Italian neighborhood bursting with bars, restaurants, and sidewalk cafés. Tucked into the valley between Russian Hill and Telegraph Hill, North Beach is best known for its excesses in literature, food, libations, and sex. This is where you will find the ghosts of the city's famed Beat past, as well as the best espressos in the city, as the neighborhood's Italian roots are still much in evidence.

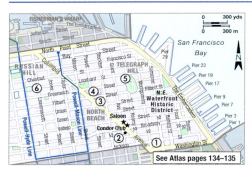

See Atlas pages 134–135

Above: the legendary bookstore, City Lights.

The Barbary Coast

Despite its name, North Beach borders no water, but when the neighborhood earned its name and reputation, the bay lay roughly at today's Bay Street.

Approaching North Beach from the Financial District, sandwiched between Jackson and Pacific streets and to the east of Montgomery Street, is **Jackson Square** ①. Built in the 1850s, its brick architecture was able to withstand the 1906 earthquake and the following fire. It is one of the best representations of mid-19th-century San Francisco. Despite its quaint, tree-lined blocks filled with chic galleries and design studios, Jackson Square was once the most notorious red-light district in the city, known as the Barbary Coast.

The intersection of Columbus Avenue, Broadway Street, and Grant Avenue gamely carries on this tradition. It is jam-packed with strip clubs, adult video parlors, and racy late-night clubs, including the Hungry I, which helped launch the careers of Woody Allen and Bill Cosby. Carol Doda made history at the **Condor Club**, performing the first topless and bottomless acts in the country (in 1964 and 1969, respectively), while descending from the ceiling atop a piano. For years, Ms. Doda's three-story visage, complete with neon red nipples, anchored the corner of Broadway and Columbus Avenue. Nearby, the gritty **Saloon**, opened in 1861, is the oldest bar in the city, and home to some of the city's best jazz and blues acts.
SEE ALSO MUSIC AND DANCE, P.93

Beats and Books

In the post-World War II period, rents were low, the jazz and coffeehouse scene was lively, and the neighborhood's character was lascivious; North Beach became the natural West Coast hub of beat poets, writers, and artists. This heritage is still visible today: **City Lights Bookstore** ②, Lawrence Ferlinghetti's National Literary Landmark, is both a bookstore and a publishing house, which first gained notoriety in 1956 when it published Alan Ginsburg's poem, *Howl* and subsequently won the obscenity case

Left: cars snake down crooked Lombard Street.

During 1906 earthquake and fire, North Beach was completely destroyed. It was quickly rebuilt with little of the architectural flourishes for which San Francisco is famous. These simple and understated Victorian and Edwardian buildings came to be fondly known as '1906 specials'.

views, and its interior is illustrated with murals, in the style of Diego Rivera.
SEE ALSO WALKS AND VIEWS, P.124

Russian Hill

To the west is the leafy and genteel Russian Hill. Named for the Russians buried here in the early days of San Francisco, it is bisected by the Powell-Hyde cable car route and lined with elegant bistros and boutiques. It is also home to heart-stopping hills, including Filbert Street, deemed the steepest in the city (along with 22nd Street between Church and Vicksburg streets), and the famous 'crookedest street in the world', **Lombard Street** ⑥, constructed with eight hairpin turns.
SEE ALSO WALKS AND VIEWS, P.127

Irish stevedores were some of the earliest inhabitants of Telegraph Hill, using the rickety network of stairs to get to and from work at the docks every day. They were replaced by Italian immigrants, and later, bohemians who liked the views and seclusion of the rustic hill.

brought against it, in a landmark ruling. Next door sits **Vesuvio Café**, a beatnik haunt that saw everyone from Bob Dylan to Dylan Thomas.

Up Columbus Avenue, in the heart of North Beach, sits **Washington Square** ③. While dogs and sunbathers dominate in the afternoon, early mornings belong entirely to Chinese tai-chi practitioners. Across the street, the 85-year-old Romanesque Church of **Sts Peter and Paul** ④, picturesque with its gleaming white twin spires, gives daily Mass in Italian, Chinese, and English. Columbus and the

narrow Grant Avenue are the two dominant commercial streets, the former filled with delis, restaurants, and cafés that spill out onto the sidewalks, while Grant retains many family-run Italian businesses and remains the center of North Beach's social world.
SEE ALSO BARS AND CAFÉS, P.35; CHURCHES, P.44; LITERATURE, P.79; PARKS AND GARDENS, P.98

Telegraph Hill

Telegraph Hill got its name in 1849 when it became the site of the first telegraph on the West Coast. Today, lush with winding staircases, gardens, and birdsong (including the famous flock of wild redheaded conures), it is one of the most exclusive districts in San Francisco.

Erected in 1933 and resembling the nozzle of a fire hose, **Coit Tower** ⑤ is a monument to the firefighters of the 1906 earthquake. It commands panoramic

Below: local character at North Beach's Caffé Trieste.

Chinatown

San Francisco's Chinatown is one of those rare tourist attractions that is also a dynamic community. With 100,000 residents tightly packed into 24 square blocks, Chinatown is as close as you can get to a city within a city, complete with its own banks, schools, law offices, video stores, and sweatshops, sadly reminiscent of those at the turn of the 20th century. Not that you see this on main thoroughfare Grant Avenue, which feels in many ways like a Disney version of 'Chinatown', but do not be fooled: behind the tourist-oriented commercialism exists a thriving, insular, and in many ways, impenetrable community.

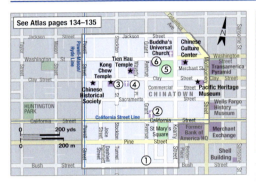

Above: checkers is a serious activity in Portsmouth Square.

'Little Canton'

Despite Chinatown's 'otherness', it has been a significant part of Chinatown's history since the earliest days of the Gold Rush. Due to political upheaval and widespread famine in Southern China in the 1850s, it is estimated that as many as 30,000 Chinese came to California to find their fortunes in the gold fields of the Sierras or to find work on the Transcontinental Railroad. As many as half decided to stay in San Francisco. These immigrants quickly set up a commercial district near the then center of town, Portsmouth Square.

By the mid-19th century, 'Little Canton,' as it was then known, was filled with hotels and boarding houses, as well

as at least six restaurants (serving Chinese and non-Chinese food), as well as 33 retail stores and 15 pharmacies. The latter's herbal remedies served a vital purpose in a quickly growing city with few doctors.

Christened 'Chinatown' in 1853 by the local press, the area was also notorious as a den of vice. Brothels, opium dens, and gambling rings were legendary, and often exaggerated to justify the anti-Chinese racism rampant in 19th-century California. This discrimination and hostility reached a boiling point in the aftermath of the 1906 earthquake and fire, which leveled the ramshackle Chinatown. Seeing the opportunity to seize the valuable downtown

real estate, as well as to eradicate what they saw as a blight on the city, San Francisco's leaders tried to relocate Chinatown to the windswept Hunter's Point in the distant southeast corner of the city. However, the residents of Chinatown refused, and due to their steadfastness and the intervention of the Dowager Empress on behalf of her distant subjects, Chinatown was rebuilt in its original spot, in the heart of the city.
SEE ALSO HISTORY AND ARCHITECTURE, P.65

Grant Avenue

The 'official' entrance of Chinatown is through the ornately decorated jade-tiled **Chinatown Gate** ① at the intersection of Bush Street and Grant

frenetic hum. Here, stores sell 'real' Chinese goodies – lychee wine, pickled ginger and herbal remedies. The **Tien Hau Temple** (125 Waverly) is believed to be the oldest Chinese temple in the country.

Portsmouth Square ⑤ is steeped in history and often considered the birthplace of San Francisco. In 1846, it was where Captain John Montgomery first raised the American flag. A year later, it was the site of San Francisco's first school. And a year after that, it was the place where Sam Brannan, owner of San Francisco's first newspaper, the *California Star*, announced that gold had been discovered in the Sierra foothills. Today, it is where children play, and old men go to spend their day arguing politics, while playing checkers and mahjong at the small tables dotting the square.

The pagoda-like former Chinese Telephone Exchange building on Washington Street, where the *California Star* was once printed, is now home to the **United Commerical Bank** ⑥.
SEE ALSO CHURCHES, P.44

Below: going to the bank, Chinatown style.

Every year in early spring, Chinatown sees the biggest Chinese New Year celebration outside of Asia, drawing thousands into the cramped neighborhood. During the festivities, firecracker wrappers litter every alleyway, as venders fill the streets, and the spectacular parade, complete with the 201ft (61m) Golden Dragon, seals the celebration.

Avenue near Union Square. A gift from Taiwan in 1970, it is modeled after a traditional village gate, and marks the beginning of Chinatown's Cantonese restaurants and stores hawking silks, jade, carved teak, and other Asian-themed bric-a-brac. The busy main drag, **Grant Avenue**, is packed with souvenir shops, but there are some respites along the way; **Old St Mary's Church** ②, at the intersection of Grant Avenue and California Street, was established in

1853, making it the oldest Catholic church in the city.
SEE ALSO CHURCHES, P.44; SHOPPING, P.112

Around Chinatown

It is worth stepping off Grant Avenue to experience the richer flavors of Chinatown. **Stockton Street** ③ is its working center, filled with Chinese-owned and -operated businesses, countless dollar stores, and open-air markets.

Many temples of different faiths sit atop buildings (to place them closer to heaven) throughout Chinatown, frequently acting as both an active house of worship and a community center. They are open to visitors, but be respectful and prepared to leave an offering. **Waverly Place** ④, just off Clay Street between Stockton Street and Grant Avenue, is known as the 'Street of Painted Balconies' and offers a brief reprieve from Chinatown's

Union Square and Financial District

B anks, designer labels, chic bars, exclusive restaurants, top-end hotels, the theater, and art galleries all define this commercial mecca. In the heart of the West Coast's financial hub in downtown San Francisco, the hum of cable cars is an atmospheric background noise to socialites shopping for their next gala and theatergoers attending the latest play. Weekdays downtown are dominated by a smart-looking set shuffling between the office, trips for lattes, the gym, and high-powered martini lunches.

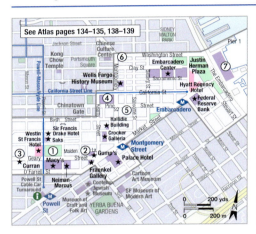

Above: multitasking on the move downtown.

Union Square ①

Gump's, Macy's, Neiman-Marcus, Saks Fifth Avenue, many international luxury retailers – from Cartier to Hermès – and hometown institutions such as Shreve & Co. give this shopping district enough swank to hold up to any other cosmopolitan city.

Redesigned in 2002, Union Square has a sleek modern look of gray and pink granite, and provides a place of repose for the weary shopper. In spite of its appearance, the square is as old as San Francisco itself. First deeded for public use in 1850, it got its name a decade later when

it was used to rally support for the Union cause during the Civil War. At the square's center is a 90ft (27m) Corinthian column, topped by a bronze Victory commemorating the successful Manila Bay campaign during the Spanish-American War.

The square is ringed by high-end hotels; particular standouts include the **Sir Francis Drake Hotel**, home of the lavish Harry Denton Starlight Room, and the **Westin St Francis Hotel**, which was built in 1904.

Nearby is Maiden Lane, a pedestrian-only alleyway studded with boutiques,

sidewalk cafés, and the Frank Lloyd Wright-designed **Xanadu Gallery** ②. Maiden Lane's tongue-in-cheek name originates from its notorious red-light past; it was known for having the cheapest prostitutes on the Barbary Coast.

Wedged between Union Square, Market Street, Civic Center, and the Tenderloin, is the city's Theater District. At its heart lies the historic **Geary Theater** built in 1910. It is home to San Francisco's **American Conservatory Theater** ③, whose season runs roughly from September through June. They perform an assortment of theater classics as well as original productions. The three other large theaters, the **Orpheum**, the **Golden Gate**, and the **Curran**,

Left: the distinctive Transamerica Pyramid.

old world **Palace Hotel**, which initially made news in 1875 for supposedly being fire proof (definitively disproved in 1906), but has since become known for its opulent Garden Court, the site of the celebration following the opening session of the United Nations; the 1930 **Pacific Stock Exchange** ⑤, illustrated by muralist Diego Rivera; and the **Transamerica Pyramid** ⑥, the tallest building in the city, which redefined San Francisco's skyline when it was built in 1972.

SEE ALSO HISTORY AND ARCHITECTURE, P.67; HOTELS, P.73; MUSEUMS AND GALLERIES, P.83

Embarcadero

Only recently has the waterfront become incorporated into the Financial District. For years the Embarcadero Freeway turned the waterfront into a mess of concrete and abandoned wharves; it collapsed during the Loma-Prieta Earthquake in 1989, opening up this vital area to redevelopment and rebirth. Since then, the Embarcadero has been lined with palm trees, given tracks for the historic F-line streetcars, and seen the renovation of the **Ferry Building** ⑦. Opened in 1898 and with a 230ft (70m) tower modeled after Seville's Cathedral, it is the transit center for ferries bringing people to and from work every day, and more recently, the epicenter of San Francisco's sustainable food movement. Redevelopment has made this landmark into a gourmet emporium with a range of dining options, as well as food merchants and a farmers' market.

SEE ALSO FOOD AND DRINK, P.56

Snaking through the Financial District is the hidden French Quarter of San Francisco. Alleyways such as Belden Place and Claude Alley are full of French bistros, and the area is particularly lively each year on Bastille Day (July 14).

---

attract larger national shows, often New York companies running performances before they debut on Broadway.

SEE ALSO HOTELS, P.72; MUSEUMS AND GALLERIES, P.83; SHOPPING, P.112; THEATER AND CABARET, P.118, 119

Financial District

Considered to be the financial capital of the West Coast, the soaring Financial District owes its great heights to the gold struck in the Sierra Nevada. The banks of 'Wall Street West' turned the miners' gold into money by minting currency. Bank of America and Wells Fargo both began

and have been headquartered here (Wells Fargo still is). The **former Bank of America Building** ④ is the second tallest building in the city; the polished black granite sculpture by Masayuki Nagare just outside it is locally known as the 'Bankers Heart'. The **Wells Fargo Museum** celebrates the bank's rich history and role in the Gold Rush.

Other historic and architectural gems include: the

Below: it is always time to eat at the Ferry Building.

13

SoMa and Civic Center

Firmly rooted in the life of the city are the grandiose Civic Center and the energetic SoMa (South of Market) districts. Awash with civic life, they are underpinned by city government, cultural institutions, public spaces, the visual and expressive arts, cutting edge restaurants, and a thriving late-night club scene. Bordering the two neighborhoods is the edgier Tenderloin district, while nearby Hayes Valley is a smart locale packed with upscale eateries and trendy design stores.

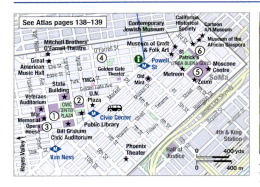

Above: performance is part of the scenery at Yerba Buena park.

Civic Center

San Francisco's Civic Center is dominated by Arthor Brown Jr's Beaux Arts **City Hall** ①. Built in 1914, it was influenced by the City Beautiful movement of the 1890s and is perhaps the grandest seat of city government in the United States, eclipsing even New York's, and representing the city's optimism at the end of the century. City Hall was the scene of the murders of Harvey Milk and Mayor George Moscone in 1978, and in February 2004 found itself at the center of nationwide controversy when Mayor Gavin Newsom granted marriage licenses to same-sex couples; around 4,000 flocked to City Hall to exchange their vows before the Supreme Court of California shut down proceedings.

Brown was also responsible for many other Civic Center buildings, including the Veterans Auditorium, home to the **Herbst Theater**, the **War Memorial Opera House** (the birthplace of the United Nations) and the **Asian Art Museum** ②, which has one of the world's largest collections of Near and Far East art.

The Civic Center also includes the Main Public Library, the State Building, the ultramodern **Louise M. Davies Symphony Hall** ③, and the Bill Graham Civic Auditorium, named for the famous promoter who was responsible for San Francisco's explosive music scene in the 1960s.

SEE ALSO MUSEUMS AND GALLERIES, P.83; MUSIC AND DANCE, P.90

The Tenderloin

Connecting the Civic Center to Market Street is the **United Nations Plaza**, host to a farmers' market every Wednesday and Sunday. This is also the tip of the gritty Tenderloin, a neighborhood that extends along Market Street to Union Square. Known for drugs, prostitution, criminal activity, and the down and out, it is also home to some great old San Francisco architecture, inexpensive but fantastic ethnic food, and historic sites, including the **Glide Memorial Methodist Church** ④, dedicated to serving the homeless while welcoming visitors to its energetic and

Left: the road to City Hall.

gradual decay began when San Francisco transferred its shipping industry to the ports of Alameda and Oakland. In the 1950s the area emerged as the center for the gay community's leather sub-culture. However, the dot-com boom of the 1990s turned the South of Market district into SoMa, a chic area filled with museums, live-work lofts, nightclubs, exciting restaurants, and a ton of artistic and entrepreneurial energy. Since the bust at the turn of the millennium, SoMa has settled down a bit, but it has forever changed into a vital part of San Francisco's cultural life.

The intersection of Mission and 3rd streets is the nexus of SoMa's museum district, anchored by the **Moscone Convention Center** and **Yerba Buena Center for the Arts** ⑤, a 22-acre (9-hectare) complex complete with rolling gardens, an art museum, the children's museum **Zeum**, performance spaces, an ice skating rink, a 15-screen movie theater at the Metreon, and a beautifully restored 1905 carousel.

Nearby **St Patrick's Church**, established in 1851, stands for a bit of history. Still serving the community, it now performs a Sunday Mass in Tagalog for the local Filipino residents. Across 3rd Street is the **San Francisco Museum of Modern Art** ⑥. Other museums include the **Museum of the African Diaspora**, the **California Historical Society**, the **Cartoon Art Museum**, and the **Contemporary Jewish Museum**.

SEE ALSO CHILDREN, P.41; MUSEUMS AND GALLERIES, P.84, 85; PARKS AND GARDENS, P.98

The Mitchell Brothers' O'Farrell Theater is a Tenderloin institution and a San Francisco legend. A pioneer in the adult entertainment industry, Hunter S. Thompson proclaimed it 'the Carnegie Hall of public sex in America.' In 1991 it became infamous when one brother was shot and killed by the other.

---

soulful Sunday sermons, and the historic **Great American Music Hall**, with voluptuous Rococo interiors that hark back to its bordello past and add flavor to this world-class music venue. The neighborhood is as edgy as it looks, so keep alert during the day and hail a cab at night.

SEE ALSO CHURCHES, P.44; FOOD AND DRINK, P.56; MUSIC AND DANCE, P.92

Hayes Valley

On the other side of the Civic Center, the newly revitalized Hayes Valley is a charming, compact neighborhood to enjoy a coffee, cocktail, or a bit of shopping before, or after, a night at the opera. It is also home to several of the city's top restaurants.

SoMa

Low-slung factories and empty warehouses once filled the wide blocks stretching from Market Street to the old working waterfront. Its

Below: the striking San Francisco Museum of Modern Art.

Nob Hill

Perched on the highest of San Francisco's many hills, the robber barons of Nob Hill have been looking down at the rest of San Francisco since the late 19th century. Nicknamed the 'hill of palaces' by Robert Louis Stevenson, it has always had a reputation for being home to privilege and refined luxury. While this attitude endures, all but one of the 'palaces' are gone, replaced by the Gothic Grace Cathedral, the beautiful Huntington Park, and elite hotels with spectacular views. Today, Nob Hill is a charming neighborhood filled with elegant apartment buildings, where the lesser mansions once stood.

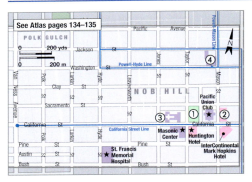

Above: the temples to luxury on Nob Hill.

Fit For a Baron

In 1873, Andrew Smith Hallidie invented the cable car, and turned the once barren 'California Street Hill' into prime real estate. No sooner had the tracks been laid when San Francisco's wealthiest began vying for the best lot, and out-doing each other building opulent and extravagant mansions. The most prominent residents occupied the apex of the hill. These were James Flood, who was one of the kings of the Comstock Silver Load, and the Big Four rail barons: Charles Crocker, Mark Hopkins, Leland Stanford, and Collis Huntington. It did not take long for the name to change to 'Nob Hill', 'nob' being a variation on 'nabob', the Indian word for Moghul

prince. But many San Franciscans gave it their own nickname, 'Snob Hill.'

Thus there was little love lost, when the fire following the 1906 earthquake consumed the neighborhood. The sole surviving mansion, the interior ravaged by the fire, belonged to James Flood. Holding court next to the genteel greenery of **Huntington Park** ①, it is now home to the **Pacific Union Club**, which keeps up the elitism of its forbearers and does not admit women.

SEE ALSO PARKS AND GARDENS, P.98

Hotels and Cathedrals

From the ashes of the great Hopkins, Stanford, and Huntington mansions have sprung world-famous luxury hotels.

Across from the old Flood mansion now stands the **Huntington Hotel** and the **InterContinental Mark Hopkins Hotel**. Between them is the imposing **Fairmont Hotel** ②, which was completed just before the 1906 earthquake. Surviving the quake but not the fire, it was quickly rebuilt, opening a year to the day after the devastating event. High rates keep these hotels exclusive, but everyone can view their elegant lobbies or enjoy a cocktail in the bar.

The estate of Charles Crocker was the only one of the Big Four not to become a hotel. Instead, the Crocker family donated the property to the Episcopal Diocese, which built **Grace Cathedral** ③. Its Gothic spires can be seen

Left: parking is for experts only on a hill this steep.

to walk and enjoy great views. Strolling the lesser streets and alleyways, it is easy to spy the neighborhood of Dashiell Hammett, who set many of his stories here, in particular, *The Maltese Falcon*. In Nob Hill, Hammett saw all the components that help define the old San Francisco: wealth, power, criminals, and style.

SEE ALSO CHURCHES, P.45; HOTELS, P.74; LITERATURE, P.78; MUSEUMS AND GALLERIES, P.87; MUSIC AND DANCE, P.92

Polk Gulch and the TenderNob

As Nob Hill slides down to the south and west, the classic apartment buildings become a little rougher around the edges. Before Castro became the city's gay center, Polk Gulch was it. Today this is where the Tenderloin nips at the well heeled Nob Hill neighborhood along Polk Street. Full of energy, Polk Gulch is filled with ethnic restaurants, eclectic shops, and several hard-rocking nightspots. East of Polk Gulch, Geary Street, and its environs host bars, cafés, and hole-in-the-wall eateries. This north-south border between Nob Hill and the Tenderloin has been dubbed by locals as 'the TenderNob.'

The walls of the 'Room of Dons' inside the InterContinental Mark Hopkins Hotel, are covered in nine 7ft (2m) -tall murals depicting early California, including a golden Queen Califa for whom the state is named.

from high spots around the city, but the Cathedral's details deserve a closer look. From the windows, which depict prominent 20th-century figures, to the bronze and gold cathedral doors cast from Lorenzo Ghiberti's *Doors of Paradise*, and Keith Haring's altarpiece in the AIDS Interfaith Memorial Chapel, it suggests a modernism and egalitarianism that is refreshing on Nob Hill.

Across the street is the **Masonic Center**. Commissioned by the California Freemasons after the end of

World War II, it is now an event center hosting cultural performances.

Located near the intersection of Chinatown and Nob Hill, at the corner of Washington and Mason streets, is the **Cable Car Museum** ④. Built in 1910, it is the nerve center of the present cable car system. It details the cars' history and shows off the inner workings of the unique mechanical system.

Centrally located, Nob Hill is a wonderful, if athletic, place

Right: the Masonic Center's distinctive stained-glass imagery.

Central Neighborhoods

Riding the city's crests and valleys from the bay to Market Street, Fillmore Street is an excellent place to penetrate San Francisco's central neighborhoods. Largely residential, these districts all contain their own thriving commercial centers with parks, cafés, restaurants, niche stores and boutiques. Whether affluent, ethnic or edgy, these districts boast some of the best examples of San Franciscan architecture and contain some of its most distinct cultural pockets. Each is unique in character, informed by their location in San Francisco's wild topography, and all deserve a trip off the beaten path.

Above: celebrating jazz in the Fillmore District.

Marina and Cow Hollow

The Marina neighborhood is popular with young professionals who make good money in the Financial District and pack out the bars at the weekend. Locals celebrate the Marina's proximity to the bay with the Golden Gate Promenade, where they push baby strollers, walk dogs, or power walk past harbors stuffed with sailboats, frisbee-throwers on the Marina Green, and native birds and plant species at the restored Crissy Field. Farther along the waterfront, the unique **Wave Organ** ① pro-

duces unearthly 'music' as waves swell against its 25 pipes that jut into the ocean.

Back on dry land, locals get their lattes on Chestnut Street, where stores, cafés, and an old theater grace this low-rise, pastel district. At the far end, by the Presidio, the **Palace of Fine Arts** ②, first built for the Pacific International Exposition in 1915, now houses the **Exploratorium**.

Union Street is another commercial hub, also called Cow Hollow for the cow pastures that used to occupy the softly sloping landscape. Here the 1920s Mediterranean

architecture gives way to older Victorians, some of which have been converted into boutiques, bars, and restaurants. **The Vedanta Temple** ③ on Webster Street is a distinctive tribute to religious tolerance; the amalgam of architectural styles is designed to convey that all religions stem from common roots.

SEE ALSO MUSEUMS AND GALLERIES, P.87

Pacific Heights

Sitting high above the Marina is the crown of Pacific Heights, the neighborhood of today's power brokers and social elite, and lined with beautiful, jaw-dropping mansions. While many remain in private hands, others have been converted to schools or

Left: the picturesque 'painted ladies' of Alamo Square.

guishing feature is its 100ft (30m) -high, five-tiered **Peace Pagoda**, given to San Francisco by Japan following World War II. Despite being settled by Japanese immigrants as far back as the 1860s, Japantown was razed during World War II as the US government expelled Japanese Americans to inland internment camps.
SEE ALSO PAMPERING, P.97

The Western Addition

An extension of the Fillmore, the Western Addition also has a long and proud African-American past, and is where you'll find the **St John Coltrane African Orthodox Church** ⑥, at 1286 Fillmore Street.

Alamo Square ⑦ is the pinnacle of the Western Addition. This sloping city park fits perfectly into an imagined 19th-century past, surrounded by fully restored Victorians. The famous **'painted ladies'** on the eastern side – also known as Postcard Row – pit a dramatic contrast against the sparkling view of the Financial District and City Hall.
SEE ALSO CHURCHES, P.45; HISTORY AND ARCHITECTURE, P.65; PARKS AND GARDENS, P.99

Built on reclaimed land and rubble from the 1906 earthquake, the Marina was one of the worst hit areas when the Loma-Prieta earthquake struck in 1989, though only the markedly newer structures give any clue to this today.

---

consulates. One of the few open to the public is the Queen Anne-style **Haas-Lilienthal House** (1886) ④, full of Victorian-era antiques.

In addition to **Alta Plaza** and **Lafayette Park**, Fillmore Street is the place to enjoy the luxury of Pacific Heights. For those lighter of pocket, it has a number of secondhand stores where the rich discard last year's fashions.
SEE ALSO PARKS AND GARDENS, P.99

The Fillmore District

It is a steep drop down to the Fillmore District, where the line between the haves and the have-nots cannot be any

clearer. Rich in cultural history, the Fillmore has seen better days. Once a thriving African American community, attracting the very best jazz stars of the 1930s and 1940s, it was destroyed by the controversial Urban Redevelopment Program of the 1950s, which filled the area with low-income housing developments. Nonetheless, it is a great neighborhood for seeing live music, particularly at the **Fillmore Auditorium** ⑤, where Bill Graham helped launch the careers of San Francisco's biggest 1960's musical acts.
SEE ALSO MUSIC AND DANCE, P.92

Japantown

Just across the street from The Fillmore is the compact Japantown. It is dominated by the **Japan Center**, an enormous complex of stores, theaters, sushi bars, restaurants, and the wonderful Japanese-style **Kabuki Springs and Spa**. Its distin-

Below: the Peace Pagoda.

Haight-Ashbury and Golden Gate Park

In 1966, at the intersection of Haight and Ashbury streets, a young, pre-beard Jerry Garcia and the rest of the Grateful Dead posed for one of the era's iconic photos, proclaiming the district to be the epicenter of the emerging counterculture. The brightly painted Victorian houses became hippies' crash pads; their presence is still felt today in this nostalgic neighborhood. Nearby, Golden Gate Park stretches to the sea over 1,000 acres (400 hectares), containing wonderful gardens, museums, and other attractions.

The Haight

Low rents initially attracted the next wave of bohemians following the Beats. By the mid-1960s the neighborhood had filled with headshops, boutiques, bookstores, musicians and artists, but it was 1967 when it gained iconic status, as tens of thousands flocked here for first the 'Human Be-In,' and then the famous 'Summer of Love.' The event catapulted the careers of such San Francisco bands as Jefferson Airplane, Big Brother, and the Holding Company, not to mention the Grateful Dead. The sense of this history is palpable as you walk around Haight Street, particularly from its intersection with **Ashbury Street** ①.

However, while The Haight, as it is known by locals, is considerably steeped in nostalgia, there are plenty of modern day fashonistas, Goths, and young alternative types

claiming the neighborhood as their own. Crowded with thrift stores, iconoclastic fashion boutiques, cheap eateries, friendly local bars, the vast **Amoeba** record store – housed in an old bowling alley – and the second-run **Red Vic Movie House**, Haight Street remains a colorful and dynamic place to hang out.

Down several residential blocks, past the city's oldest park, **Buena Vista**, and Divisadero Street, the Lower Haight is considerably grimier and less nostalgic, but some feel it is a more exciting version of the Haight and today it is certainly more progressive. Edgy music and fashion stores sit alongside hip bars and eateries here. At the corner of Page and Scott streets is **Jack's Record Cellar** ②, the oldest record store in the city.

For a change of tempo and a sunnier neighborhood, visit Cole Valley. Winding up

Above: hippies still congregate in the Haight.

the hill from Upper Haight toward University of California San Francisco Medical School, Cole Valley is filled with charming gingerbread houses, young families, and fabulous places to grab coffee or brunch. A climb up **Tank Hill** offers spectacular views of the city.

SEE ALSO FASHION, P.52; HISTORY AND ARCHITECTURE, P.67; MOVIES, P.81; MUSIC AND DANCE, P.93;

Left: the Conservatory of Flowers in Golden Gate Park.

trees and fountains, the Music Concourse is an outdoor summer music venue seating 20,000 people. Surrounding it are the new **M.H. de Young Memorial Museum** ③, with a striking exterior, home to an impressive collection of art from around the world, ranging from antiquity to the modern era; the recently reopened **California Academy of Sciences** ④, featuring an aquarium, **planetarium** and living green roof; and the **Japanese Tea Garden** ⑤, a favorite for its subtlety and beauty. Also nearby is the 70-acre (28-hectare) **Strybing Arboretum** and the **Conservatory of Flowers**; the latter is housed in the oldest building in the park, an elegant copy of the Palm House in London's Kew Gardens.

Crossing 19th Avenue, the park is dotted with a series of lakes and contains horse stables, archery facilities, fly-fishing ponds, playgrounds, tennis and bocce ball courses, a polo field, and two windmills, once used to pump water for the entire park.

SEE ALSO CHILDREN, P.42; MUSEUMS AND GALLERIES, P.87; PARKS AND GARDENS, P.99, 100, 101

Filled with grand Victorians and large backyards, Haight-Ashbury began as the suburbs, linked by the Haight Street Cable Railroad to the Financial District. In the housing shortage during World War II, many of these single homes were divided into apartments, which were vacated once the war was over, as families left for the suburbs in the 1950s mass 'white flight.'

PARKS AND GARDENS, P.99; WALKS AND VIEWS, P.127

Golden Gate Park

One of the civic wonders of San Francisco, **Golden Gate Park** is eight blocks wide and 52 blocks long. It represents the aspirations of late-19th century civic leaders who sought to build a city (and a park) rivaling New York. The dedicated and talented William Hammond Hall converted the once windswept sand dunes into a verdant wonderland, hailed for its botanical variety and naturally unfolding topography. Today it is home to a vast collection of cultural attractions and countless places to picnic, play frisbee, or catch some sun.

The eastern end of the park has the highest concentration of cultural sites. Built at the turn of the 20th century and landscaped with

Below: Bob Dylan gets a nod in a local mural.

Mission and Castro

Pride and Viva La Raza! define these two adjoining neighborhoods, which in many ways provide San Francisco's political and artistic heartbeat. The well-groomed Castro, considered by many to be the gay capital of the world, showcases beautifully restored Victorian and Edwardian homes, while draping its thriving nightlife, love of shopping, and political activism in rainbow flags. Farther east, the Mission district dresses itself with colors of the Americas. This working-class Latino neighborhood has lured artists, musicians, and hipsters to create one of the most dynamic and diverse districts in the city.

See Atlas pages 136–139

Above: the symbol of Pride flies over a street in the Castro.

The Castro

It was only 40 years ago that the Castro shifted from a working-class, Irish-Catholic neighborhood to being the gay hub of the city, but it is hard now to imagine it any differently. Its tightly packed commercial strip largely caters to the gay community, but there is something for everyone, in particular the **Castro Theater** ①, which exhibits the glamour and class of the neighborhood. Designated a US National Historic Landmark in 1977, this ornate Spanish Baroque theater, complete with Art Deco flourishes, is a revival movie house, and often the host to one of San Francisco's many film festivals. On special nights it features a live organist who plays on an ascending platform before the start of the film. **Twin Peaks** ②, a friendly neighborhood joint, sits proudly at the corner of Castro and Market, and was the first openly gay bar in the US.

The Castro's dedication to community and civil rights is represented at the Charles M. Holmes Campus at **The Center** ③. Located at 1800 Market near the intersection with Hayes Valley, The Center is the nexus for community events, classes, support groups, and information about the local LGBT (Lesbian, Gay, Bisexual, Transgender) community.

During the annual Pride celebration in June, this civic commitment becomes a party lasting all weekend. Attracting half a million people, Pride is the highest of high holidays of the gay community, including a huge parade festooned with queens, floats, and high-stepping frivolity.

SEE ALSO GAY AND LESBIAN, P.58, 60, 61, 62; MOVIES, P.81

The Mission

Castro and Mission residents come to sunbathe and walk their dogs at sunny **Mission Dolores Park** ④, where the district begins, its namesake only two blocks away on the palm-lined Dolores Street. Modestly situated next to the impressive Basilica is the Misión San Francisco de Asís, commonly known as the **Mission Dolores** ⑤. The city's oldest

consciousness as well as a deep connection to *'La Raza'* (the race, or the people). The **Galeria de la Raza** ⑥ on 24th Street is largely considered the most important Chicano art center in the country.

Meanwhile, the **Women's Building** ⑦ is festooned with brilliant murals and is an important community center. The Women's Movement also took root in the Mission, while one-time lower rents in this part of the city attracted a strong lesbian community that many credit with shifting the character of this once-rough neighborhood.

Since then, the Mission has become a hub for those trying to make it in the art world; it is seen as the new bohemian center, the main neighborhood where young hipsters choose to live. Its numerous bars, cafés, and bookstores are representative of this trend, as well its emerging chic culinary scene.

SEE ALSO CHURCHES, P.45; GAY AND LESBIAN, P.62; MUSEUMS AND GALLERIES, P.88; PARKS AND GARDENS, P.101; WALKS AND VIEWS, P.128

Co-founded by author Dave Eggers, 826 Valencia is a non-profit organisation dedicated to helping and encouraging young people to write. It also doubles as a pirate store.

---

building, it was completed just days before the signing of the Declaration of Independence in 1776.

From Dolores Street, the Mission spreads east. Valencia Street is the hipster and bohemian center of the Mission, and is aptly filled with great bookstores, boutiques, bars, cafés, and the site of the **New College of California**, an ultra-liberal university. Mission Street's numerous Art Deco marquees speak of a more prosperous time, but the street is still rich in culture and artistic energy. Full of discount stores, Mexican groceries, and more late-night spots, it is a dynamic neighborhood,

though a bit less salubrious after dark. While it is a diverse area, the Latino culture for which this area is especially famous can be seen particularly on 24th Street, from Mission to Folsom. Lined with trees and *taquerias*, it has the feeling of being lodged deep in the heart of Latin America.

Murals throughout the Mission express its political

Below: the Misión San Francisco de Asís (or Mission Dolores) gives the city its name.

Around San Francisco

Less visited than their central cousins, San Francisco's outlying districts hark back to the city's military and working class foundations. These fringe areas provide green areas and astonishing views of the city, while giving an insight into the lives of many working San Franciscans. They also reach back to San Francisco's natural history. Western places such as Land's End and Ocean Beach preserve the water's wild edge, while the city's south-eastern peaks blossom with wildflowers in Spring. Meanwhile, stretching out from the Presidio and South Beach respectively are the photogenic, iconic Golden Gate Bridge and the busy, impressive Bay Bridge.

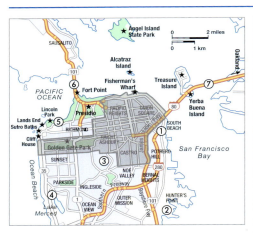

Above: shopping in trendy Noe Valley.

South Beach

The Embarcadero promenade, offering spectacular views of the bay and its namesake bridge, leads to the neighborhood of South Beach, full of redeveloped warehouses and startup companies. The water line leads from Fisherman's Wharf to the new **AT&T Park** ①, home to the San Francisco G ants.

The **49ers'** home is **Monster Park** ②. It is located in Hunter's Point, the site of the once bustling Naval Shipyard, after whose departure the neighborhood has never quite recovered.
SEE ALSO SPORT, P.117

Potrero Hill to Twin Peaks

Overlooking Hunter's Point, Potrero Hill is a one-time working class neighborhood and a great spot for dinner while enjoying the south end views of the city. Nearby residential neighborhoods include Bernal Heights, packed with families and narrow streets, and Noe Valley, whose 24th Street has a charming assortment of gourmet stores, cafés, and bistros. **Twin Peaks** ③ has an overlook to take in the panoramic view; residents who are wealthy enough enjoy the views year round.
SEE ALSO WALKS AND VIEWS, P.126

Ocean Beach

The 4 miles (6.4km) of Ocean Beach are a wonderful place to play in the sand or take in a sunset. Be aware though, the water is very cold and the undertow strong enough to catch even the most experienced swimmers off guard.

The **San Francisco Zoo** ④ anchors the south end, with a constant stream of new and exciting exhibits, while the **Sutro Baths** and the **Cliff House** overlook the north. The Cliff House has gone through a number of incarnations, but now houses **Sutro's**, an upscale restaurant with killer views. Public walkways allow appreciation of these without the need for a fat wallet.
SEE ALSO CHILDREN, P.41; RESTAURANTS, P.111

At sea level, Treasure Island is a great place to ride a bike, take in the phenomenal views of the city, and come eye to eye with the giant cargo ships coming into the Port of Oregon.

Sunset and Richmond

Known as the Avenues, the Sunset and Richmond districts run along either side of **Golden Gate Park**. Both are vast residential neighborhoods full of working-class famililes of various ethnicities, and commercial districts filled with bookstores, groceries, and Asian restaurants.

Bisecting the Richmond is **Lincoln Park**, home to the **Palace of the Legion of Honor** ⑤. Housed in a Beaux Arts building, the Legion showcases 4,000 years of ancient and European art. From here, it is a short walk to **Lands End**, the city's wildest bit of coastline, with arresting views of the Golden Gate.

SEE ALSO MUSEUMS AND GALLERIES, P.88; PARKS AND GARDENS, P.101; WALKS AND VIEWS, P.125

The Presidio

Almost 1,500 acres (607 hectares) in size, the Presidio occupies the northwest corner of the city. For more than 200 years, the Presidio was an active military installation, and was turned over to Golden Gate National Parks in 1995. Today the vast swath of land is a rich collection of historic buildings, residential neighborhoods, and hiking trails.

Out in the bay, to the north, sit **Alcatraz** and **Angel Island**, both accessible by ferry from **Fisherman's Wharf**. Once the Quarantine and Immigration stations for the west coast, Angel Island processed thousands of Asians attempting to immigrate here, often holding them for several months. The buildings of the station still exist and can be visited on a docent-led tour. Today it is a

Left: catching some waves at the Presidio's beach.

state park with 13 miles (21km) of trails.
SEE ALSO PARKS AND GARDENS, P.101; WALKS AND VIEWS, P.126

Iconic Bridges

The **Golden Gate Bridge** ⑥ is perhaps the most photographed bridge in the world. Crews work continually from one end to the other and back, sandblasting rust and repainting. Hidden below the bridge is the impenetrable **Fort Point**, a Civil War-era fortification built to protect the San Francisco Bay from any potential Confederate attack.

The **Bay Bridge** ⑦ is the longest steel high-level bridge in the world, and one of its busiest. On its journey downtown from Oakland, it passes through **Yerba Buena Island** and the adjacent man-made **Treasure Island**. The latter was created in the late 1930s for the Golden Gate International Exposition and taken over by the Navy shortly thereafter; it has been recently returned to the city. Alongside the Bay Bridge, a replacement bridge is being built, due for completion in 2013.
SEE ALSO HISTORY AND ARCHITECTURE, P.66

Below: a monument to the Giants in South Beach.

Oakland, Berkeley, and the Bay Area

From the Black Panthers to Chez Panisse, the East Bay is in many ways the revolutionary center that San Francisco gets so much credit for. With its lively political culture, vast parklands and outdoor spaces, museums and intellectual centers, and widely diverse demographics, the East Bay is a thriving metropolitan center independent of its scene-stealing neighbor to the west. Oakland and Berkeley are an easy trip across the Bay Bridge, and the BART system makes them highly accessible.

Above: Jack London's haunt, First and Last Chance Saloon.

Oakland ①

Much has changed in **Oakland** since the indignity of Gertrude Stein's quip, 'There is no there there.' During World War II the industry and ports of Oakland boomed, as did its population, creating the diversity responsible for Oakland's uniquely textured culture. Today, it is one of the most diverse cities in the state with 30 percent of its population African American, 25 percent Caucasian, 25 percent Hispanic, and 16 percent Asian.

Oakland is not a city defined by its skyline, but by its parks and diverse cultural attractions. Near downtown sits **Lake Merritt**, a 155-acre (64-hectare) natural salt-water lake, popular with wildlife, picnickers, and joggers. Close by are the **Oakland Museum of California**, the **African American Museum and Library**, and the restored Art Deco **Paramount Theater**.

On the waterfront is **Jack London Square**, perhaps Oakland's biggest tourist draw. Named for the city's

most famous son, it is a complex of stores, seafood restaurants, and one of London's frequent haunts, the First and Last Chance Saloon. Here also is the legendary **Yoshi's** jazz club.

Farther south on the Nimitz Freeway is the **Oakland-Alameda County Coliseum and Oracle Arena**, home to the Oakland A's, the Golden State Warriors, and the Oakland Raiders.
SEE ALSO LITERATURE, P.78; MUSIC AND DANCE, P.93; MUSEUMS AND GALLERIES, P.89; SPORT, P.117

Berkeley ②

Since the Free Speech Movement in 1964, the **University of California, Berkeley** has been a hotbed of political activism. The university cam-

The Marin Headlands are accessible by public transit from San Francisco. Golden Gate Transit makes the trip, as does the number 76 bus.

surrounding open space. The magnificent **Marin Headlands** across the Golden Gate from San Francisco attest to this. It is one of several parks in Marin County, which include the **Muir Woods** and the **Point Reyes National Seashore** ④. In the west, open space gives way to dairy farms, ranch land and a windswept coast, while the east is home to upper-middle class communities, many of whom travel daily into the city.

Around the Bay Area

In Palo Alto, south from San Francisco, is **Stanford University** ⑤, UC Berkeley's major rival in sports, academics, and prestige. Major points of interest include the **Hoover Tower** and the **Rodin Sculpture Garden**, which displays 20 bronze castings.

Nearby **Silicon Valley** was once called the Valley of Heart's Delight, but it is now famed for and synonymous with innovation in technology.

Below: taking the scenic way to Point Reyes.

pus, the 'crown of the UC system,' is a sprawling temple to education, full of earnest students and Nobel Prize-winning professors. The focal point of campus is the 307ft (94m) **Sather Tower**, known as the Campanile, which can be seen from across the bay. The on-site **Berkeley Art Museum** is one of the largest university art collections in the country.

Intersecting the campus at Sproul Plaza is **Telegraph Avenue**, long known to be one of the landmarks of the counterculture, as is nearby **People's Park**, the site of a legendary student-police confrontation in 1969. In north Berkeley, Alice Water's **Chez Panisse** remains a mecca for devotees of California cuisine. Berkeley is a beautiful city filled with elegant Craftsman style homes; a stroll through its leafy streets is a highly recommended treat.

SEE ALSO MUSEUMS AND GALLERIES, P.89; RESTAURANTS, P.111

Marin County

A drive over the Golden Gate Bridge or a ferry ride from the Ferry Building or Fisherman's Wharf takes you into Marin County, which boasts beautiful coastline, rugged hills and attractive towns. **Sausalito** ③ is one of the most worthwhile to visit; it is known as the 'French Riviera' of the West Coast, due to its equable climate, art galleries, and restaurants, all with great views.

The Bay Area is a rare example of a major metropolitan area that has succeeded in preserving vast amounts of

Perhaps Oakland's most famous export in the early 1970s was the Black Panthers, who formed in response to police brutality in Oakland's African American neighborhoods. They quickly spread to other big cities and became key figures in that turbulent era.

Wine Country

In need of wine for their sacramental duties, the Spanish padres of the California missions can be credited with bringing viticulture to the Napa and Sonoma valleys. However, it was a Hungarian nobleman, Count Agoston Haraszthy, who saw the area's full potential. In 1857, he opened the region's first winery, Sonoma's Buena Vista Winery, which is still in operation. Since then, many winemakers have followed in his footsteps, producing vino recognized around the world for its excellence. A trip to the wine country is a worthwhile excursion from San Francisco, for the region's beauty, cuisine, and sunshine, as well as for its wine.

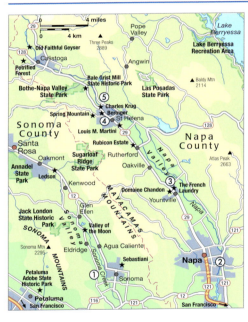

Above: vines at the Ledson Winery in Sonoma County.

Sonoma

Home to the last mission, established in 1832, **San Francisco de Solano Mission** ① in Sonoma is integrally tied to the state of California's earliest beginnings. This will come as no surprise when strolling through Sonoma's 8-acre (3.2-hectare) central main square. Surrounding it is a collection of historic sites, including where the first California Republic flag was raised, a collection of Mexican army barracks, and several 19th-century houses, which have been tastefully converted into stores and restaurants. Sonoma was nicknamed **Valley of the Moon** by founding father Mariano Vallejo, and author Jack London used this moniker as a title to one of his books about the area. **Jack London State Historic Park** is the location of the writer's grave and last home, now a museum.

Napa

Just over the Mayacamas Mountains, Napa Valley stretches along the floodplain of the Napa River and State Highway 29. At the base of the valley, Napa has several expensive restaurants, a visitor's center, and a depot to catch the Napa Valley Wine Train, which allows visitors to fully enjoy the best wineries and tasting rooms in relaxed luxury. **Copia** ②, sitting near downtown, is a museum and education center devoted to food, wine, and art. The wine gardens here are both a gar-

dener's and an oenophile's delight, designed to represent all the flavors and aromas used to describe different varietals of wine.

Farther north, **Yountville** is where the wine country begins in earnest. Here visitors will find the **Napa Valley Museum** ③, in addition to epicurean institutions such as Thomas Keller's internationally renowned restaurant, **The French Laundry**, and the nearby **Domaine Chandon Winery**, French makers of sparkling wine.

SEE ALSO RESTAURANTS, P.111

Right: the Ledson vineyard.

St Helena

The next stop on Highway 29, also called The Great Wine Way, is **St Helena**. The carefully preserved 19th-century downtown is full of chic stores, restaurants, and galleries, including the **Silverado Museum** ④, which celebrates Robert Louis Stevenson, a one-time resident of the area.

The surrounding area is filled with country inns, beautiful parks, and nearly 40 wineries. Historic wineries include **Louis M. Martini Winery**, run by one of the valley's oldest

Left: at the Sebastiani Winery in Sonoma County.

The Rubicon Estate in Rutherford is owned by the filmmaker, Francis Ford Coppola, and worth a stop for the movie memorabilia he has on display here, including his Oscars.

wine-making families, and **Beringer Vineyards**, started by two brothers in 1876 and whose Rhine House, the location of a tasting room, was built in 1883. **Charles Krug Winery** is also housed in a historic building (1874) and is the oldest winery in the Napa Valley, having opened its doors in 1861.

Of additional historical and culinary note is the **Greystone Mansion** ⑤, a stone winery built in 1883 by mining magnate William Bourne. It is now the West Coast headquarters for the New York-based Culinary Institute of America.

Calistoga

Rich in mineral springs and hot, therapeutic mud, **Calistoga** offers a decadent reprieve from the valley's Bacchanalian excesses. Throughout the one-street downtown, day spas mix with bookstores and cafés. At **Old Faithful Geyser**, 2 miles (3.2km) north of town, visitors can feel (for a fee) the power of Calistoga's subterranean water.

A–Z

In the following section,
San Francisco's attractions and
services are organized by theme,
under alphabetical headings. Items
that link to another theme are
cross-referenced. All sights that are
plotted on the atlas section at the
end of the book are given a page
number and grid reference.

Alcatraz

Tales of The Rock and its legendary inmates have fascinated Americans since the golden years of the American gangster. Now operated by the National Park Service, anyone can come and go to Alcatraz and explore its famous cellblocks, notorious Segregation Unit, and the 19th-century military garrison standing beneath it all. What is less known about the island is that it was also the site of one of the most significant and prolonged Native American protests in American history, and is now home to a rare and unique variety of plant, animal, and bird life.

'The Rock'

Somber by day and eerily illuminated at night, Alcatraz is a haunting presence in the San Francisco Bay. For prisoners of The Rock, the sounds of the city, from the clang of the cable cars to the light chatter of evening cocktail parties, would float across the water into their cells as haunting reminders of the world outside. Alcatraz was once home to some of the most hardened criminals of the 20th century. But today, the cells of Chicago mob boss Al Capone, the bootlegger 'Machine Gun' Kelly, and Robert Shroud, played by Burt Lancaster in the film *The Birdman of Alcatraz*, are available for all to see.

Originally built as a military garrison in the mid-18th century, Alcatraz was prized for its strategic significance. It began its life as a prison in 1895, when it imprisoned Modoc and Hopi tribe leaders. Responding to the crime wave sweeping the country in the 1920s and 1930s, the federal government decided Alcatraz was fortified enough

to house the most violent offenders, and took over the prison in 1934. Alcatraz Federal Penitentiary quickly gained a reputation for its harsh system of earned privileges for the most basic rights, its deadening solitary confinement, and the cold, damp weather. Its severity lead to 36 attempted escapes, none of which succeeded – 23 were caught alive, six were shot and killed during their escape, two drowned and five were presumed drowned. In 1963, Attorney General Robert Kennedy shut down the

Below: Alcatraz's most famous inhabitant: Al Capone.

crumbling and expensive prison, and it was turned over to the National Park Service.

Indian Occupation

Six years later, with a trace of irony, a large group of Native Americans under the banner 'Indians of All Tribes' laid claim to the island and occupied it until 1971. Mounted as a protest against the many treaties with Native Americans broken by the US government, the group demanded title to Alcatraz and funds to build an Indian center and university. While the occupation ended with no demands met, it jumpstarted the Pan-Indian Movement and prompted the US

Recently, the Alcatraz Historic Gardens Project has been busy rebuilding the gardens and natural landscape surrounding the prison. Once tended by inmates and prison personnel as a popular pastime, these gardens provided color, as well as hope and reprieve from the harsh world behind the penitentiary's locked doors.

Left: 'The Rock', from the air.

special activities. It is recommended to purchase tickets in advance as they sell out quickl, particularly during the summer, on weekends, and on holidays.

Visiting the Park

Once on Alcatraz, there are park rangers to provide assistance and information regarding the variety of tours, which include kid-friendly programs and guided walks through the island's gardens and natural landscape. There is also a museum, two book-stores, and a visitor center located both on the dock and at the main level.

Weather and terrain is another consideration. Located in the middle of the bay, both the island and the ride out there can be plagued with cold and foggy weather, regardless of the time of year. Be sure to wear layers, and comfortable walking shoes to negotiate the uneven walkways and steep, uphill climb from the dock to the main level. An accessible shuttle runs between the dock and prison building for those unable to walk the ¼-mile (400m) climb. For more information visit www.parksconservancy. org/visit/alcatraz/index.asp and www.nps.gov/alcatraz.

Alcatraz

Pier 33; information tel: 561-4926, tickets tel: 981-7625; tickets and tours: www. alcatrazcruises.com; daily; entrance charge; metro: F to The Embarcadero and Bay Street; bus: 10; map p.135 C4

---

government to adopt a policy of Indian self-determination. Lasting markers of the occupation include graffiti, and the shell of the warden's house that was destroyed by a fire in 1970. The group was helpless to extinguish the blaze as only a few weeks before, the government had cut off their only water source.

Getting to Alcatraz

The most visited attraction in San Francisco, Alcatraz is open daily and easily accessible. Leaving from Pier 33, **Hornblower Cruises** run the ferry service to the island. All tickets can be purchased online, by phone, or at the ticket office at Pier 33 *(see box, above, for more details)*. Ferries leave roughly every half hour from 9am to

3.55pm and take about 15 minutes each way. Visitors may take any return ferry until 6.15pm. It is advised to allow at least 2½ hours for the entire trip to get the full experience.

Tickets are pricey ($26 for adults, $16 for kids 5–11, kids under 5 are free), but cover the transit cost and the 45-minute cellhouse audio tour, which is available at Pier 33 and at the dock at Alcatraz. Night Tours are also available ($19.50–33) Thursday through Monday and depart at 5.55pm and 6.45pm. It includes a narrated boat tour around the island, guided island tours, and a variety of

---

Below: cells at the former ultimate maximum-security prison.

Bars and Cafés

According to at least one study, residents of San Francisco spend more per capita on alcohol than any other urbanites in the US. That figure would hardly surprise locals – with mixologist-minded cocktail lounges, hipster dives, Irish pubs, and all manner of low-key neighborhood watering holes, San Francisco is clearly a city that enjoys a good buzz. It also loves its café culture; the importance of artisan coffee micro-roasting, organic teas, and ready Wi-Fi access should not be underestimated. The line between cafés and restaurants, or bars and clubs, is often blurry, so see also *Food and Drink, p.54*, *Nightlife, p.94*, and *Restaurants, p.102*.

Fisherman's Wharf

Fiddler's Green
1333 Columbus Avenue; tel: 441-9758; daily 9.30am–2am; metro: F to Fisherman's Wharf; bus: 10, 30, 47; cable car: Powell-Hyde, Powell-Mason; map p.134 B4
Over shepherd's pie and pints of Guinness, Irish natives mix freely with tourists in this unassuming little bar. The reasonably priced breakfasts are cause enough to come by and escape the area's mayhem.

North Beach, Telegraph Hill, and Russian Hill

Café Brioche
201 Columbus Avenue; tel: 822-2287; Mon–Sat 7am–8pm; bus: 9X, 30, 41, 45; map p.135 C2
Enjoy an expertly made espresso drink with one of Brioche's pastries or sandwiches, made fresh in their South San Francisco bakery. The floor-to-ceiling windows let in plenty of light, but its warmth comes directly from the friendly service. Cash only.

Caffe Trieste
601 Vallejo Street; tel: 392-6739; www.caffetrieste.com; Fri–Sat 6.30am–midnight, Sun–Thur 6.30am–11pm; bus: 9X, 30X, 45, 41; map p.135 C3
Its rust-colored interior is reminiscent of 1950s North Beach, as are the locals who take up residence at most of the café's small round tables. Live music fills the space on Saturdays, and the beer and wine selection keep Trieste full late into the evening. Cash only.

Mario's Bohemian Cigar Store
566 Columbus Avenue; tel: 362-0536; daily 10am–11pm; bus: 9X, 30, 45, 41; map p.134 C3
Inside this small slice of a

Below: Vesuvio's highly distinctive signage.

café, Mario's serves up delicious small pizzas and baked focaccia sandwiches, as well as espressos, beer, and wine.

San Francisco Art Institute Café
800 Chestnut Street; tel: 749-4567; www.sfai.edu; Sept–May Mon–Thur 8.30am–5pm, Fri until 4pm, June–Aug 9am–2pm; bus: 30; cable car: Powell-Hyde, Powell-Mason; map p.134 B3
Perched on top of the school, this casual café with organic coffee and teas has spectacular views of the Golden Gate, Alcatraz, Angel Island, and the East Bay.

Spec's 12 Adler Museum Café
12 William Saroyan Place, off Columbus Avenue; tel: 421-4112; Mon–Fri 4.30pm–2am, Sat–Sun 5pm–2am; bus: 9X, 30, 41, 45; map p.135 C2
Since the 1940s, seamen have been leaving behind salty trinkets from their adventures, giving Spec's the right to call itself a museum. Popular with bohemians, Beats, and hippies since it opened, Spec's is a friendly place full of character. Cash only.

Left: alfresco café culture in North Beach.

Chinatown

Li Po Cocktail Lounge

916 Grant Avenue; tel: 982-0072; daily 2pm–2am; bus: 1, 12, 30, 45; map p.134 C2

Passing through the big red doors, patrons will not be surprised to learn that this funky dive bar use to be an opium den. Named for the famous Chinese poet, Li Po is a favorite haunt of both locals and tourists. Cash only.

Union Square and Financial District

Blue Bottle Co. Mint Plaza Café

66 Mint Street; tel: 495-3394; http://bluebottlecoffee.net; Mon–Fri 7am–7pm, Sat 8am–6pm, Sun 8am–4pm; bus: 5, 21, 27, 31; cable car: Powell-Hyde, Powell-Mason; map p.139 C4

Coffee connoisseurs adore this airy, high-ceilinged café, which takes freshness and small-batch roasting to the extreme. Try single-origin espresso drinks or brewed coffee from a halogen-powered siphon bar, paired with small tasty sandwiches.

Bourbon and Branch

501 Jones Street; tel: 346-1735; www.bourbonandbranch.com; daily 5pm–3am; bus: 2, 3, 27, 76; map p.134 B1

Full of legends, **Caffe Trieste** is believed to be the first place to serve espresso on the west coast. It was opened in 1956 by an Italian émigré who wanted to bring the tastes and smells of Italy to his adopted home. It is also thought to be where Frances Ford Coppola penned *The Godfather*.

Stella

446 Columbus Avenue; tel: 986-2914; www.stellapastry.com; Mon–Thur 7.30am–7pm, Fri–Sat 7.30am–midnight, Sun 8.30am–7pm; bus: 9X, 30, 39, 41, 45; map p.134 C3

Few pastries hold a candle to Stella's light, buttery, and delicate concoctions. With an ample espresso machine and cozy tables, this tiny store makes savoring these Italian delicacies a real treat.

Tosca

242 Columbus Avenue; tel: 986-9651; www.toscacafesf.com; Tue–Sun 5pm–2am; bus: 9X, 30, 41, 45; map p.134 C3

Classy and harking back to the jazz era, Tosca's red vinyl booths and long elegant bar attracts self-styled bohemians and yuppies alike. Knowledgeable bartenders mix up drinks including the house coffee and brandy. Hunter S. Thompson once broke his arm here pirouetting off the bar.

Vesuvio

255 Columbus Avenue; tel: 362-3370; www.vesuvio.com; daily 6am–2am; bus: 9X, 30, 45, 41; map p.134 C3

The best time to go to Vesuvio is late in the day, when locals gather to enjoy an afternoon drink or espresso. The narrow, two-story bar is rich in literary history, complete with pictures of James Joyce and the voice of Jack Kerouac booming over the loudspeakers.

Below: wine time at Café de la Presse *(see p.36)*.

Legend has it that this historic San Francisco hotel bar was carved from a single redwood tree. Redesigned by Philippe Starck, it still retains its elegance, but now with a modern twist. Well-heeled beauties sip their cocktails while digital art lights up plasma screens.

Sears Fine Food
439 Powell Street; tel: 986-0700; www.searsfinefood.com; daily 6.30am–10pm; BART and metro: all lines to Powell; bus: 2, 30, 38, 45; cable car: Powell-Hyde, Powell-Mason; map p.134 C1
The Swedish pancakes are the legend here, but the rest of the menu is tasty as well, from gourmet burgers to fresh seafood. Daily brunch until 3pm.

SoMa and Civic Center

21st Amendment
563 2nd Street; tel: 369-0900; www.21st-amendment.com; Mon–Sat 11.30am–2am, Sun 10am–2am; metro: N to 2nd and King; bus: 10, 12, 30, 45, 76; map p.139 E4
With a small beer garden and a lofted, industrial interior, there is plenty of space for beer and baseball enthusiasts to enjoy the charms of this famed SoMa brewery. It also serves excellent pub food made from seasonal and local ingredients.

Hemlock Tavern
1131 Polk Street; tel: 923-0923; www.hemlocktavern.com; daily 4pm–2am; bus: 1, 2, 19, 47, 49; map p.134 B1
Cavernous and selling hot peanuts for $1 a bag, this is the natural home for the hipsters who haunt Polk Gulch. Live music in the back room and the outdoor heated smoking lounge, complete with tables and barstools, are extra bonuses.

A dark, sultry speakeasy without signage (look for the door below the Anti-Saloon League sign), where masterfully mixed libations are poured. Passwords 'books' or 'cigar' get you into the 'Library' and 'Russel's Room'; reservations are required for the main bar.

Café de la Presse
352 Grant Avenue; tel: 398-2680; www.cafedelapresse. com; Mon–Thur 7.30am–9.30pm, Fri 7.30am–10pm, Sat–Sun 8am–10pm; bus: 2, 9X, 30, 45; map p.135 C1
Join the European literati at this charming French café's

sidewalk tables for excellent bistro fare, shots of espresso and glasses of beer or French and Spanish wine. Inside, you can buy international magazines and newspapers. Free Wi-Fi.

Edinburgh Castle
950 Geary Street; tel: 885-4074; www.castlenews.com; daily 5pm–2am; bus: 2, 3, 4, 19, 27; map p.134 B1
A cultural gem in the gritty Tenderloin, this Scottish-run bar hosts local bands and poetry readings upstairs, has a pool table and dart board downstairs, is packed on quiz nights, and has a fantastic Scotch inventory to go with the best fish and chips in the city (served until 11pm), delivered from around the corner.

Redwood Room at the Clift Hotel
495 Geary Street; tel: 929-2372; www.clifthotel.com; Sun–Thur 5pm–2am, Fri–Sat 4pm–2am; BART and metro: all lines to Powell; metro: F, J, K, L, M, N, T to Powell; bus: 2, 3, 9X, 76; map p.134 C1

> Likened to Ferlinghetti's City Lights during the 1950's, the **Edinburgh Castle** is considered the current hub of underground literature in San Francisco. Hosting regular readings and the city's annual festival, **Litquake**, it attracts aspiring writers, artists and musicians, alongside literary luminaries such as Irvine Welsh.

MOMA Caffé Museo
151 3rd Street; tel: 357-4000; www.sfmoma.org; Mon–Sun 10am–6pm, Thur until 9pm, closed Wed; BART and metro: all lines to Montgomery; bus: 5, 9X, 30, 45, 71; map p.139 D4

Accessible from the street, the museum's café is a destination in its own right. Stylish and airy, with plenty of sidewalk seating, it serves up coffee, beer, wine, and light Italian-inspired fare.

Paragon
701 2nd Street; tel: 537-9020; www.paragonrestaurant.com; Mon–Fri 11.30am–2pm, 5.30–10pm, Sat 5.30–10pm; metro: N to 2nd and King; bus: 10, 30, 45, 76; map p.139 E4

Sit at the polished bar, or at the outside tables on warm evenings, and order from the little black book of a bar menu. Inside, patrons are treated to a list of house cocktails, classic standbys, an impressive collection of spirits, and unmissable small plates.

Nob Hill

Amelie
1754 Polk Street; tel: 292-6916; www.ameliesf.com; daily 6pm–2am; bus: 1, 12, 19, 27; map p.134 B2

This sultry, crimson-walled wine bar features a French-heavy menu, stylish clientele, and an inviting atmosphere.

Nook Café
1500 Hyde Street; tel: 447-4100; www.nookcafe.com; Mon–Fri 7am–10.30pm, Sat 8am–10.30pm, Sun 8am–9pm; cable car: Powell-Hyde; bus: 19, 27; map p.134 C2

Sunny café by day, cozy candlelit wine bar by night, this low-key spot on the cable car line offers fresh, flavorful sandwiches and great happy hour deals, like $3 glasses of wine.

Top of the Mark
1 Nob Hill; tel: 616-6916; www.topofthemark.com; Mon–Thur 6.30am–11.30pm, Fri–Sat 6.30am–12.30am, Sun 10am–10pm; bus: 1; cable car: California; map p.134 C1

To get the authentic Nob Hill experience, come and sip cocktails in this most elegant of bars. With spectacular views overlooking all of San Francisco, it makes any visitor feel like a true baron.

Tunnel Top
601 Bush Street; tel: 986-8900; Mon–Sat 5pm–2am; bus: 2, 30, 45, 76; cable car: California; map p.134 C1

Despite its shady exterior, this bar, hidden appropriately on top of the Stockton tunnel, is full of thriving thirtysomethings listening to the sounds of live DJ's and sipping very reasonably priced drinks.

Central Neighborhoods

Arlequin To Go
384 Hayes Street; tel: 626-1211; Mon–Fri 8am–8pm, Sat 9am–7pm, Sun 9am–6pm; metro: F to Market Street and Van Ness Avenue; bus: 9, 21, 47, 49, 66; map p.138 A3

Do not let the name fool you: this small café opens up to a wide, lush garden patio in the back, and is a great place to enjoy top quality café food (sandwiches, salads, burgers) with espresso or a glass of wine.

Bus Stop
1901 Union Street; tel: 567-6905; Mon–Fri 10am–2am, Sat–Sun 9am–2am; bus: 22, 41, 45; map p.134 A2

In the heart of Cow Hollow, this sports bar quickly fills up with twenty- and thirtysomethings drinking well poured drinks and affordable beer while watching sports and each other.

Cav Wine Bar and Kitchen
1666 Market Street; tel: 437-1770; www.cavwinebar.com; Mon–Thur 5–11pm, Fri–Sat 5pm–midnight; metro: all lines to Van Ness; bus: 6, 7, 71; map p.138 B3

Sit at the sleek zinc bar alongside sleek professionals and connoisseurs enjoying Cav's exceptional 300-plus wine list.

Crissy Café
603 Mason Street; tel: 561-7690; www.parksconservancy.org; daily 9am–5pm; bus: 28, 29, 76; map p.132 C3

Enjoy a latte or a grilled sandwich made from local and organic ingredients while overlooking the newly restored Crissy Field. Sunny weekends can be particularly busy.

Noc Noc
557 Haight Street; tel: 861-5811; www.nocnocs.com; daily

Below: locals aren't shy about lingering over coffee.

37

5pm–2am; bus: 6, 7, 22, 71; map p.137 E2

The highly stylized interior (aboriginal/Flintstones-esque circa 1986) attracts an easy-going, fun-loving crowd. With wine, sake, and 18 beers to choose from, it can be standing room only on weekends.

Haight-Ashbury and Golden Gate Park

The Alembic
1725 Haight Street; tel: 666-0822; www.alembicbar.com; daily noon–2am; bus: 7, 71; map p.137 C2

One of the best cocktails bars in the city, with exceptional drinks, speakeasy-style decor, and delicious Southern-infused food.

Cole Valley Café
701 Cole Street; tel 668-5282; www.colevalleycafe.com; daily 6.30am–8.30pm; metro: N to Cole and Carl; bus: 6, 33, 37, 43, 71; map p.137 C2

For neighborhood denizens and tourists alike, this sunny place serves up coffee and light café fare with colorful, hippie flair.

Hobson's Choice
1601 Haight Street; tel: 621-5859; www.hobsonschoice.com; Mon–Fri 2pm–2am, Sat–Sun noon–2am; metro: N to Haight Street; bus: 6, 33, 37, 43, 71; map p.137 D2

Many San Franciscan cafés have wireless internet access, and a few have online computers. To log in from your own laptop, ask at the register for the network's password. The public libraries (www.sfpl.lib.ca.us) also have access to the Internet, as do the ubiquitous Starbucks, which are particularly concentrated in the Financial District.

Populated by good-looking young people lounging on couches, amid dripping chandeliers, red walls, and Victorian flair, drinking glasses of rum-infused punch.

Magnolia
1398 Haight Street; tel: 864-PINT; www.magnoliapub.com; Mon–Thur noon–midnight, Fri noon–1am, Sat 10am–1am, Sun 10am–midnight; bus: 6, 7, 33, 37, 43; map p.137 D2

If the Grateful Dead opened a brewpub, this would be it. Despite the great food and relaxed atmosphere, it is Magnolia's magnificent drafts, which routinely change and are served in glasses designed to best draw out their qualities, that steal the show.

Pork Store Café
1451 Haight Street; tel: 864-6981; www.porkstorecafe.com; Mon–Fri 7am–3.30pm, Sat–Sun 8am–4pm; bus: 6, 7, 33, 37, 71; map p.137 D2

First opened in 1916 as a butcher shop, the Pork Store is now a classic diner, with a good lunch but an epic breakfast. Window seats provide amusing people-watching in the Haight; avoid on the crowded weekends.

Rosamunde Sausage Grill
545 Haight Street; tel: 437-6851; www.rosamundesausagegrill.com; daily 11.30am–10pm; bus: 6, 7, 22, 71; map p.137 E2

Not much happens here besides sausage, but that is enough. With unique and mouth-watering flavors, such as wild boar, duck, chicken cherry, smoked pork, and spicy vegan, this is a great spot to grab a quick bite to eat.

Zazie
941 Cole Street; tel: 564-5332; www.zaziesf.com; Mon–Fri 8am–2.30pm, Sat–Sun 9am–3pm, Sun–Thur 5.30–9.30pm, Fri–Sat 5.30–10pm; metro: N to Carl and Cole; bus: 6, 37, 43; map p.137 D1

This charming, well-priced, local bistro-cum-café offers plenty of outdoor seating. Standouts among a French-influenced menu are the deservedly popular breakfasts and brunches.

Below: the home-grown drinking options are numerous: produce from the nearby wine country, locally brewed beer, and the martini, which some claim was first mixed in San Francisco.

Mission and Castro

Café Flore
2298 Market Street; tel: 621-8579; www.cafeflore.com; daily 7am–2am, kitchen closes at 10pm; metro: F, K, L, M, T to Castro; bus: 24, 22, 37; map p.137 E1
Café Flore has everything you could need or want in a café: a full bar, a well-used espresso machine, a light bistro menu, lush garden seating and an airy interior. Its atmosphere encourages its patrons to stay and chat, or quietly read.

Casanova Lounge
527 Valencia Street; tel: 863-9328; www.casanovasf.com; daily 4pm–2am; bus: 14, 22, 33, 49, 53; map p.138 B1
A rotating lineup of varied DJ's keep tattooed hipsters happy as they lounge beneath velvet nude paintings in this low-lit Mission hotspot. Cash only.

Dolores Park Café
501 Dolores Street; tel: 621-2936; www.doloresparkcafe.org; Sat–Thur 7am–8pm, Fri 7am–10pm; metro: J to Church and 18th streets; bus: 22, 26, 33; map p.138 A1
With wide windows opening on to the sunny Dolores Park, this café, patronized by the requisite strollers, dog walkers, and Mission hipsters in tight black jeans, is obviously a favorite at this neighborhood crossroads.

Laszlo Bar
2534 Mission Street; tel: 648-7600; www.foreigncinema.com/laszlo; Tue–Sun 6pm–2am; bus: 14, 26, 49
Attached to the Foreign Cinema, Laszlo has high ceilings and a modern interior with movies continuously playing on the back wall. Its mixed crowd represents Foreign Cinema's respectability and Mission Street's hipster grunginess. Nightly DJ's add to the experience.

Ritual Coffee Roasters
1026 Valencia Street; tel: 641-

Above: a Mexican lunch in the Haight.

1024; www.ritualroasters.com; Mon–Fri 6am–10pm, Sat 7am–10pm, Sun 7am–9pm; bus: 14, 26, 49
From the square tables in the front to the lounge-like couches in the rear, it is usually difficult to find a seat in this epicenter of Mission trendiness. Although the selection of coffee, teas, and pastries is enticement enough to give it a try. Free Wi-Fi.

Zeitgeist
199 Valencia Street; tel: 255-7505; daily 9am–2am; metro: all lines to Van Ness; bus: 14, 26, 37, 49; map p.138 A2
Everyone is welcome at this punk/biker bar. Its stark interior studded with beer kegs and playing loud punk rock, gives way to a beer garden. At its long communal tables, bike messengers mix with thirtysomething punk types, twentysomething hipsters and rocker girls.

Around San Francisco

Connecticut Yankee
100 Connecticut Street; tel: 552-4440; www.theyankee.com; Mon–Sat 11am–2am, Sun 10am–2am; bus: 10, 19, 22; map p.139 D1

Built as a saloon in 1907, it has been serving Potrero Hill for 100 years. Today, locals gather in the beer garden to enjoy the bar's menu during the day, or inside where live music is played most nights.

Java Beach Café
1396 La Playa Street; tel: 665-5282; www.javabeachcafe.com; Mon–Fri 5.30am–11pm, Sat–Sun 6am–11pm; metro: N to Ocean Beach; bus: 18
Sitting on the Great Highway facing the Pacific Ocean, this small café is filled with surfers and locals who would be at home near any California beach. It is perfect for lunch or breakfast on a sunny day, or for an espresso to warm up when the fog rolls in.

Park Chalet
1000 Great Highway, off John F. Kennedy Drive; tel: 386-8439; www.beachchalet.com; Mon–Thur noon–9pm, Fri–Sat noon–11pm, Sun 10am–9pm; bus: 5, 18, 31, 38
Located at the western end of Golden Gate Park, the Park Chalet spills out into the park's greenery with outdoor seating, live music, house-brewed beer, a full bar, flatbread pizzas, and BBQ specialties.

Children

One of the great things about traveling with children in San Francisco is that many of the city's attractions are suitable for people of all ages. A stroll across the Golden Gate Bridge, exploring the markets of Chinatown, cresting a hill aboard a cable car, or zigzagging down legendary Lombard Street are all crowd pleasers for young and old alike. San Francisco is a very kid-friendly city with an abundance of state-of-the-art playgrounds, restaurants that offer children's menus (and often crayons), bathrooms equipped with changing tables for babies, and lots of wide open spaces for running around.

Attractions

ALCATRAZ

While older kids will appreciate the excellent audio tour, little ones might be spooked, but everyone will enjoy the ferry trip across the bay.

SEE ALSO ALCATRAZ, P.32–3

FISHERMAN'S WHARF

Pier 39 is a major tourist attraction, second only in California to Disneyland. Despite the kitsch, children will enjoy visiting the fabled sea lions on the north side of Pier 39 near K dock. For the very young, the vintage carousel delights. The following attractions found here are also popular with kids:

Aquarium of the Bay
Pier 39; tel: 623-5301; www.aquariumofthebay.com; June–Aug daily 9am–8pm, Sept–May Mon–Fri 10am–6pm, Sat–Sun 10am–7pm; entrance charge; metro: F to The Embarcadero and Beach Street; bus: 10, 47; map p.134 C4

Kids of all ages are fascinated by sharks and other marine life displayed here. Moving walkways through clear tunnels give you a diver's-eye view of the Bay.

Jeremiah O'Brien
Liberty Ship
Pier 45; tel: 544-0100; www.ssjeremiahobrien.com; daily 10am–4pm; entrance charge; metro: F to Jefferson and Taylor streets; bus: 10, 30, 47; cable car: Powell-Mason; map p.134 B4

Tour the engine room and barracks of this faithfully restored ship that saw service in World War II.

Musèe Mèchanique
Pier 45 Shed A; tel: 346-2000; www.museemechanique.org; Mon–Fri 10am–7pm, Sat–Sun 10am–8pm; free; metro: F to Jefferson and Taylor streets; bus: 10, 30, 47; cable car: Powell-Mason; map p.134 B4

Bring a pocket full of change to play antique penny-arcade games assembled at this quirky collection of more than 300 vintage mechanical games and toys, including

---

Most hotels allow children to stay in parents' rooms at no additional charge (though sometimes there is an age limit) and will provide a rollaway bed or portable crib as needed.

Below: the city reflected in Zeum's facade.

Left: under the sea at the Aquarium of the Bay.

Childcare

Most hotel concierges can arrange for childcare or recommend a babysitting service. Reputable services include:

American ChildCare Service
Tel: 285-2300; www.american childcare.com ($20 per hour; 4 hour minimum)

The Core Group
Tel: 206-9046; www.thecore group.org ($15–$20 per hour)

Town & Country Resources
Tel: 567-0956 or 800-398-8810; www.tandcr.com ($20 per hour; 4 hour minimum)

Family Dining

Chow
215 Church Street; tel: 552-2469; www.chowfoodbar.com; $$; Sun–Thur 8am–11pm, Fri–Sat 8am–midnight; metro: F, J, K, L, M, T to Church; bus: 22, 37; map p.138 A2

Comfort food with a pedigree, in a cozy, welcoming atmosphere. Choose from a superb roasted chicken, pork chops, macaroni and cheese, chicken pot pie, spaghetti and meatballs, noodle dishes, salads, and daily specials. Some dishes can be ordered in

antique slot machines, hand-cranked music boxes, and coin-operated pianos.

The Wax Museum
145 Jefferson Street; tel: 885-4834; www.waxmuseum.com; daily 10am–9pm; entrance charge; metro: F to Jefferson and Taylor streets; bus: 10, 47; map p.134 B4

The creepy cast of some 200 wax figures includes celebrities and political figures.

YERBA BUENA GARDENS AND CENTER FOR THE ARTS

Beautiful gardens, outdoor events, a theater, bowling alley, art gallery, vintage carousel, ice skating rink, and playground are all part of this complex that also includes:

Zeum
221 Fourth Street; tel: 820-3320; www.zeum.org; Wed–Fri 1–5pm, Sat–Sun 11am–5pm; entrance charge; BART: to Powell; metro: all lines to Powell; bus: 12, 14, 30, 45, 76; map p.139 D4

At this hands-on multimedia arts and technology museum, geared toward older kids and teenagers, learn about animation, digital technology, and electronic

media, and create movies, music, and art. The Metreon next door houses restaurants, an IMAX theatre, and 15 movie screens.

SEE ALSO PARKS AND GARDENS, P.98

AROUND SAN FRANCISCO
San Francisco Zoo
1 Zoo Road; tel: 753-7080; www.sfzoo.org; Mid-Mar–Oct 31 daily 10am–5pm, Nov 1–mid-Mar daily 10am–4pm; entrance charge; metro: L to SF Zoo; bus: 18, 23

The zoo is home to some 700 animals in 100 acres (40 hectares) on the edge of the Pacific. The African Savannah and Grizzly Gulch are two of the newer habitats. The Lemur Forest and big cats remain perennial favorites. Also here is a Children's Zoo and an historic miniature steam train.

Average price for a three-course meal and a half-bottle of house wine for the parents:

$$$$	more than $100
$$$	$50–$100
$$	$25–$50
$	less than $25

Below: giraffes watch their visitors at San Francisco Zoo.

smaller portions. Also at: Park Chow; 1240 Ninth Avenue; tel: 665-9912; $$; Sun–Thur 8am–10pm, Fri–Sat 8am–11pm; metro: N to 9th Avenue; map p.136 B1.

Giorgio's Pizzeria
151 Clement Street; tel: 668-1266; www.giorgiospizza.com; $; Mon–Thur 11am–10pm, Fri–Sat 11am–11pm, Sun 11am–9pm; bus: 1, 2, 3, 4; map p.136 B4

A San Francisco favorite for pizza and calzones, this laid-back old-school Italian atmosphere includes red-and-white checkered vinyl tablecloths and a jukebox in the back. Staff are friendly and very accustomed to dealing with children. On Wednesday from 4–6pm, children can make their own mini pizzas with some coaching from the staff during the weekly 'Kids' Happy Hour.'

Health and Necessities

Walgreens, a discount drug-store chain, is ubiquitous in San Francisco. Here you will find everything from diapers and sweatshirts to sunscreen and film. Many also have a limited grocery selection and children's toys.

If a child accidentally swallows something that could cause harm, call the State Poison Control hotline (tel: 800-876-4766).
SEE ALSO ESSENTIALS, P.49

Museums

Cartoon Art Museum
655 Mission Street; tel: 227-8666; www.cartoonart.org; Tue–Sun 11am–5pm; entrance charge, under 6 free, 1st Tue of month 'Pay What You Wish Day'; BART and metro: all lines to Montgomery; bus: 9, 14, 30, 45, 71; map p.135 D1

A museum dedicated to the cartoon as art form. Exhibits range from illustrators like Edward Gorey and Charles Shultz to political satirists and local talents like Keith Knight and Paul Madonna.
SEE ALSO MUSEUMS AND GALLERIES, P.84

Exploratorium
3601 Lyon Street; tel: 561-0360; www.exploratorium.edu; Tue–Sun 10am–5pm; entrance charge, under 4 free, 1st Wed of month free; bus: 28, 30, 43; map p.133 D3

Located inside the landmark Palace of Fine Arts building, this cutting-edge museum offers more than 650 hands-on science, technology, art, nature, and human perception exhibits, including the popular Tactile Dome, a pitch-black labyrinth navigated by touch. Even kids who bore easily will find something to be mesmerized with here.
SEE ALSO MUSEUMS AND GALLERIES, P.87

Randall Museum
199 Museum Way; tel: 554-9600; www.randallmuseum.org; Tue–Sat 10am–5pm; donation suggested; metro: F, K, L, M, T to Castro; bus: 24; map p.137 E1

A small, worthwhile gem in Corona Heights. Appreciated by locals but often over-looked by visitors, it includes a petting zoo and drop-in arts and crafts classes.
SEE ALSO MUSEUMS AND GALLERIES, P.88

Outdoors

The consistently mild climate in San Francisco lends itself to a myriad of outdoor activities, from flying kites at Ocean Beach, to renting bikes and discovering the treasures of Golden Gate Park, to simply taking an urban hike and conquering some of the city's renowned hills.
SEE ALSO PARKS AND GARDENS, P.98–101; WALKS AND VIEWS, P.124–9

GOLDEN GATE PARK
Bordered by Fulton Street, Lincoln Way, Great Highway and Stanyan Street; tel: 831-2700; metro: N to Irving Street and 9th Avenue; bus: 7,18, 21, 44, 71; map p.136–7

Though they may not be particularly interested in the art collection at the de Young Museum, for kids, this 1,017-acre (412-hectare) park is a goldmine. A vintage 1912 carousel stands adjacent to the large, recently refurbished **Koret Children's Corner** playground on the southeast side. Due west, a walking path with stone bridges and weeping willows encircles picturesque **Stow Lake** and leads to a waterfall on top of **Strawberry Hill**. At the boat-house, pedal boats can be rented for a leisurely tour of the lake, as well as bikes and inline skates.

Below: the vintage carousel at Yerba Buena Gardens.

In the northeast corner, the **Conservatory of Flowers** is a magnificent wood and glass greenhouse that houses rare tropical plants, orchids, and trees, including carnivorous flora, always a hit with kids. Golden Gate Park is also home to **Strybing Arboretum** – an amazing 55-acre (22-hectare) botanical garden (children love the succulent garden and the teaching garden) – as well as a herd of buffalo, two windmills, a chain of lakes, horse stables, tennis and bocce courts.

OCEAN BEACH
Great Highway; tel: 556-8371; free; metro: N to Ocean Beach; bus: 5, 18, 31
San Francisco's largest beach, 3 miles (5km) of sand and wild coastline stretching south from the Cliff House. It is not a place for swimming: tides and currents are powerfully strong and the water is very cold, but the beach is perfect for kids to run around, build sandcastles, and have picnics.

Stores

A few areas stand out when shopping for kids. In Laurel Heights, **Sacramento Street**, between Presidio Avenue and Spruce Street, is home to stylish baby boutiques as well as stores for children's furnishings, shoes, educational toys, and unique clothing. Look out for **Snippety Crickets**, a hair salon for kids. A block south on California Street, some of the big chains, such as **Gap Kids**, **Gymboree**, and **Stride Rite**, are found at Laurel Village. **Union Street** in Cow Hollow,

Some good Internet resources for family travel are www.familytravelforum.com and www.familytravelnetwork.com.

Above: enjoying the playground at Golden Gate Park.

24th Street in Noe Valley and **Chestnut Street** in the Marina are also good spots to find cool indie stores for kids.
The Ark
3845 24th Street; tel: 821-1257; www.thearktoys.com; daily 10am–7pm; metro: J to Church and 24th streets; bus: 24, 48
3325 Sacramento Street; tel: 440-8697; daily 10am–7pm; bus 1, 3, 4, 43; map p.133 D1
Two locations of this family-owned business offer high-quality, well-crafted wooden and classic toys, games and crafts designed to spark the imagination.
Citikids
152 Clement Street; tel: 752-3837; www.citikids.com; Mon–Sat 10am–6pm, Sun 11am–5pm; bus: 2; map p.136 B4
A children's department store, geared mostly toward babies and toddlers. A large selection of gear including strollers, car seats, highchairs, and boosters, plus clothing, furniture, books, toys, and other necessities.

Cover to Cover Booksellers
1307 Castro Street; tel: 282-8080; http://covertocover.book sense.com; Mon–Sat 10am–9pm, Sun 10am–6pm; bus: 24, 48, metro: J to Church and 24th streets
A cozy neighborhood bookstore that holds signings by well-known authors.
Gamescape
333 Divisadero Street; tel: 621-4263; www.gamescapesf.net; Mon–Sat 10am–7pm, Sun 11am–5pm; bus: 6, 7, 24, 71; map p.137 E2
An encyclopedic collection of board, card, role-playing, and miniature games.
Kids Only
1608 Haight Street; tel: 552-5445; Mon–Fri 10.30am–6.30pm, Sat 10am–6pm, Sun 11am–5pm; bus: 6, 7, 71; map p.137 D2
Looking for a Johnny Cash-inspired onesie reading 'Crawl the Line', or a mini tutu? This eclectic little store is full of offbeat apparel, along with blankets and slings.

Churches

San Francisco's religious structures and the services they host are a varied mix of the traditional and unconventional. Sts Peter and Paul Church in North Beach is an old-fashioned favorite for Roman Catholic Italian weddings, while the progressive Glide Memorial United Methodist Church attracts boisterous crowds to soul-raising Sunday Celebrations, and Buddha's Universal Church is the largest Buddhist Church is the US. Still other places of worship offer intimate temples, soaring cupolas, and even labyrinths for meditative walking. Check service schedules ahead of time to avoid stumbling into one in progress.

North Beach, Telegraph Hill, and Russian Hill

Sts Peter and Paul Church

666 Filbert Street; tel: 421-0809; www.stspeterpaul.san francisco.ca.us/church; Sun–Fri 7.30am–4pm, Sat 7.30am–6pm; free; bus: 30, 39, 41, 45; map p.134 C3

Crowning Washington Square with its Romanesque facade and frothy twin spires, this Catholic church, built in 1924, is popular for traditional Italian weddings. Baseball legend Joe DiMaggio and Marilyn Monroe even had their wedding photos snapped here, although their ceremony actually took place at City Hall.

Chinatown

Buddha's Universal Church

720 Washington Street; tel: 982-6116; www.bucsf.com; call for public tours; free; bus: 1, 9X, 30, 41; map p.135 C2

The largest Buddhist church in the US, filled with gold leaf and mosaic tiles, an altar resembling the ship of the Dharma, and a rooftop garden and terrace.

Above: the soaring spires of Sts Peter and Paul Church.

Old St Mary's Church

660 California Street; tel: 288-3800; www.oldsaintmarys.org; Mon–Fri 7am–4.30pm, Sat 10am–6pm, Sun 8.30am–1pm; free; bus: 1, 30; cable car: California; map p.135 C2

This Paulist-led parish church was San Francisco's Catholic cathedral for most of the second half of the 19th century, until its location amidst ill-reputed neighbors (note the inscription under the clock reading 'Son Observe the Time and Fly from Evil') led to a new cathedral being built at a better-respected address.

Tien Hau Temple

125 Waverly Place; Mon–Sun 10am–4pm; donation suggested; bus: 1, 9X, 30, 45; cable car: California; map p.135 C2

Climb to the third floor to reach this historic temple dedicated to the Queen of the Heavens and Goddess of the Seven Seas (said to protect travelers, sailors, artists, and prostitutes), where red paper lanterns flood the ceiling and incense fills the air.

Union Square and Financial District

Glide Memorial Methodist Church

330 Ellis Street; tel: 674-6000; www.glide.org; service Sun 9am and 11am; free; BART and metro: all lines to Powell; bus: 27, 31, 38; map p.138 C4

In the thick of the Tenderloin, Reverend Cecil Williams and his devoted staff and volunteers have cared for the poor and homeless for more than 40 years. Sunday Celebrations feature the 100-member Glide Ensemble singing jazz, blues, gospel, and spirituals.

Left: the intricate bronze doors at Grace Cathedral.

cupola marked with a giant golden cross. Beneath, up to 2,400 worshippers flank three sides of the altar. Music pipes from a fine Fratelli Ruffatti organ from Padua, Italy, and above the altar a large, suspended sculpture by Richard Lippold shimmers with reflected light.

St John Coltrane African Orthodox Church
1286 Fillmore Street; tel: 673-7144; www.coltranechurch.org; Sun service noon; free; bus: 22, 31; map p.137 E4
This church – perhaps the world's only one dedicated to a jazz musician – draws a diverse crowd of Christians, jazz lovers, and novelty-seekers to its three-hour Sunday services, which though untraditional, express heartfelt sentiments.

Mission and Castro
Misión San Francisco de Asís (Mission Dolores)
3321 16th Street; tel: 621-8203; www.missiondolores.org; Mon–Sun 9am–4pm; donation suggested; metro: F, K, L, M, T to Church, J to 16th and Church streets; bus: 22, 37; map p.138 A1
Founded in 1776 by Spanish missionary Father Junipero Serra, Misión San Francisco de Asís (commonly referred to as 'Mission Dolores') is San Francisco's oldest intact building. Carved Mexican altars stand at the front of a narrow, elongated adobe church; above, a restored ceiling is decorated with bright Ohlone Indian designs. The peaceful cemetery doubles as a blooming garden, where more than 5,000 Native Americans are buried, as well as famed namesakes of city streets, such as the first Mexican governor, Luis Antonio Arguello.

On the first Sunday of October, Sicilian parishioners from Sts Peter and Paul Church conduct a procession honoring Maria Santissima del Lume (Mary, Most Holy Mother of Light). They head along Columbus Avenue down to Fisherman's Wharf for the traditional Blessing of the Fleet.

Nob Hill
Grace Cathedral
1100 California Street; tel: 749-6300; www.gracecathedral.org; free; Mon–Fri 7am–6pm, Sat 8am–6pm, Sun 8am–7pm; free; bus: 1, 27; cable car: California; map p.134 B1
The stately Episcopal Grace Cathedral sits on land gifted by the Charles Crocker family. Completed in 1964, the Gothic-style church (resembling Paris' Notre Dame) features famed east entrance doors that are gilded bronze replicas of Lorenzo Ghiberti's 15th-century *Gates of Paradise*, sculpted for the Baptistery in Florence. Two winding labyrinths, one inside of limestone, and one outside of terrazzo stone, provide paths for traditional meditative walking.

Central Neighborhoods
Cathedral of St Mary of the Assumption (St Mary's Cathedral)
1111 Gough Street; tel: 567-2020; www.stmarycathedralsf.org; Mon–Fri 6.45am–4.30pm, Sat 6.45am–5.30pm, Sun 7.30am–3.30pm, concert 3.30pm; free; bus: 2, 3, 4, 38; map p.138 A4
The architecture of this strikingly modern structure soars 19 stories heavenward, creating a cavernous, coffered

Below: orthodox worship at an unorthodox church.

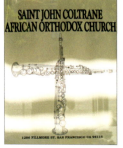

Environment

With an extensive recycling and composting program, a bike-riding and hybrid-driving population, a sustainability-focused food movement, and countless efforts to 'green' the city by planting trees and native species on its rooftops and public spaces, San Francisco has rightly developed a reputation for being an eco-friendly, carbon footprint-conscious city. But as much as it tries, it is also a densely populated metropolitan area that carries the inevitable environmental concerns, ranging from air quality to water shortage. However, San Francisco's greatest threat lies just below the surface, in the network of seismic faults.

Tremors Beneath

From its plunging cliffs to its dramatic peaks and valleys, the astounding natural beauty of the Bay Area is the result of the shifting tectonic plates that ensure residents are kept on their toes. Sitting between two major fault lines, the San Andreas skirting the edge of the city and the Hayward running up the East Bay, San Francisco is continually under threat of violent earthquakes. Fortunately, better building codes, and retrofitting efforts have stabilized many bridges, highway overpasses, and downtown buildings that have suffered in previous quakes. Landfill is still an issue, however. Today builders dig deep, reaching bedrock to anchor their skyscrapers, but neighborhoods such as the Marina still illustrate what can happen to filled-in bay or wetlands: in the 1989 Loma Prieta earthquake, this upmarket district's ground liquefied and its million-dollar homes collapsed.

Despite the threat, San Franciscans handle the subject of earthquakes with great aplomb. 'What can you do about it?' they will say, throwing up their hands. Still, there are basic rules every Californian school kid learns: If an earthquake occurs, stay indoors, preferably under something sturdy like a piece of furniture or in a door frame; and if outside, avoid trees, power lines, buildings, and bridges. Sometimes a rolling undulation, sharp crack, or violent shaking, earthquakes can last anywhere from a few short seconds to a couple of long minutes. For further instructions, refer to http://earthquake.usgs.gov.

Catching Like Wildfire

In arid California, fire is serious business. Every summer, wildfires rip through the state and occasionally destroy homes and communities. The Oakland Hills Fire of 1991 killed 25 people, injured 150 others and caused an estimated $1.5 billion in damages. It demonstrated that even the populated Bay Area is not immune to a fire's destruction. Whenever traveling outside the cities anywhere in California, it is

Below: the 1989 Loma Prieta quake caused great damage to the Marina district.

Left: bicycles and recycling bins – but is it enough?

tered tap flowing from the Hetch Hetchy Resevoir.

Congestion

San Francisco is the second most densely populated major city in the US, and is a part of the larger Bay Area, home to 7.4 million people. Despite large municipal transit agencies and the state of the art BART system, millions of Bay Area residents get in their cars every day to drive to work, and the Bay Area is among the highest in the country for the length of its average commute and the amount of time drivers sit waiting in traffic. The air pollution caused by this congestion is blown into the South Bay and Sacramento Valley, away from San Franciscan eyes and noses. Fortunately, there are organizations such as the Bay Area Air Quality Management District working on ways to get people out of their cars and onto their feet, bikes, or hybrid vehicles. It also sponsors 'Spare the Air' days that provide free Bay Area transit on days when air pollution has a high risk of exceeding federal and state safety levels.

Below: a familiarly busy sight on the Golden Gate Bridge.

From its basement to its 2.5-acre (1-hectare) living roof, the new California Academy of Sciences in Golden Gate Park was built with the environment in mind. The world's greenest museum, it holds a Platinum-level LEED (Leadership in Energy and Environmental Design) certification.

essential to be extremely aware of fire hazards. During the dry summer and autumn months there are strict laws regarding campfires, and in some instances, they are not allowed at all. Cigarettes should never be put out on the ground or thrown from a car window.

Water Fights

Contrary to the common misconception of a lush California, much of it is, in fact, a semi-desert. Its Mediterranean climate, where 98 percent of its annual rainfall occurs between November and March, leaves it open for severe drought and fights over water. The movie *Chinatown* documented this in Southern California, but San Francisco is also known for its own dramatic battle for water. In the early 20th century, the city proposed damming the Hetch Hetchy River high above Yosemite National Park to meet its growing needs. The contest pitted the entire city of San Francisco against the legendary environmental champion, John Muir, who died shortly thereafter.

During the major drought of the mid-1980s to the early 1990s, California residents were forced to ration water; this included restaurants making water service at the table by request only. Conservation remains a hot topic, especially as global warming continues to dry out California, but the new water battle in San Francisco is bottled versus tap. Due to environmental concerns pertaining to waste and its resulting carbon footprint, Mayor Gavin Newsom signed an executive order prohibiting the city from purchasing bottled water. Instead, city workers must rely on the fil-

Essentials

Whatever your 'must-see' list when visiting San Francisco, needs such as posting a letter, checking your email, or finding a pharmacy may well demand your attention at some point. The following listings give an overview of practical information for visitors to San Francisco, from entering the US to calling home, so that you can dedicate your time to getting on with the fun stuff. If you suffer any major problems, there are listings of embassies and consulates, as well as the city's main hospitals. Bear in mind too, that your hotel concierge can be a goldmine of useful information, as can the Visitor Information Center.

Baggage Restrictions

There are detailed restrictions on traveling with liquids, medicines, and dangerous items. For the latest information, refer to the **US Transportation Security Administration** (tel: 866-289-9673; www.tsa.gov).

File claims for damaged or missing luggage before leaving the airport. For queries and complaints, contact the **Federal Aviation Administration Consumer Hotline** (tel: 866-835-5322; www.faa.gov) or the **Aviation Consumer Protection Division** (tel: 202-366-2220; http://airconsumer.ost.dot.gov).

Climate

San Francisco weather can change significantly from hour to hour and between neighborhoods. Springs are warm and sunny, with an average high in April of 64°F (18°C) and

> To carry liquids, gels, and aerosols in your carry-on bag, they must be in containers 3oz (85ml) or smaller, and all the containers must be put together in one quart-size, zip-top, clear plastic bag.

low of 48°F (9°C), while summers are cool and overcast, with the city blanketed in fog, with an average high in July of 71°F (22°C) and low of 54°F (12°C). Come September and October, the summer chill is replaced with beautifully mild and sunny days, with an average high in September of 73°F (23°C) and low of 55°F(13°C). Rain storms (no snow) appear from December to February, though crisp, sunny days offer breaks from the damp and dreary ones. The average high in January is 56°F (13°C) and average low is 43°F (6°C).

Clothing

Plan ahead for varied weather and bring easy-to-layer clothes. The hills are hard to climb in sky-high heels. A raincoat and sturdy umbrella are vital for winter months: rain storms are no drizzle affair.

The city's casual, come-as-you-are vibe means jeans, T-shirts, and tennis shoes are ubiquitous, including in many restaurants and entertainment venues. However, snazzier eateries and nightclubs warrant something smarter.

Above: how to identify your local cops.

Customs

Adult visitors staying longer than 72 hours may bring along the following items duty free: 1 liter of wine or liquor; 100 cigars (non-Cuban), or 3lbs of tobacco, or 200 cigarettes; and gifts valued under $100.

Absolutely no food (even in cans) or plants of any type are permissible. Visitors may also arrive and depart with up to $10,000 currency without declaration. For the most up-to-date information on what may be brought with you, refer to the US Customs and Border Protection website (www.cbp.gov).

Left: make your trip as easy as possible, so you can get on and enjoy the local attractions.

1189 Potrero Avenue; tel: 647-1397; bus: 9, 33, 48.
3201 Divisadero Street; tel: 931-6417; bus: 28, 30, 30X, 43, 76. Additional Walgreens and Rite Aid (www.riteaid.com) branches are open late into the evening.

INSURANCE AND HOSPITALS

Healthcare can be very expensive, especially hospitalization. Foreign visitors should always ensure that they have full medical insurance covering their stay before traveling to the US. Below are hospitals with 24-hour emergency rooms.

California Pacific Medical Center

Castro Street at Duboce Avenue; tel: 415-600-6000; www.cpmc.org; metro: N to Duboce; bus: 24, 37; map p.137 E2

Saint Francis Memorial Hospital

900 Hyde Street; tel: 353-6300; www.saintfrancismemorial.org; bus: 1, 2, 19, 27, 76; map p.134 B1

San Francisco General Hospital

1001 Potrero Avenue; tel: 206-8000; www.sfdph.org; bus: 9, 33, 48

UCSF Medical Center

505 Parnassus Avenue; tel: 476-1000; www.ucsfhealth.org; metro: N to UCSF; bus: 6, 43, 66; map p.136 C1

Holidays

National US holidays are: **New Year's Day** (January 1); **Martin Luther King Jr. Day** (3rd Monday in January); **President's Day** (3rd Monday in February); **Memorial Day** (Last Monday in May); **Independence Day** (July 4); **Labor Day** (1st Monday in September); **Columbus**

Electricity

Electricity in the US is 110 Volts, 60 Hertz AC. Outlets are generally for flat blade, two-prong plugs. Most foreign appliances require a transformer and/or plug adaptor.

Embassies and Consulates

Details for other embassies and consulates can be found in the Yellow Pages.
Australia
Tel: 536-1970; www.dfat.gov.au
Canada
Tel: 834-3180;
www.sanfrancisco.gc.ca
Ireland
Tel: 392-4214;
www.irelandemb.org
New Zealand
Tel: 399-1255; www.nzemb.org
South Africa
Tel: 202-242-4400;
www.saembassy.org
UK
Tel: 617-1300;
www.britainusa.com/sf

Emergency Numbers

Ambulance, fire, or police: dial 911 from any telephone, no coins needed

Police (non-emergency): tel: 553-0123

Health

DRUGSTORES (PHARMACIES)
Some medicines that are available over the counter in your home country may require a prescription in the US. 24-hour locations of the useful Walgreens drugstore chain (www.walgreens.com) can be found at the following locations:
498 Castro Street; tel: 861-3136; metro: F, K, L, M, T to Castro; bus: 33, 34, 35, 37.

Below: one of the most useful places in San Francisco.

Above: points to note before you set out on Golden Gate Bridge...

Day (2nd Monday in October); **Veteran's Day** (November 11); **Thanksgiving Day** (4th Thursday in November); and **Christmas Day** (December 25).

Information

Visitor Information Center of San Francisco
900 Market Street; tel: 391-2000; www.onlyinsanfrancisco.com; May–Oct Mon–Fri 9am–5pm, Sat–Sun 9am–3pm, Nov–Apr Mon–Fri 9am–5pm, Sat 9am–3pm; BART and metro: all lines to Powell; bus: 6, 7, 27, 30, 45; cable car: Powell-Hyde, Powell-Mason; map p.138 C4
The center is down the stairs near the cable car turntable at Market and Powell streets and supplies brochures, maps, and helpful answers. Call for a listing of monthly events.

Internet

Internet cafés include:
H Café
3801 17th Street; tel: 487-1611; www.hcafesf.com; Mon–Fri 6am–9pm, Sat–Sun 7am–8pm; metro: F, K, L, M, T to Castro; bus: 22, 33, 37; map p.138 A1

Quetzal Internet Café
1234 Polk Street; tel: 673-4181; www.quetzal.org; Mon–Fri 6.30am–10pm, Sat–Sun 7.30am–10pm; bus: 1, 4, 19, 27, 31; map p.134 B1
Also, many cafés have WiFi hotspots, and public library branches provide free Internet access (San Francisco Public Library; tel: 557-4400; http://sfpl.org)

Media

The largest regional newspaper is the *San Francisco Chronicle* (www.sfgate.com/chronicle). The Sunday *Datebook* section lists art, music, and entertainment events. Free alternative weeklies are found in newspaper boxes, cafés, and bars. The four main weeklies are *The San Francisco Bay Guardian* (www.sfbg.com), *SF Weekly* (www.sfweekly.com), *San Francisco Bay Times* (www.sfbaytimes.com), and *Bay Area Reporter* (BAR; www.ebar.com). The latter two are gay- and lesbian-oriented, and most easily found in and around the Castro neighborhood. The city's

magazines include *San Francisco Magazine* (www.sanfran.com) and *7x7* (www.7x7sf.com). Web-based city guides include www.sfstation.com.

Money

ATMs
ATMs are at banks, some stores, and bars, and charge usage fees. Debit card use on purchases at major grocery and drugstores allows you to get cashback; check with your bank before traveling.

BANKS AND CURRENCY EXCHANGE
Bank hours are generally Monday through Friday, from about 9am to 5pm. Some are open Saturday mornings. ATMs can be used to obtain currency; change foreign currency at airports, major banks downtown, or American Express offices.

CREDIT CARDS
Credit cards are accepted at most restaurants, hotels, and stores.

CURRENCY
The dollar ($) is divided into 100 cents (¢). The coins are the penny (1¢), nickel (5¢), dime (10¢), quarter (25¢), and the less-common half dollar (50¢) and $1 coin. Common banknotes are the $1, $5, $10, $20, $50, and $100 bills.

SALES TAXES
In San Francisco, a 9.5 percent sales tax is added to the prices of goods and services; in surrounding cities, the sales tax is 8.25 percent. Hotels charge a 14 percent tax.

TRAVELER'S CHECKS
With the popularity of ATMs, credit cards, and debit cards, traveler's checks are increasingly less common. However, banks, stores, restaurants, and hotels generally accept

US dollar-denominated traveler's checks. If yours are in foreign denominations, they first must be changed to dollars. Unexchanged checks should be kept in your hotel safe. Record the checks' serial numbers in a separate place to facilitate refunds of lost or stolen checks.

Postal Services

Post offices open at 8–9am and close at 5–6pm, Monday through Friday; the post office in the Macy's department store on Union Square is also open on Sunday, 11am–5pm. Use the Civic Center post office for general-delivery mail (poste restante).

Civic Center Post Offiice
101 Hyde Street; tel: 563-7284; Mon–Fri 9am–6pm, Sat 8am–3pm; BART and metro: all lines to Civic Center; bus: 6, 7, 9, 21, 49; map p.138 B4

US Postal Service
Tel: 800-275-8777; www.usps.com

Telephone

Local calls are inexpensive; long distance calls are decidedly not. Public phones accept coins and credit cards, but the latter charge exorbitant rates. The San Francisco

Below: be aware of California's strident smoking laws.

Be careful where you light-up in San Francisco: the city may be blanketed in fog, but the air is quite smoke-free. Smoking laws are strict, and it is banned in many public places such as offices, shops, restaurants, and bars. The minimum legal age for smoking is 18 years old.

---

area code is 415, which you only need to dial from outside of the city; the country code is 1. Toll-free numbers begin 1-800, 1-888, 1-877, or 1-866.
Directory enquires: 411
US calls outside your area code: 1 + area code + phone number
International Calls: 011+ country code + number
Operator: 0 for assistance with local calls; 00 for international calls

Time Zone

San Francisco is on Pacific Standard Time. PST is three hours behind Eastern Standard Time (New York) and eight hours behind Greenwich Mean Time (London).

Tipping

Restaurants: 18–20 percent. Most restaurants add a service charge automatically for parties of six or more.
Taxis: 10–15 percent
Bars: 10–15 percent, or at least $1–2 per drink
Coat check: $1–2 per coat
Doormen: $1–2 for hailing a cab or bringing in bags
Porters: $1 per bag (more if you packed bricks)
Valet parking: $2–3
Concierge: $5–10
Maids: $3–5 per day

Visa Information

US citizens returning to the US by air or land from Canada, Mexico, the Caribbean, and Bermuda will need a passport or other accepted ID.

Under the current Visa Waiver Scheme, for nationals of 35 countries (including the UK, Australia, and New Zealand) no visa is needed for US stays of less than 90 days (for business or pleasure). For these travelers, a valid ESTA (Electronic System for Travel Authorization) approval is required; applications can be completed online at https://esta.cbp.dhs.gov. A machine-readable passport is also required. For passports renewed or extended between October 26, 2005 and October 25, 2006 a digital photograph printed on the data page or an integrated chip containing the information from the data page (an e-Passport) is required. Passports renewed on or after October 26, 2006 must be e-Passports. Nationals of the Czech Republic, Estonia, Hungary, Latvia, Lithuania, Malta, the Republic of Korea, and the Slovak Republic require e-Passports.

All other foreign citizens need visas. Application forms and information are available at US embassies and consulates. Plan several weeks in advance. Double check current requirements at http://travel.state.gov.

Below: the always-handy ATM, found all over the city.

Fashion

A singular parade of styles strut San Francisco's streets, ranging from ultra-casual to edgy hipster to boho-chic. Emporiums and high-end designer outposts flood Union Square, but style hounds find more fashion fuel in boutiques and thrift stores. Fillmore, Union, and Chestnut streets cater largely to luxe label-addicts; the Mission sells independent labels and vintage thrift to hipsters; Hayes Valley delivers cool contemporary designs; and the Haight specialize in casuals and offbeat secondhand. Stores are generally open Monday–Saturday 11am–6pm, and Sunday noon–6pm.

Local Fashions and Designers

San Francisco fashion is a mixed bag. Casuals dominate, and jeans, T-shirts, and sneakers are ubiquitous. Runway looks are rarely seen; instead current trends are toned down in varied ways. Carefully coifed styles and designer threads are popular in the northern neighborhoods, while the Mission and Haight are dominated by alternative looks and secondhand finds.

Union Square is stuffed with major department stores and retail outlets, while well-known, high-end designers are clustered on Post, Stockton, and Geary Streets, Grant Avenue, and Maiden Lane.

Excellent local independent designers include: **Dema** (1038 Valencia Street; tel: 206-0500; www.godemago.com; Mon–Fri 11am–7pm, Sat noon–7pm, Sun noon–6pm; bus: 14, 26, 49); **House of Hengst** (924 Valencia Street; tel: 642-0841; www.houseofhengst.com; Mon–Sat noon–7pm, Sun noon–6pm; bus: 14, 26, 49); and **Sunhee Moon** (3167 16th Street; tel: 355-1800; www.sunheemoon.com; Mon–Fri noon–

Above: high-end names decorate Maiden Lane.

7pm, Sat–Sun noon–6pm; map p.138 A1). All three are found in the hip Mission District.

Fashion also grabs the city's attention during San Francisco Fashion Week (www.fashionweek-sf.com), initiated in 2004.

SEE ALSO SHOPPING, P.112–4

Apparel and Accessories

AB Fits
1519 Grant Avenue; tel: 982-5726; www.abfiit.com; Tue–Sat 11.30am–6.30pm, Sun noon–6pm; bus: 15, 20, 30, 41; map p.134 C3
Premium denim destination.

Ambiance
1458 Haight Street; tel: 552-5095; www.ambiancesf.com; Mon–Sat 10am–7pm, Sun 11am–7pm; bus: 6, 7, 33, 71; map p.137 D2
Romantic, funky, and vintage-inspired girly goodies.

Anica
2418 Polk Street; tel: 447-2878; www.anicaboutique.com; Tue–Fri noon–7pm, Sat 11am–6pm, Sun 11am–5pm; bus: 19, 41, 45, 47, 49; map p.134 A3
Finely-picked progressive line-up for sophisticated females.

Behind the Post Offiice
1510 Haight Street; tel: 861-2507; Mon 11am–7pm, Tue noon–6pm, Wed–Sat 11am–7pm, Sun 11am–6pm; bus: 6, 7, 33, 44, 71; map p.137 D2
Emerging and established names for trendy, urban ladies.

Citizen Clothing
536 Castro Street; tel: 575-3560; www.citizenbody.com; Mon–Sat 10am–8pm, Sun 11am–7pm; metro: K, L, M, T to Castro; bus: 24, 33, 35, 37; map p.137 E1
Well-picked men's hip casuals.

Gap
890 Market Street; tel: 788-5909; www.gapinc.com; BART and metro: all lines to Powell; bus: 4, 30, 38, 45, 76; cable car: Powell-Hyde, Powell-Mason; map p.139 C4

Left: made in San Francisco: the flagship Levi's store.

Shoes

Gimme Shoes
416 Hayes Street; tel: 864-0691; www.gimmeshoes.com; Mon–Sat 11am–7pm, Sun noon–6pm; bus: 5, 7, 21, 42, 49; map p.138 A3
Global, fashion-forward footwear. Also at 2358 Fillmore Street; tel: 441-3040.

Shoe Biz
1420 Haight Street; tel: 861-3797; www.shoebizsf.com; Mon–Sat 11am–7pm, Sun 11am–6pm; bus: 6, 33, 43, 71; map p.138 A2
Stylish sneakers jostle for shelf space alongside sky-high stilettos, boots, and strappy sandals. Also at 877 Valencia Street; tel: 550-8655.

Lingerie

Alla Prima
1420 Grant Avenue; tel: 397-4077; Tue–Sat 11am–7pm, Sun 12.30–5pm; bus: 30, 45; map p.134 C3
Pretty palette of European lingerie. Also at 539 Hayes Street; tel: 864-8180.

Belle Cose
2036 Polk Street; tel: 474-3494; Mon–Fri 11am–6.30pm, Sat 11am–7pm, Sun noon–5pm; bus: 12, 19, 47, 49, 76; map p.134 B2
Vintage and vintage-inspired glamour.

Below: trying it on in a Mission boutique.

Many streets sparkle with gorgeous jewelry, but Union Square is especially dazzling. Splurge at **De Vera** (29 Maiden Lane; tel: 788-0828; http://de veraobjects.com; Tue–Sat 10am–6pm; bus: 2, 3, 4, 30, 45; map p.135 C1), veteran **Shreve and Co**. (200 Post Street; tel: 421-2600; www.shreve.com; Mon–Sat 10am–6pm, Sun noon–5pm; bus: 2, 3, 4, 30, 45; map p.135 C1), or many Powell and Sutter Street offerings.

This US behemoth started in San Francisco in 1969.

Levi's
300 Post Street; tel: 501-0100; www.levisstore.com; Mon–Sat 10am–9pm, Sun 10am–6.30pm; bus: 2, 3, 4, 30, 45; map p.135 C1
For the basics, snag San Francisco-based attire at the flagship Levi's store, the company that gave birth to blue jeans in 1873.

My Roommate's Closet
3044 Fillmore Street; tel: 447-7703; www.myroommates closet.com; Mon–Fri 11am–6.30pm, Sat 11am–6pm, Sun noon–5pm; bus: 22, 41, 45; map p.133 E2

Ever-changing racks of chic, discounted designer duds.

Ooma
1422 Grant Avenue; tel: 627-6963; www.ooma.net; Tue–Sat 11am–7pm, Sun noon–5pm; bus: 15, 30, 45; map p.135 C3
Brightly-colored bastion for feminine, feisty fabulousness.

Villain's
1672 Haight Street; tel: 626-5939; www.villiansf.com; daily 11am–7pm; bus: 6, 7, 33, 71; map p.137 D2
Scores of hip, funky looks for the fellas.

Secondhand

American Rag Cie
1305 Van Ness Avenue; tel: 474-5214; www.amrag.com; Mon–Sat 11am–7pm, Sun noon–7pm; bus: 2, 3, 47, 49; map p.134 B1
Pricey but trendy second-hand and vintage-inspired pieces.

Buffalo Exchange
1555 Haight Street; tel: 431-7733; www.buffaloexchange. com; Sun–Thur 11am–7pm, Fri–Sat 11am–8pm; bus: 6, 7, 33, 43, 71; map p.137 D2
Broken-in looks that do not break the bank. Also at 1210 Valencia Street; tel: 647-8832.

Food and Drink

It is fortunate that San Francisco has so many hills, so residents and visitors alike can quickly burn off the many culinary enticements this city has to offer. With delicate pastries at cafés, delectable small plates at fashionable bars, and esteemed fine dining establishments helmed by celebrity chefs, it is virtually impossible to abstain in the 'Paris of the West.' Blessed with thriving immigrant communities, year-round natural abundance, a love of all things local and organic, and a slight spirit of rebellion, San Francisco has emerged as one of the culinary capitals of the world.

'Gastronomic Orgies'

Nothing has changed since Gertrude Stein made reference to San Francisco's culinary excesses. The Bay Area is known for its farmers, growing everything from rare heirloom tomatoes to raising heritage herds of beef cattle. But its original claim to fame was the sea's bounty and its inspired dishes like Chioppino, a seafood stew derived from a traditional Italian dish.

While Fisherman's Wharf is always crowded with seafood lovers, mid-November through May is particularly busy, enticing locals eager to snag the favorite Dungeness crabs off the boats. In San Francisco, crab is enjoyed steamed, cracked, and drowned in butter, accompanied only by a loaf of San Francisco's famous sourdough.

In recent years, celebrity chefs and food artisans have turned eclectic San Francisco into the epicenter of the American sustainable food movement. Based upon the idea that food should be produced locally and from techniques derived of age-old traditions, it has given the city an impressive assortment of boutique charcuteries, cheese makers, bakeries, farmers' markets, and cuisine that highlights the Bay Area's natural cornicopia and diverse population.

Immigrant Influences

Coming from all around the world in the mid-19th century, immigrants added vast diversity to the city's culinary character. In addition to the Mexican and American traditions already here, French, Irish, German, Basque, Spanish, Italian, and Chinese immigrants brought with them the tastes of home. Poised at the edge of the Pacific, San Fran-

---

With yeast in short supply, the settlers who arrived in the Gold Rush utilized fermented dough as the basis of their bread. This technique hardly originated with this generation of gold seekers, but San Francisco is home to natural yeasts and bacteria circulating in the air that create the chewy texture and highly sour taste that define San Franciscan sourdough.

---

cisco boasts especially strong and diverse pan-Asian cuisine. Still to this day, immigrants continue to bring food secrets that broaden the city's palate, as in the Ethiopian, Arabian, Moroccan, Afghan, and Turkish restaurants.

Eating Out

There is something for everyone here: eateries encompass all price ranges for every type of food available. Breakfast is generally between 7am to 10am, except on the weekends when brunch service runs until 1 or 2pm. Weekday lunch is between 11.30am to 2.30pm and dinner starts around 5.30pm.

Drinking

San Franciscans pay attention to both what they eat and what washes it down. This is a drinking city. Early on, residents began brewing their own beer. Today, there are many microbreweries around the city with the strength and complexity to rival any cocktail or glass of wine, including the **Anchor Steam Brewery** on Potrero Hill which not only

54

Left: the famed San Francisco sourdough bread.

This local coffee roaster peddles strictly coffee beans, not cups. However, the smell alone will lure even the most adamant tea drinker into this tiny storefront.

Liguria Bakery
1700 Stockton Street; tel: 421-3786; Mon–Fri 8am–2pm, Sat 7am–2pm, Sun 7am–noon; bus: 9X, 30, 39, 41, 45; map p.134 C3
Get here early, as the ladies at Liguria bakery quickly sell out of their melt-in-the-mouth focaccia, and once it is gone, they close the doors. Only available in a few flavors, it drips with olive oil and is easily the best focaccia in the city.

Molinari Delicatessen
373 Columbus Avenue; tel: 421-2337; www.molinarisalame.com; Mon–Fri 9am–5.30pm, Sat 7.30am–5.30pm; bus: 9X, 30, 39, 41, 45; map p.134 C2
Cranky Italians serve up the city's best deli fare. Imported cheese, cured meats, and canned goods compliment Molinari's own selection of sausage, salamis, and raviolis made in Hunter's Point.

Trader Joe's
401 Bay Street; tel: 351-1013; www.traderjoes.com; daily 9am–9pm; bus: 10, 39, 47; cable car: Powell-Mason; map p.134 B4

makes beer, but gin and rye bourbon as well.

Surrounded by excellent wine country, San Francisco is an easy access point for visiting the many acclaimed vineyards and trying an excellent selection of local wine, from traditional varietals such as Chardonnay and Cabernet, to lesser-known specialties like Gamay Beaujolais.
SEE ALSO WINE COUNTRY, P.28–9

Fisherman's Wharf

Baker's Hall at Boudin Bakery
160 Jefferson Street; tel: 928-1849; www.boudinbakery.com; daily noon–6pm; metro: F to Pier 39; bus: 10, 30, 39; map p.134 B4
In the heart of Fisherman's Wharf, the Boudin bakery hawks its original San Francisco sourdough near the site of its first bakery. From chutneys to chocolate, Baker's Hall sells locally crafted goods that compliment the famous bread.

Ghirardelli Chocolate Soda Fountain at Ghirardelli Square
900 North Point Street; tel: 474-3938; www.ghirardelli.com; daily 10am–11pm; bus: 10, 19,

30, 47; cable car: Powell-Hyde; map p.134 A4
It is rumored that so much chocolate was made here that when it rains the walls ooze chocolate. But even when it is not raining, the Soda Fountain's ice cream sundaes still ooze with chocolate, caramel, and plenty of whipped cream. The store sells a wide variety of Ghirardelli's products.

Chinatown

Gourmet Delight
1045 Stockton Street; tel: 392-3288; daily 8am–6pm; bus: 1, 12, 30, 41, 45; map p.134 C2
Complete with darkly burnished poultry in the windows, this is the place for Chinese deli food. Always crowded, its counters heave with chow mein, Cantonese-style deep-fried chicken, sweet-and-sour pork, and piles of cooked vegetables. Cash only.

North Beach, Telegraph Hill, and Russian Hill

Graffeo Coffee
735 Columbus Avenue; tel: 986-2420; www.graffeo.com; Mon–Fri 9am–6pm, Sat til 5pm; bus: 9X, 30, 39, 41, 45; map p.134 C3

Below: the food temple that is the Ferry Building.

Left: Italian specialties at Molinari's Delicatessen *(see p.55)*.

prepared food venders and more. Tuesday and Thursday are smaller, but still bountiful.

John Walker and Co.
175 Sutter Street; tel: 986-2707; www.johnwalker.com; Mon–Fri 10am–6.30pm, Sat noon–5pm; BART and metro: all lines to Montgomery; bus: 2, 30, 38, 45, 76; map p.134 C1
In this small downtown store, you can find anything from Italian Candoli grappa, to a bottle of 1980 Opus One, to hand-crafted, single-barrel Noah's Mill Kentucky Bourbon.

SoMa and Civic Center
Blue Bottle Coffee
315 Linden Street; tel: 510-653-3394; www.bluebottlecoffee.net; Mon–Fri 7am–5pm or 6pm, Sat–Sun 8am–5pm or 6pm; bus: 6, 21, 47, 49, 71; map p.138 A3
Perhaps no other roaster in the Bay Area has quite the same devotion to the bean as Blue Bottle. Roasted everyday, each roast is as different and complex as a varietal of wine. Come by their tiny kiosk in Hayes Valley to sample it.

Civic Center Farmers' Market
1182 Market Street; tel: 558-9455; www.hocfarmersmarket.org; Sun 7am–5pm, Wed 7am–5.30pm; BART and metro: all lines to Civic Center; bus: 5, 6, 21, 47, 49; map p.138 B3
The least expensive farmers' market in the city, this market excels at fresh vegetables, particularly Asian varieties.

Miette
449 Octavia Street; tel: 837-0300; http://miettecakes.com; daily 11am–7pm; bus: 6, 21, 47, 49, 71; map p.138 A3
French for 'little crumb,' Miette is a charming pastry shop selling deliciously unique cakes, such as their bestselling gingerbread cake

This small, national chain grocery store offers quality goods at reasonable prices. It is a local staple, and usually crowded.

XOX Truffles
754 Columbus Avenue; tel: 421-4814; www.xoxtruffles.com; Mon–Sat 9am–6pm, Sun 10.30am–6pm; bus: 9X, 30, 39, 41, 45; map p.134 C3
Tiny and handmade, their flavors range from cognac to honey vodka to pistachio and everything in between. There are even vegan soy varieties.

Union Square and Financial District
Ferry Building Market
1 Ferry Building, Market and the Embarcadero; tel: 693-0996;

Despite the amount of homegrown wine and beer, San Francisco will never give up its cocktails. Claiming to be the home of the first martini, the city has a fine tradition of drinking hard. Scotch, gin, and vodka – poured with minimal fuss or dressed up by mixologists – are particular favorites.

www.ferrybuildingmarketplace.com; Mon–Fri 10am–6pm, Sat 9am–6pm, Sun 11am–5pm; BART and metro: all lines to Embarcadero; bus: 1, 2, 12, 14, 21; map p.135 E2
The Ferry Building is a highlight of any trip to San Francisco. Food lovers crowd to the high temple of the Bay Area sustainable food movement, to browse local chocolatiers, olive-oil makers, produce stands, meat counters, the Acme Bakery, and the Cowgirl Creamery. There's also a wine store and excellent sit-down eateries.

Ferry Plaza Farmers' Market
1 Ferry Building, Market and the Embarcadero; tel: 291-3276; www.ferryplazafarmersmarket.com; Tue and Thur 10am–2pm, Sat 8am–2pm; BART and metro: all lines to Embarcadero; bus: 1, 2, 12, 14, 21; map p.135 E2
Voted one of the best farmers' markets in the country by The New York Times, the Saturday market has everything; fresh seasonal vegetables, naturally nested eggs, artisan coffee, charcuterie,

Despite this city's food obsession, dining in San Francisco is rarely a fancy affair. Ease and comfort are the guiding principals in this city where locals are not shy about spending hours lingering over coffee, and rarely venture out to dinner before 7pm. Few restaurants have dress codes or serve past 10pm.

(made with dark stout beer, molasses, spices, and a sweet cream cheese frosting), as well as lemon, lime meringue, and banana cream tarts, and old-fashioned and imported candies.

Central Neighborhoods

Real Food Company
2140 Polk Street; tel 673-7420; www.realfoodco.com; daily 8am–9pm; bus: 12, 19, 41, 45; map p.138 B4

This local chain has a great and affordable inventory of natural foods, local bread, a diverse cheese and meat counter, and the best produce section in the city. Also at 3060 Fillmore Street; tel: 567-6900.

Mission and Castro

Bi-Rite Market and Creamery
3639 18th Street; tel: 241-9760; www.biritemarket.com; daily 9am–9pm; BART: 16th Street;

Below: take-out pizza is popular wherever you go.

metro: J to Church and 18th streets; bus: 22, 33, 36; map p.138 A1

With its own creamery across the street (with flavors like salted caramel or honey lavender) Bi-Rite Market is the one-stop shop for anyone looking for natural foods with a little indulgence on the side.

La Palma Mexicatessen
2884 24th Street; tel: 647-1500; www.lapalmafoods.com; daily 9am–5pm; BART: to 24th Street Mission; bus: 12, 27, 48, 67

A great stop for Mexican canned and dried goods and corn tortillas hand-made daily. Two-meal burritos and fresh tacos are also available at the service counter.

Mission Pie
2901 Mission Street; tel: 282-1500; www.missionpie.com; Mon–Thur 7am–9pm, Fri 7am–10pm, Sat 8am–10pm, Sun 9am–9pm; BART: 24th Street; bus: 14, 48, 49

The daily pies here are local favorites. About a half dozen flavors are available each day, ranging from walnut to pear blueberry to sweet potato to banana cream.

Mitchell's Ice Cream
688 San Jose Avenue; tel: 648-2300; www.mitchellsice cream.com; daily 11am–11pm; bus: 14, 26, 49, 67

No matter what time it is, Mitchell's is always packed with locals satisfying a sweet tooth.

Tartine Bakery
600 Guerrero Street; tel: 487-2600; www.tartinebakery.com; Tue–Wed 7.30am–7pm, Thur–Fri 7.30am–8pm, Sat 8am–8pm, Sun 9am–8pm; bus: 26, 33; map p.138 A1

Locals love the eclairs, tarts, freshly baked bread, and other assorted treats – try the frangipane croissant or the gougère – from this small bakery with James Beard Award-winning chefs.

Around San Francisco

24th Street Cheese Company
3893 24th Street; tel: 821-6658; Mon–Fri 10am–7pm, Sat until 6pm, Sun until 5pm; metro: J to Church and 24th streets; bus: 24, 48

This Noe Valley institution has one of the most reputable cheese counters in the Bay Area. The choice is extensive, and anything can be tasted.

Arizmendi Bakery
1331 9th Avenue; tel: 566-3117; www.arizmendibakery.org; Tue–Fri 7am–7pm, Sat 7.30am–6pm, Sun 7.30am–5pm; metro: N to Judah Street and 9th Avenue; bus: 6, 43, 44, 66; map p.136 B1

One of four related co-ops in the Bay Area, it sells fresh bread, delicious pastries, and artisan shortbread in the inner Sunset's main drag. Many would say their pizza, a special made daily on a sourdough crust, is worth a trip across the city. Cash only.

Noe Valley Bakery and Bread Company
4073 24th Street; tel: 550-1405; www.noevalleybakery.com; Mon–Fri 7am–7pm, Sat–Sun until 6pm; metro: J to Church and 24th streets; bus: 24, 48

For Noe Valley residents, this bakery is their daily bread, literally. Long lines form early as locals wait for the breads, cakes, and pastries.

Below: fresh produce at the Civic Center Farmers' Market.

Gay and Lesbian

S an Francisco is internationally known as one of the world's most welcoming places for gays and lesbians. The lively hub of this thriving and politically-influential community is the Castro neighborhood, where rainbow flags adorn brightly colored Victorian houses. The Castro is especially popular with younger gay men, but women, families, and straights are also present in strong numbers. Another hotspot is SoMa, still home to large clubs, leather bars, and specialty stores. For lesbians, Noe Valley, Bernal Heights, and Valencia Street are particularly popular neighborhoods.

Arts and Entertainment

San Franciscans are an artsy crowd, and the gay and lesbian community is no exception. Queer comedy is supplied by **QComedy**, music by the **San Francisco Gay Men's Chorus**, and innovative performance art, comedy, musicals, and drama by **Theater Rhinoceros**, the oldest gay and lesbian theater company in the US. Another theater option is **Brava! for Women in the Arts**.

The landmark **Castro Theatre** hosts special events like the **San Fran**cisco International Gay and Lesbian Film Festival (www.frameline.org/festival), which is held in June.
SEE ALSO MOVIES, P.81

Brava! for Women in the Arts
2789 24th Street; tel: 641-7657; www.brava.org; BART: 24th Street; bus: 12, 27, 48

Qcomedy
www.qcomedy.com

San Francisco Gay Men's Chorus
Tel: 865-3650, box offiice: 865-2787; www.sfgmc.org

Theater Rhinoceros
1360 Misson Street, #200 (performance locations vary); tel: 800-838-3006; www.therhino.org

Bars and Nightclubs

Badlands
4121 18th Street; tel: 626-9320; www.badlands-sf.com; Mon–Sun 2pm–2am; metro: F, K, L, M, T to Castro; bus: 24, 33, 35, 37; map p.137 E1
Badlands packs its dance floor to the gills with a young crowd loving the Top 40 and 80s hits. TV screens around the dance floor blast music videos.

Bar on Church
456 Castro Street; tel: 861-7499; www.thebarsf.com; Mon–Sat 4pm–2am, Sun 2pm–2am; metro: F, K, L, M, T to Castro; bus: 33, 35, 37; map p.137 E1
Bar on Church has a small dance floor jam-packed with a friendly crowd of pretty boys, dancing to current pop mashups and downing strong, cheap drinks.

The Café
2369 Market Street; tel: 861-3846; www.cafesf.com; metro: F, K, L, M, T to Castro; bus: 24, 35, 37; map p.137 E1
A large, young mixed crowd (guys and girls) dance, drink,

Below: the colors of gay pride decorate the Castro.

Left: gay couples are part of the mainstream in San Francisco.

on. Tan, muscled bartenders mix cocktails heavy in rum and infused vodka with the requisite muddled lime.

Lone Star Saloon
1354 Harrison Street; tel: 863-9999; www.lonestarsaloon.com; Mon–Sun noon–2am; bus: 12, 19, 27, 47; map p.138 C2
The Lone Star Saloon was the first 'bear' bar in the US. For the smoker's den, head out to the big backyard patio, which gets especially busy for weekend Beverage Benefits.

Marlena's
488 Hayes Street; tel: 864-6672; www.marlenasbarsf.com; daily 3pm–2am; bus: 21; map p.138 A3
A diverse group (gay, lesbian, transgender, transvestite, and drag queens) turns out for popular weekend drag shows.

Martuni's
4 Valencia Street; tel: 241-0205; http://martunis.ypguides.net; daily 2pm–2am; metro: F to Market and Gough streets; bus: 6, 7, 26, 71; map p.138 A2
A mixed crowd packs in on weekends to this fun and friendly piano bar. The martinis are dangerously large and potent.

and flirt the night away to Top 40 tunes at this upscale spot. Third Saturday of the month is for lesbians.

The Eagle Tavern
398 12th Street; tel: 626-0880; www.sfeagle.com; daily noon–2am; bus: 9, 12, 27, 47; map p.138 B2
A leather bar with cruisey, anything-goes Beer Busts on the outdoor patio, as well as occasional mud-wrestling, and live bands.

El Rio
3158 Mission Street; tel: 282-3325; www.elriosf.com; Mar–Nov Mon–Thur 5pm–2am, Fri 4pm–2am, Sat–Sun 3pm–2am, Dec–Feb Mon–Thur 5pm–2am, Fri 4pm–2am, Sat–Sun 5pm–2am; BART: 24th Street; bus: 12, 14, 26, 49, 67
A funky Mission bar for 'chiquitas, bananas, and mixed fruits,' El Rio draws diverse crowds with live and DJ music, film and art showings, drag, spoken word, and fundraisers. The outdoor patio and 'Salsa Sundays' are especially popular.

Lexington Club
3464 19th Street; tel: 863-2052; www.lexingtonclub.com; daily

> Walking tours like the **FOOT! 'Come Out to the Castro'** tour (tel:793-5378; www.foottours.com) or the **'Cruisin' the Castro Tour'** (tel: 255-1821; www.cruisinthecastro.com) deliver fun history and culture lessons over the course of an easy stroll.

5pm–2am; bus: 14, 26, 49; map p.138 B1
One of the few real lesbian bars in the city, this Mission dive for dykes draws a chill, mostly younger (and sometimes cliquey) crowd.

Lime
2247 Market Street; tel: 621-5256; www.lime-sf.com; Sun–Thur 5pm–midnight, Fri–Sat until 1am, brunch: Sat 11am–3pm, Sun 10.30am–3pm; metro: F, K, L, M, T to Castro; bus: 22, 24, 37; map p.137 E1
It is impossible to escape the feeling that you have stepped into *A Clockwork Orange* entering Lime, especially as the mini TVs scattered throughout the all-white interior with neon lighting grow increasingly naughty as the night goes

Below: the local bars offer something for everyone.

Midnight Sun
4067 18th Street; tel: 861-4186; Mon–Fri 2pm–2am, Sat–Sun 1pm–2am; metro: F, K, L, M, T to Castro; bus: 33, 35, 37; map p.137 E1

Big-screen televisions are the draw for this video bar where gay men gather to watch a mix of popular shows like *Glee* and *The Simpsons*.

Mix
4086 18th Street; tel: 431-8616; daily 6am–2am; metro: F, K, L, M, T to Castro; bus: 24, 33, 35, 37; map p.137 E1

This neighborhood hang-out with an open-air back patio lives up its name, with a mixed crowd that's lesbian- and hetero-friendly.

Moby Dick's
4049 18th Street; tel: 861-1199; www.mobydicksf.com; Mon–Fri 2pm–2am, Sat–Sun noon–2am; metro: F, K, L, M, T to Castro; bus: 33, 35, 37; map p.137 E1

A friendly, casual neighborhood bar where you can play pool, pinball, and touchscreen trivia while enjoying daily drink specials.

Pilsner Inn
225 Church Street; tel: 621-7058; www.pilsnerinn.com; Mon–Sun 10am–2pm; metro: F, J, K, L, M, T to Church Street; bus: 22, 37; map p.138 A2

Locals guys enjoy the relaxed vibe, extensive draft beer selection, pool tables and pinball machines, and the smoker-friendly heated back patio. Sometimes diners from the nearby popular restaurant, Chow, come to kill time waiting for tables.

Powerhouse
1347 Folsom Street; tel: 552-8689; www.powerhouse-sf.com; Wed–Sun noon–2am; bus: 12, 19; map p.138 C3

A popular, very cruisey SoMa bar filled with loads of hunky men and not many shirts.

The Stud
399 9th Street; tel: 863-6623; www.studsf.com; bus: 12, 14, 14L, 19, 26; map p.138 C2

Mostly gay men party here, but certain nights and events, such as live bands every Thursday, draw many other types too.

Truck
1900 Folsom Street; tel: 252-0306; www.trucksf.com; Mon–Fri 11am–2am, Sat–Sun 2pm–2am; bus: 12, 22, 33, 53; map p.138 B2

A young, hipster Mission spot with truckish touches. Mixed crowds stop in throughout the night for drinks, burgers, fried food, and the eye-candy on both sides of the bar.

Twin Peaks Tavern
401 Castro Street; tel: 864-9470; www.twinpeaks tavern.com; Mon–Fri noon–2am, Sat–Sun 8am–2am; metro: F, K, L, M, T to Castro; bus: 33, 34, 35, 37; map p.137 E1

A longtime Castro fixture on the corner of Castro and Market Streets, Twin Peaks Tavern opened in the 1970s and was one the first gay bars in the US to have clear, rather than opaque glass windows. It is a quiet spot to chat and people-watch through the glass front.

Wild Side West
424 Cortland Avenue; tel: 647-3099; Mon–Sun 1pm–2am; bus: 24

This cozy, welcoming neighborhood bar in Bernal Heights draws a primarily lesbian and local clientele, who relax and chat in the large garden out back.

SEE ALSO BARS AND CAFÉS, P.34–9; NIGHTLIFE, P.94–5; THEATER AND CABARET, P.119

Cafés

Baghdad Café
2295 Market Street; tel: 621-4434; daily 24 hours; $; metro: F, K, L, M, T to Castro; bus: 24, 35, 37; map p.137 E1

A decent 24-hour diner, popular with post-clubbing crowds with the munchies who come for burgers and fries, meaty sandwiches, and breakfast standards.

Just for You Café
732 22nd Street; tel: 647-3033;

Below: entertainment of all sorts is available.

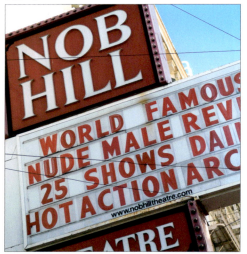

Above: a performer dances on Market Street at the LGBT Pride Festival.

www.justforyoucafe.com;
Mon–Fri 7.30am–3pm, Sat–Sun
8am–3pm; $; metro: T to 23rd
Street; bus: 48

A diverse crowd raves about
the hearty, homemade
breakfasts, especially the
giant, powdered-sugar-
dusted beignets and other
New Orleans and Mexican
specialties.

Samovar

498 Sanchez Street; tel: 626-
4700; www.samovarlife.com;
daily 10am–10pm; metro: F, K,
L, M, T to Castro; bus: 24, 33;
map p.139 A1

As a change from the area's
many bars, this is a popular
and relaxed spot selling a
wide selection of teas, with
small plates providing a further temptation to linger.

SEE ALSO BARS AND CAFÉS, P.34–9

Festivals and Events

The annual **San Francisco
LGBT Pride Festival** (tel: 864-
0831; www.sf-pride.org) each
June is the world's largest,
featuring the ever-popular
Pride Parade. SoMa hosts the
Up Your Alley leather and
fetish fair in July (www.folsom

streetfair.com/alley) and then the
Folsom Street Fair – the
'grand-daddy of all leather
events' – in September (www.
folsomstreetfair.com). Come
October, arts and craft vendors and community groups
gather at the **Castro Street
Fair** (www.castrostreetfair.org).
Aids awareness and activist
events include an annual **Aids
Walk San Francisco**
(www.aidswalk.net/sanfran), and
various events on World Aids
Day (www.artistsagainstaids.com).

Health and Fitness

Gold's Gym

2301 Market Street; tel: 626-
4488; www.goldsgym.com;
metro: F, K, L, M, T to Castro; bus:
24, 33, 35, 37; map p.137 E1
1001 Brannan Street; tel: 552-
4653; www.goldsgym.com; bus:
19, 27; map p.139 C2

The Castro and SoMa loca-
tions of Gold's Gym are
largely used by gay men. Call
for hours and daily rates.

Magnet

4122 18th Street; tel: 581-1600;
www.magnetsf.com; Tue 11am–
6pm, Wed–Fri 2–9pm, Sat
11am–6pm; metro: F, K, L, M, T

to Church; bus: 24, 33, 33, 37;
map p.137 E1

Taking a holistic approach to
gay men's health, Magnet
provides anonymous testing,
counseling, seminars, dance
lessons, art shows, and other
events in a friendly setting.

Information and Resources

The best source for information on the latest shows,
films, events, clubs, and gay
news are two free weekly
newspapers: the *Bay Area
Reporter* (BAR; www.ebar.com)
and the *Bay Times* (www.sfbay
times.com). These are
found in cafés, bars, bookstores, and street-corner

61

boxes, especially in and around the Castro.

The San Francisco Bay Guardian and *SF Weekly* are two non-gay-specific alternative weeklies with useful listings and information. Further resources can be found at websites such as: www.onlyinsanfrancisco.com/gay-travel and at the centers, museums, and locations listed below.

The Center (San Francisco LGBT Community Center, Charles M. Holmes Campus)

1800 Market Street; tel: 865-5555; www.sfcenter.org; Mon–Thur noon–10pm, Fri noon–6pm, Sat 9am–6pm; free; metro: F to Market Street and Laguna Street; bus: 6, 7, 26, 71; map p.138 A2

The Center is a vital nexus for the LGBT (Lesbian, Gay, Bisexual, Transgender) community, and supplies a general information desk, library, Internet access, community bulletin boards, and café.

Community United Against Violence (CUAV)

170A Capp Street; tel: 777-5500, hotline 415-333-4357; www.cuav.org; map p.138 B1

An anti-violence organization that offers a 24-hour crisis line, free counseling, and legal advocacy.

GLBT Historical Society Museum

657 Mission Street, Suite 300; tel: 777-5455; www.glbt history.org; Tue–Sat 1–5pm; BART and metro: all lines to Montgomery; bus: 9, 14, 30, 45, 71; map p.135 D1

Engrossing, varied exhibits focus on GLBT history, art, and culture.

James C. Hormel Gay and Lesbian Center, Main Library

100 Larkin Street, Third Floor; tel: 557-4400; http://sfpl.org; Mon 10am–6pm, Tue–Thur 9am–8pm, Fri noon–6pm, Sat 10am–6pm, Sun noon–5pm; free; BART to Civic Center; metro: all lines to Civic Center; bus: 6, 7, 19, 21, 71; map p.138 B3

Books, photographs, films, and memorabilia document LGBT history and culture in this resource center, the first of its kind to be located in a public institution.

Lavender Youth Recreation and Information Center (LYRIC)

127 Collingwood Street; tel: 415-703-6150; www.lyric.org; metro: K, L, M to Castro; bus: 24, 33; map p.137 E1

A community center for lesbian, gay, bisexual, transgender, queer, and questioning youth.

The Women's Building

3543 18th Street; tel: 431-1180; www.womensbuilding. org; Mon–Sun 9am–5pm, additional evening hours vary; BART: 16th Street Mission; metro: J to Church and 18th streets; bus: 14, 22, 26, 33, 49; map p.138 A1

The beautiful *MaestraPeace* mural colorfully decorates the outside of this 'multi-ethnic, multi-cultural, multi-service center for women and girls.'

Below: a colorful gay pride mural in the Castro.

Left: flamboyant style at a Ferry Building cook-off.

outfits, and home decor.

Nancy Boy

347 Hayes Street; tel: 552-3802; www.nancyboy.com; Mon–Fri 11am–7pm, Sat–Sun 11am–6pm; bus: 21, 47, 49; map p.138 A3

'Tested on Boyfriends – Not Animals' is the playful motto of this high-end Hayes Valley boutique that specializes in skincare and beauty products for men, including a popular shaving line.

Rolo Castro

2351 Market Street; tel: 431-4545; www.rolo.com; Mon–Sat 11am–7pm, Sun noon–6pm; metro: F, K, L, M, T to Castro; bus: 24, 37; map p.137 E1

A go-to spot for edgy and very-of-the-moment designer clothing, Rolo Castro is the place to find top-shelf trends, generally at top-dollar prices.

Under One Roof

549 Castro Street; tel: 503-2300; www.underoneroof.org; Mon–Wed 10am–8pm, Thur–Sat 10am–9pm, Sun 11am–8pm; metro: F, K, L, M, T to Castro; bus: 24, 33, 35, 37; map p.137 E1

Profits from the sales of this store's odds and ends are donated to organizations providing HIV/Aids education and support services.

The Wild Card

3989 17th Street; tel: 626-4449; daily 11am–8pm; metro: F, K, L, M, T to Castro; bus: 24, 33, 35, 37; map p.137 E1

A gay-themed stationery store with risqué cards and naughty novelties. Fun for gifts.

Restaurants

2223

2223 Market Street; tel: 431-0692; www.2223restaurant. com; Mon–Thur 5.30–9.30pm, Fri–Sat 5.30–11pm, Sun 10am–2.30pm, 5–9.30pm; $$; metro: F, J, K, L, M, T to Church; bus: 9, 22, 37; map p.137 E1

A chic neighborhood favorite for comfort food in a fun, lively setting; also a great bet for Sunday brunch.

Catch

2362 Market Street; tel: 431-5000; www.catchsf.com; daily 11.30am–9.30pm, with exceptions; $$; metro: F, K, L, M, T to Castro; bus: 24, 35, 37; map p.137 E1

A casual, cozy seafood spot with a heated outdoor patio, view of Market Street, nightly live piano music, and a lively, fun atmosphere.

Home

2100 Market Street; tel: 503-0333; www.home-sf.com; daily 5pm–midnight and Sat–Sun 10am–2pm; $$; metro: F, J, K, L, M, T to Church Street; 22, 33, 37; map p.138 A2

Good value, welcoming restaurant specializing in tasty versions of American favorites and other comfort foods. Also boasts a fun patio bar.

SEE ALSO RESTAURANTS, P.102–11

Stores

A Different Light Bookstore

489 Castro Street; tel: 431-0891; www.adlbooks.com; Sun–Thur 10am–10pm, Fri–Sat 10am–11pm; metro: F, K, L, M, T to Castro; bus: 33, 34, 35, 37; map p.137 E1

San Francisco's biggest gay bookstore supplies gay and lesbian oriented books, magazines, and newspapers.

Cliff's Variety

479 Castro Street; tel: 431-5365; www.cliffsvariety.com; Mon–Fri 8.30am–8pm, Sat 9.30am–8pm, Sun 11am–6pm; metro: F, K, L, M, T to Castro station; bus: 24, 33, 35, 37; map p.137 E1

This unique hardware store sells just about everything you might need for a costume, with aisles of tools, craft supplies, fancy-dress

Average price for a three-course meal and a half-bottle of house wine:	
$$$$	more than $100
$$$	$50–$100
$$	$25–$50
$	less than $25

63

History and Architecture

BC 13000

The Farallon Islands, covered in cedar and pine forests, mark the ocean's edge and the beginning of the vast savannah that is now the San Francisco Bay.

BC 8,000

Ancestors of the Ohlone and Miwok tribes begin settling the shores of the recently filled-in bay.

1579

Sir Francis Drake lands just north of the Golden Gate, missing the bigger bay to the south presumably due to fog. At the present-day Drake's Bay, he claims the surrounding land for England, to no avail.

1769

Cresting Sweeney Ridge above present-day Pacifica, the governor of California, Gaspar de Portola, and his party discover the San Francisco Bay whilst looking for the port of Monterey.

1776

The Spanish arrive and build a garrison at the site of the Presidio. More than 200 years later, it retains the best array of American military architecture in the country. On the other side of the peninsula, near a lagoon called Nuestra Senora de los Dolores, the padres established the Misión San Francisco de Asís. Built with adobe in the Spanish style of its day, the mission, commonly known as the Mission Dolores, is San Francisco's oldest building and the only one left representing this era.

1822

When Mexico wins its independence from Spain, California becomes a Mexican territory and its mission system is secularized.

1835

William Richardson, an English sea captain, pitches his tent at Yerba Buena Cove and founds a settlement with the same name.

1839

Swiss settler Jean-Jacques Vioget drafts a layout for Yerba Buena based on a grid. Less than 10 years later, Jasper O'Farrell 'creates' Market Street.

1846

Early in the Mexican-American War, John Montgomery sails the USS *Portsmouth* through the Golden Gate, and raises the Stars and Stripes in the present day Portsmouth Square.

1847

Yerba Buena is renamed San Francisco.

1848

James Marshall discovers gold at John Augustus Sutter's mill in the Sierra Nevada foothills on January 24. Nine days later on February 2, the Treaty of Guadalupe Hildago is signed, making California American.

1849

The Gold Rush ignites the greatest mass migration in history, turning what was a 2,000-person town into a rugged city with a population of 20,000.

1850

The US Congress grants California statehood, skipping the intermediate stage of territory.

1855

At the corner of Pacific and Battery, a brick hotel building is constructed over the hull of a landlocked ship used as a saloon. Still called 'Old Ship Saloon,' it represents the look of the Barbary Coast era.

1859

With the discovery of the Comstock Load, a vast silver deposit in Virginia City, Nevada, San Francisco once again becomes a boomtown.

1862

The electrical telegraph is invented, linking San Francisco with the rest of the country.

1869

The Transcontinental Railroad is completed, making millionaires of the 'Big Four' barons: Charles Crocker, Collis P. Huntington, Mark Hopkins, and Leland Stanford.

1870

William Hammond Hall begins the difficult task of turning the city's western sand dunes into Golden Gate Park.

1873

Cable Cars are invented, allowing for the development of San Francisco's steepest hills and outer western areas.

1875

Anti-Chinese riots raze Chinatown. The Pacific Coast Stock Exchange and the grand Palace Hotel are both built.

1882

The Chinese Exclusion Act is passed in Congress.

1886

The first brownstone west of the Mississippi is built for tycoon James Flood atop Nob Hill.

1895

The famous 'Painted Ladies' lining Alamo Square represent the city's Victorian architecture. Queen Anne's, known for their asymmetrical style and arresting turrets, are also popular at this time, as are Edwardians, distinguished by their narrow and rectangular bay windows.

1906

At 5.12am on April 18th, an earthquake measuring an estimated 8.3 on the Richter Scale hits San Francisco. The earthquake causes considerable damage, including the destruction of City Hall, and its disruption of gas and water lines results in blazing fires all over the city that burn for three days, destroying much of San Francisco and leaving thousands of people dead or homeless.

1907

Complete with a classic copper facade, the flatiron Sentinal Building is finished, despite damage from the earthquake and fire. It represents the architectural style of San Francisco's downtown before the great quake.

1908

Chinatown is rebuilt, designed by white architects with an eye on extenuating its exotic Beijing-inspired architecture to attract tourism and tame its perceived excesses.

1910

The Angel Island Immigration Station opens. Known as the 'Ellis Island of the west' it goes on to process 175,000 Asian immigrants, often holding them for several months.

1912

The San Francisco Municipal Railway is created and becomes one of the first publicly owned transit companies in the nation.

1914

Influenced by the City Beautiful movement of the late 19th century, Arthur Brown Jr completes the new City Hall, designed in the beaux arts style.

1915

To mark the opening of the Panama Canal and the rebirth of the city, San Francisco hosts the Panama-Pacific Exposition on waterfront filled in with the refuse left from the 1906 earthquake. Afterward, it is christened the Marina and developed in the Mediterranean architectural style sweeping California in the 1920s. The only structure to remain from the Exposition is the Palace of Fine Arts.

1918

The Gothic Hallidie Building is completed during a boom in downtown development.

1926

Unique for its Romanesque and French Chateau ornamentation, the Hunter-Dulin Building opened its doors. Its most famous tenent is Dashiell Hammett's fictional Sam Spade.

1930

Diego Rivera paints murals at the Pacific Stock Exchange and the San Francisco Art Institute.

1933

The fluted Coit Tower, deeded to the city by Lilly Hitchcock Coit, is completed. Its interior is illustrated with frescoes depicting working class San Francisco.

1934

The West Coast Waterfront Strike lasts 83 days and shuts down San Francisco's port, prompting violent collisions with the police and National Guard, and inspiring a four-day general strike throughout the city.

1937

The Golden Gate Bridge opens at the cost of $35 million and the lives of 11 construction workers, six months after the Bay Bridge is completed.

1940

Known as the 'Harlem of the west', the Lower Fillmore jazz clubs begin attracting big names such as Ella Fitzgerald, Duke Ellington, Billie Holiday, Charles Mingus, and Charley Parker.

1941–5

As 1.6 million American military men pass through Fort Mason on their way to the front, Bay Area industry booms with the war effort.

1942

The US government rounds up Japanese residents, including 3rd generation citizens, and moves them to internment camps deep in the country's interior.

1945

World War II is declared over. The UN charter is signed in the War Memorial Opera House.

1955

Alan Ginsburg reads his poem *Howl* at the Gallery Six, igniting the San Francisco Poetry Renaissance.

1957

San Francisco columnist Herb Caen coins the phrase 'Beatnik' at a bar, while listening to Beat poetry the night Sputnik is launched.

1951–9

In the Fillmore district, Justin Herman's controversial Urban Renewal Program demolishes African-American owned businesses and some 200 homes, replacing them with low-rise, low-income apartment blocks.

1964
On the ashes of the Crocker mansion on Nob Hill, the French Gothic inspired Grace Cathedral is completed.

1965
The Grateful Dead debut at the Fillmore Auditorium.

1967

Haight-Ashbury blossoms with the Summer of Love, launching the city and its music into the center of the counterculture.

1969
In Presidio Heights, the Zodiac killer commits his only murder in San Francisco, while continuing to taunt the SFPD and the *San Francisco Chronicle*.

1971
Inspired by the Chicano civil rights movement, artists begin a series of murals on Balmy Alley; today, there are nearly 500 murals in the Mission district. Modern Movement proponent Pietro Belluschi designs the arresting Cathedral of Saint Mary of the Assumption.

1972
The Transamerica Pyramid is finished, both redefining the skyline and initiating a boom in downtown construction. With the advent of the flexible steel corset, buildings in the earthquake-prone downtown are no longer restricted to 20 stories. Galvanized city leaders begin the 'Manhattanization' of the area, which carries on for another 15 years.

1977
Harvey Milk is elected to city supervisor for the Castro district. The 'Mayor of Castro Street' is the first openly gay person ever elected to public office in the United States.

1978
The city is gripped in tragedy as Supervisor Harvey Milk and Mayor George Moscone are shot and killed at City Hall by former Supervisor Dan White.

1979
Dan White's defense in his murder trial, widely derided as the 'Twinkie Defense', delivers him seven years for manslaughter. The light sentence ignites the violent White Night Riots at City Hall.

1989

During the opening of the World Series at Candlestick Park, a 7.1 earthquake rocks the Bay Area, killing 67 people and causing billions of dollars worth of damage.

1995–2001
The 'New Economy' of the dot-com era dominates much of San Franciscan life. The optimism, inflated living costs, and get-rich mentality are reminiscent of the city's earlier boom times.

2000
The San Francisco Giants play their first season in the new Pacific Bell Park, now AT&T Park.

2002
The dot-com bubble finally bursts, leading to one of the largest crashes ever in the stock market.

2003
200,000 San Franciscans are part of the largest international anti-war demonstration in history.

2004
Mayor Gavin Newsom begins issuing marriage licenses for same-sex couples, putting this controversial issue on the national stage.

2005
The new de Young Museum opens in Golden Gate Park. Its modern architecture, synthesized with the natural landscaping, receives widespread praise.

2006

San Francisco Representative Nancy Pelosi becomes the first female Speaker of the House of Representatives.

2009
San Francisco buys former naval base Treasure Island from the US government for a guaranteed $55 million, with plans to develop a cutting-edge green community.

2014
Scheduled completion date of the Pelli Clarke Pelli-designed Transbay Transit Center, which will accomodate nine transportation systems and include a multi-use skyscraper, a raised park and eventually a high-speed rail line to Los Angeles.

Hotels

There is no shortage of somewhere to lay your hat here: San Francisco possesses a dizzying array of hotels, motels, bed-and-breakfasts, and inns that range from the mundane to the dramatic. All of the major chains are well represented, but the more interesting rooms can be found in the boutique hotels. These small, amenities-rich properties are sometimes developed around a theme, such as literature, art deco architecture or the 1960s, giving the hotel a definable personality. When making reservations at the larger hotels, always inquire about special packages and discounts.

Fisherman's Wharf

Argonaut Hotel

495 Jefferson Street; tel: 563-0800, toll-free: 866-415-0704; www.argonauthotel.com; metro: F to Jones and Beach streets; bus: 10, 30, 47; cable car: Powell-Hyde; $$; map p.134 B4
Directly opposite the Wharf's Hyde Street Pier, this spot boasts a maritime theme and suites with sea views, tri-pod telescopes and hot tubs.

Tuscan Inn

425 North Point Street; tel: 561-1100, toll-free: 866-648-4626; www.tuscaninn.com; metro: F to Jefferson and Taylor streets; bus: 10, 30, 47; cable car: Powell-Mason; $$; map p.134 B4
This pleasant Italian-themed hotel has an enthusiastic concierge, attractive rooms that are well-sized by local standards and an appealing location for families who wish to be near Pier 39.

Wharf Inn

2601 Mason Street; tel: 673-7411; www.wharfinn.com; metro: F to Jefferson Street and Powell Street: bus: 39, 47; cable car: Powell-Mason; $; map p.134 B4
In the thick of the Wharf, this family-friendly gem has good service and rooms with balconies overlooking Pier 39.

North Beach, Telegraph Hill, and Russian Hill

Hotel Boheme

444 Columbus Avenue; tel: 433-9111; www.hotelboheme.com; bus: 30, 39, 41, 45; $$; map p.134 C3
A flight of narrow stairs brings you inside this delightful small hotel located in the heart of North Beach. Iron beds and brightly painted walls grace the small but lovely bedrooms, and the bathrooms are well-stocked with toiletries. The front desk staff are happy to assist with rental cars, dinner reservations, and tours. All rooms have free Wi-Fi.

San Remo Hotel

2337 Mason Street; tel: 776-8688, toll-free: 800-352-7366; www.sanremohotel.com; bus: 30, 39, 41; cable car: Powell-Mason; $; map p.134 B3
Built right after the 1906 earthquake, this originally served as a boardinghouse for sailors, poets and seniors; during Prohibition, it was a speakeasy. Today, it is a bargain, with a stellar location

Left: a smart welcome at the Four Seasons.

Left: the discreet luxury of the Campton Place Hotel.

5555; www.tajhotels.com; bus: 2, 4, 30, 45, 76; cable car: Powell-Hyde, Powell-Mason; $$$$; map p.135 C1

Elegant, luxurious, and intimate, this is one of the most renowned and refined hotels in the city. The service is excellent, the amenities are top-notch, and the hotel restaurant consistently wins high ratings.

Chancellor Hotel
433 Powell Street; tel: 362-2004, toll-free: 800-428-4748; www.chancellorhotel.com; bus: 2, 3, 27, 38, 71; $$; map p.134 C1
Family owned since 1917, this charming hotel is within a stone's throw of Union Square's major department stores. Rooms are comfortably furnished; bathrooms are small but well-stocked.

Clift Hotel
495 Geary Street; tel: 775-4700, toll-free: 800-697-1791; www.clifthotel.com; bus: 2, 4, 27, 38, 76; $$$; map p.134 C1
An historic hotel redesigned by Philippe Starke, the Clift is a fusion of old-world elegance and contemporary hipness and home to the über-cool Asia de Cuba restaurant and the Redwood Room.

Four Seasons
757 Market Street; tel: 633-3000; www.fourseasons.com; BART: to Powell; metro: all lines to Powell; bus: 30, 38, 45, 76; cable car: Powell-Hyde, Powell-Mason; $$$$; map p.135 C1

> Your concierge is a treasure trove of local info. Use him for questions of every kind. You need not tip him for every tip he gives you, but if he hooks you up well, show your appreciation with a gratuity.

and immaculate rooms. Some share bathroom facilities. The penthouse is a treat and Fior d'Italia, the restaurant on the first floor, is the stuff of North Beach legend.

Washington Square Inn
1660 Stockton Street; tel: 981-4220, toll-free: 800-388-0220; www.wsisf.com; bus: 30, 39, 41; $$; map p.134 C3
A European-style bed-and-breakfast right on one of San Francisco's most scenic urban parks, Washington Square. A great place for an extended soaking in North Beach's legendary cuisine and nightlife.

Chinatown

Grant Plaza Hotel
465 Grant Avenue; tel: 434-3883, toll-free: 800-472-6899; www.grantplaza.com; bus: 30, 45; cable car: California; $; map p.135 C1

A good bet in Chinatown: immaculately clean, small rooms equipped with the very basics. Location is the prime sell here, as it is ideal for the active traveler, hill walker, and dim-sum afficianado.

Royal Pacific Motor Inn
661 Broadway; tel: 781-6661, toll-free: 800-545-5574; www.royalpacificmotorinn.com; bus: 9, 14, 30, 41, 45; $; map p.135 C2
Amenities at this budget motel on the threshold of North Beach and Chinatown. Amenities include a Finnish sauna, satellite TV, and free parking.

Union Square and Financial District

Andrews Hotel
624 Post Street; tel: 563-6877, toll-free: 800-926-3739; www.andrewshotel.com; bus: 2, 3, 27, 38, 76; $; map p.134 C1
A 1905 Victorian well-located two blocks west of Union Square. The rooms and baths are on the small side, but rates include a continental breakfast and a glass of wine in the downstairs restaurant. Smoking is not allowed.

Campton Place Hotel
340 Stockton Street; tel: 781-

> Prices per night for a standard double room, exclusive of taxes (14 percent) in high-season. Prices do not include parking or breakfast unless noted and are liable to change, so always check before you book.
> $$$$ over $350
> $$$ $225–350
> $$ $150–225
> $ under $150

Left: funky design in the lobby of Hotel Triton.

With a giant club with indoor pool and spa and an ultra-convenient location Downtown close to high-end stores, this sleek highrise knows how to cater to its sophisticated and fairly exclusive clientele.

Galleria Park Hotel
191 Sutter Street; tel: 781-3060, toll-free: 800-792-9639; www.galleriapark.com; metro: all lines to Montgomery; bus: 30, 38, 45; $$; map p.135 D1
A contemporary boutique hotel with 17 suites and a comfortable, stylish ambiance. Convenient to both Union Square and the Financial District, it features complimentary Wi-Fi, an evening wine reception, and the popular brasserie-style Midi restaurant downstairs.

Prices per night for a standard double room, exclusive of taxes (14 percent) in high-season. Prices do not include parking or breakfast unless noted and are liable to change, so always check before you book.

$$$$	over $350
$$$	$225–350
$$	$150–225
$	under $150

Golden Gate Hotel
775 Bush Street; tel: 392-3702, toll-free: 800-835-1118; www.goldengatehotel.com; bus: 2, 3, 4, 76; cable car: Powell-Hyde, Powell-Mason; $$; map p.134 C1
A cozy family-run hotel near Union Square and two blocks from the Chinatown Gate. The pretty rooms contain few amenities, but the hotel's rates include a continental breakfast and afternoon tea. Smoking is not allowed in the hotel. Some rooms with private bath. Pet friendly.

Handlery Union Square Hotel
351 Geary Street; tel: 781-7800, toll-free: 800-843-4343; www.handlery.com/sf; bus: 2, 4, 27, 38; $$; map p.134 C1
A good choice for families, the hotel has a heated outdoor pool, morning and evening room service, and on-demand movies and video games. Club rooms, located in an adjacent building, are larger and offer views, dressing areas, robes, newspapers, and fresh decor.

Hotel Bijou
111 Mason Street; tel: 771-1200, toll-free: 800-771-1022; www.hotelbijou.com; BART: to Powell; metro: all lines to Powell; bus: 27, 31; $; map p.138 C4
This 65-room hotel is dedicated to cinephiles. Rooms are awash in jewel tones, and walls are covered in black-and-white images of old cinema marquees. A mini-theater with vintage cinema seating screens free nightly movies.

Hotel Frank
386 Geary Street; tel: 986-2000, toll-free: 800-553-1900; www.maxwellhotel.com; bus: 2, 3, 27, 38, 71; $; map p.134 C1
This theatre district hotel offers cosmopolitan style with bold, black-and-white houndstooth carpets and emerald green accents. Rooms include 32-inch flatscreen TVs and iPod docking stations, and room service features deli fare courtesy of Max's on the Square.

Hotel Metropolis
25 Mason Street; tel: 775-4600, toll-free: 800-553-1900; www.hotelmetropolis.com; BART and metro: all lines to Powell; bus: 27, 31; cable car: Powell-Hyde, Powell-Mason; $$; map p.138 C4
This eco-friendly hotel with a 'four-elements' theme, vivid color schemes and a loft library is a good, centrally located bargain for families.

Hotel Monaco
501 Geary Street; tel: 292-0100, toll-free: 866-622-5284; www.monaco-sf.com; bus: 2, 3, 27, 38, 76; $$$; map p.134 C1
An elegant, renovated Beaux-Arts building with hand-painted ceiling domes and grand Art Nouveau murals in the common areas. Rates include morning coffee, afternoon tea, and wine receptions. Rooms are comfortable and glamorous, with canopied

> Views can make or break a hotel room in SF, especially the high-rise hotels. Booking online often means you cannot request where your room faces, which might be the Golden Gate Bridge or the back alley. Booking by phone allows you to specify your view.

beds, colorful decor, iHomes, and Frette linens. The Grace Slick suite is filled with original memorabilia from her Jefferson Airplane days.

Hotel Nikko
222 Mason Street; tel: 394-1111, toll-free: 800-248-3308; www.hotelnikkosf.com; BART and metro: all lines to Powell; bus: 27, 38; cable car: Powell-Mason, Powell-Hyde; $$$; map p.134 C1
An elegant and sophisticated Japanese hotel with decent rooms and, more importantly, great spa facilities.

Hotel Rex
562 Sutter Street; tel: 433-4434, toll-free: 800-433-4434; www.jdv hospitality.com; bus: 2, 3, 30, 45, 76; cable car: Powell-Hyde, Powell-Mason; $$; map p.134 C1
With a nod to the 1930s, the sophisticated Rex is dedicated to the literati and hosts book signings, poetry readings and jazz on Fridays in the library bar. An evening wine hour is complimentary.

Hotel Triton
342 Grant Street; tel: 394-0500, toll-free: 800-800-1299; www.hoteltriton.com; bus: 2, 3, 30, 45, 76; $$$; map p.135 C1
This trendy, eco-friendly hotel across from the Chinatown Gate features wild designs and mod lobby furniture. Decor in the small rooms ranges from creamy whites to cherry reds. A pioneer in green hotels, the Triton employs a sophisticated recycling program and uses biodegradable cleaning

products and energy efficient systems.

Hotel Vertigo
940 Sutter Street; tel: 885-6200, toll-free: 800-553-1900; www.hotelvertigosf.com; bus: 2, 3, 4, 27, 76; $$; map p.134 B1
The setting for Hitchcock's *Vertigo* has recently been renovated with lots of white decor and tangerine-orange accents. A deluxe continental breakfast and Wi-Fi are included in the reasonably priced room rates.

Hotel Vitale
8 Mission Street; tel: 278-3700, toll-free: 888-890-8688; www.hotelvitale.com; BART and metro: all lines to Embarcadero; bus: 2, 14, 21, 31, 71; $$$; map p.135 E2
A waterfront hotel, with a slew of amenities, including free car service within one mile and private rooftop soaking tubs. The Americano restaurant is downstairs.

Hyatt Regency
5 Embarcadero; tel: 788-1234 www.sanfranciscoregency. hyatt.com; BART and metro: all lines to Embarcadero; bus: 1, 10; map p.135 D2
Conveniently located across from the Ferry Building in the Financial District, this waterfront hotel's 802 rooms feature 32-inch flatscreen LCD TVs, iHome stereos, granite bathrooms, and rich cherry wood work desks. Unwind at the 24-hour gym, or with specialty cocktails in the lounge.

Inn at Union Square
440 Post Street; tel: 397-3510, toll-free: 800-288-4346; www. unionsquare.com; bus: 2, 3, 27, 38, 76; $$; map p.134 C1
This 30-room hotel goes the extra distance with bottled spring water on the nightstand, early evening wine and hors d'oeuvres in front of the fireplace, and overnight shoe-shining services. The nearby full-service

fitness club has a heated pool and Pilates classes.

Kensington Park Hotel
450 Post Street; tel: 788-6400, toll-free: 800-553-1900; www. kensingtonparkhotel.com; bus: 2, 3, 27, 38, 76; $; map p.134 C1
Opened in 1912, with rooms renovated in 2008, this British hotel champions old-fashioned rates and hospitality combined with up-to-date services. Free tea and sherry are served each evening.

Larkspur Hotel Union Square
524 Sutter Street; tel: 421-2865, toll-free: 800-919-9779; www.larkspurhotelunion square.com; bus: 2, 3, 30, 45, 76; cable car: Powell-Hyde, Powell-Mason; $; map p.134 C1
Rooms in this genteel hotel are tastefully decorated in dark woods, beiges, and creams, and feature LED flatscreen TVs and free wireless Internet. A continental breakfast is included. Suites are available, a plus for families. Pets are welcome.

Mandarin Oriental
222 Sansome Street; tel/toll-free: 800-622-0404; www. mandarinoriental.com/san francisco; BART and metro: all lines to Montgomery; bus: 10, 41; cable car: California; $$$$; map p.135 D2

Below: breakfast in style at the Mandarin Oriental Hotel.

Above: spectacular views from the Mandarin Oriental over North Beach and the Financial District.

This Financial District luxury hotel features extraordinary views and decadent service. Some suites have private terraces or glass bathtubs near the windows.

Ritz-Carlton
600 Stockton Street; tel: 296-7465, toll-free: 800-542-8680; www.ritzcarlton.com; bus: 1, 30, 45; cable car: California; $$$$; map p.135 C1

Opened in 1991 and recently renovated, this giant neo-classical luxury hotel caters to deep-pocketed travelers. The Ritz offers enormous rooms decorated in dark woods and beiges, Italian marble bathrooms, a fitness center, fine dining restaurant, and prime service.

The Serrano
405 Taylor Street; tel: 885-2500, toll-free: 866-289-6561; www.serranohotel.com; bus: 27, 38; cable car: Powell-Hyde, Powell-Mason; $$; map p.134 C1

A 17-story Spanish Revival building with an ornate, Moorish-style lobby, 236 rooms and suites in the heart of the Theater District. Pet- and kid-friendly with a good Pan-Asian restaurant, Ponzu, downstairs.

Sir Francis Drake
450 Powell Street; tel: 392-7755, toll-free: 800-795-7129; www.sirfrancisdrake.com; bus: 2, 3, 27, 30, 76; $$; map p.134 C1

Glide past the uniformed valets into the grand lobby of this 1928 landmark building. A recent $20 million renovation refurbished all guestrooms and public spaces, casting them in a lovely cream, sage green, and plum color scheme. The excellent Scala's Bistro is located next door, and on the top floor there is a small fitness room and a popular nightclub with a spectacular view.

Warwick
490 Geary Street; tel: 928-7900, toll-free: 800-203-3232; www.warwicksf.com; bus: 2, 3, 27, 30, 76; $$; map p.134 C1

Guests receive all the amenities expected of a much larger hotel, like twice-daily maid service, marble-tiled baths, afternoon tea and cookies, same-day laundry service and 24-hour room service. Quiet guest rooms are elegantly appointed with Louis XVI decor. The Union Square location is especially convenient for theatergoers.

Westin St Francis
335 Powell Street; tel: 397-7000, toll-free: 866-500-0338; www.westinstfrancis.com; bus: 2, 3, 4, 30, 76; cable car: Powell-Hyde, Powell-Mason; $$$; map p.134 C1

The location, across the street from Union Square, adds to the excitement of staying at this legendary hotel. If the historic aspects interest you, reserve a room in the original building. Baths are small and guest rooms rather dark, but they are furnished with handsome reproductions and chandeliers. An on-site fitness center, room service, and chef Michael Mina's

Prices per night for a standard double room, exclusive of taxes (14 percent) in high-season. Prices do not include parking or breakfast unless noted and are liable to change, so always check before you book.

$$$$	over $350
$$$	$225–350
$$	$150–225
$	under $150

> If you will have a car in SF, be sure to find out if parking at your hotel is free, or available for a fee. Fees can easily add up to $150 for a week.

acclaimed restaurant complete the package.
SEE ALSO RESTAURANTS, P.105

SoMa and Civic Center

Bay Bridge Inn
966 Harrison Street; tel: 397-0657; www.baybridgeinn.com; bus: 12, 27, 47; $; map p.139 C3
Nothing but the basics here, but one attraction for party animals is that the clean, motel-style rooms are convenient to the nightclub scene in SoMa.

Harbor Court Hotel
165 Steuart Street; tel: 882-1300, toll-free: 866-792-6283; www.harborcourthotel.com; BART and metro to Embarcadero; bus: 2, 12, 14, 31, 71; $$; map p.135 E2
Across from the Rincon Center, this 1907 building with bay views has been converted into an elegant boutique hotel with comfortable rooms and varied luxury amenities. Guests have complimentary access to the state-of-the-art fitness center next door.

Hotel Adagio
550 Geary Street; tel: 775-5000; toll-free: 800-228-8830; www.jdvhotels.com; bus: 27, 38; $$; map p.134 C1
Handsome and chic, the Adagio Hotel has Internet access, a fitness center, and superb customer service.

Hotel Milano
55 5th Street; tel: 543-8555; toll-free: 800-398-7555; www.hotelmilanosf.com; BART and metro: all lines to Powell; bus: 14, 26, 27; $$; map p.139 C4
The location – next door to the San Francisco Centre, a few blocks from Yerba Buena Gardens and Moscone Center, and close to an underground Muni station – makes this hotel a good pick for energetic tourists who like to shop. An on-site fitness room, restaurant, and full service make up for the spare decor.

Inn at the Opera
333 Fulton Street; tel: 863-8400, toll-free: 800-325-2708; www.shellhospitality.com; bus: 5, 21, 47, 49; $$; map p.138 A3
A favorite spot for the performing artists who appear nightly in San Francisco's nearby arts centers. Good for opera and symphony goers, but the surrounding neighborhood is a bit sketchy.

InterContinental San Francisco
888 Howard Street; tel: 616-6500; toll-free: 888-811-4273; www.intercontinentalsanfrancisco.com; bus: 14, 27; $$$; map p.139 C4
This towering blue-green glass hotel, the latest in SoMa's skyline redesign, is located near the Moscone West Convention Center and represents a new benchmark in local luxury.

Mosser
54 4th Street; tel: 986-4400; www.themosser.com; BART and metro: all lines to Powell; bus: 30, 45, 76; $$; map p.139 C4
An ornate stained-glass window in the lobby, antique

Above: the imposing facade of the Westin St Francis.

phone booths, and an incredibly slow elevator are quirky reminders of this hotel's past, but the good linens, latest gadgets, prime SoMa location and good rates make it an affordable choice for young sophisticates. It features a state-of-the-art recording studio, with packages for beginners and pros.

Palace Hotel
2 New Montgomery Street; tel: 512-1111, toll-free: 888-627-7196; www.sfpalace.com; BART and metro: all lines to Montgomery; bus: 3, 9, 10, 45, 71; $$$; map p.135 D1
An historical landmark just South of Market, and home of the magnificent Garden Court restaurant. Truly one of the city's most opulent returns to

Below: a deluxe room at the Hotel Adagio.

Above: the Garden Court at the Palace Hotel.

a guilded age. Enjoy a cocktail under the Maxfield Parrish mural in the Pied Piper bar.

Phoenix Hotel
601 Eddy Street; tel: 776-1380, toll-free: 800-248-9466; www.jdvhotels.com; bus: 19, 31; $; map p.138 B4

Popular with touring bands and edgy celebrities, the Phoenix has funky rooms with bamboo furniture and a tropical oasis touch. The adjoining Bambuddah restaurant and bar serves Asian-themed delights poolside.

W Hotel
181 3rd Street; tel: 777-5300, toll-free: 800-946-8357; www.whotels.com; bus: 9, 14, 30, 45, 76; $$$$; map p.139 D4

Sparse elegance and minimalist design lures the hip to SoMa. The delectable XYZ restaurant downstairs is topnotch. The modernity extends to the well-stocked rooms, each with CD players, 32-inch TVs, Wi-Fi, iPod shuffles, and goose-down duvets.

Nob Hill

Fairmont Hotel and Tower
950 Mason Street; tel: 772-5000; toll-free: 800-257-7544; www.fairmont.com/sanfrancisco; bus: 1; cable car: California; $$$; map p.134 C2

A favorite set location for filmmakers and an elegant experience, the Fairmont was about to open when the 1906 earthquake struck.

Undaunted, the hotel opened exactly a year later. Experience the opulence of turn-of-the-century SF, or take in the playful classicism of the rotunda in the Laurel Court.

Huntington Hotel
1075 California Street; tel: 474-5400, toll-free: 800-227-4683; www.huntingtonhotel.com; bus: 1; cable car: California; $$$$; map p.134 C1

A refined family-owned hotel built in 1924 at the top of Nob Hill, known for discreet, understated luxury. Originally an apartment building, rooms are larger than average. For the best views, ask for a room above the eighth floor. Grace Cathedral and Huntington Park are just across the street, the latter making the location especially pleasant for families with young children. The **Nob**

Since San Francisco is a very popular convention and tourist town, it is imperative to make reservations well ahead of time. If you have not done so, phone SF Reservations, tel: (800) 677-1500 (toll-free in US) or 510-628-4400 or visit www.hotelres.com.

Hill Spa on the premises is one of the city's best.
SEE ALSO PAMPERING, P.97

InterContinental Mark Hopkins
1 Nob Hill; tel: 392-3434, toll-free: 877-834-3613; www.ichotelsgroup.com; bus: 1; cable car: California; $$$; map p.134 C1

At the summit of Nob Hill, with grand views in all directions, this hotel offers luxury rooms on the site of the original Mark Hopkins mansion. The rooftop cocktail lounge, **Top of the Mark**, has been a

Below: fluttering flags at the Fairmont Hotel.

city staple since 1939, and an atmosphere of quiet refinement prevails throughout.
SEE ALSO BARS AND CAFÉS, P.37

Petite Auberge
863 Bush Street; tel: 928-6000, toll-free: 866-365-3004; www.jdvhotels.com; bus: 2, 3, 4, 76; cable car: Powell-Hyde, Powell-Mason; $; map p.134 C1
A small, cozy French-style inn. There is a pretty parlour and evening wine and hors d'oeuvres, and the room rate includes a gourmet breakfast.

Renaissance Stanford Court
905 California Street; tel: 989-3500, toll-free: 800-227-4736; www.mariott.com; bus: 1; cable car: California; $$; map p.134 C2
An elegant renovation credited with setting the standard for San Francisco grand-hotel revivals. Great views, and you can hear the ding-dinging of the cable cars out your window.

White Swan Inn
845 Bush Street; tel: 775-1755, toll-free: 800-999-9570; www.jdvhotels.com; bus: 2, 3, 4, 76; cable car: Powell-Hyde, Powell-Mason; $$; map p.134 C1
A cozy English-style bed-and-breakfast inn. The romantic rooms and suites all have fireplaces to combat the infamous San Francisco chill. A gourmet breakfast buffet is served daily. Complimentary evening wine and hors d'oeuvres are served in the parlor.

Central Neighbourhoods

Chateau Tivoli
1057 Steiner Street; tel: 776-5462, toll-free: 800-228-1647; www.chateautivoli.com; bus: 21, 22; $$; map p.137 E3
On Alamo Square, this plush Victorian bed-and-breakfast inn brimming with antiques and curios has nine attractive suites.

Above: one of the elegant bathrooms at the Inter-Continental Mark Hopkins.

Hotel Del Sol
3100 Webster Street; tel: 921-5520, toll-free: 877-433-5765; www.jdvhotels.com; bus: 22, 43, 76; $; map p.133 E3
Once a boring, ordinary motel, the Del Sol has had a radical make-over and now proves that looks are almost everything. Color is used to great effect, splashed on walls, fabrics, and mosaic tiles that decorate tabletops and walkways. Comfortable medium- to large-sized rooms surround a heated swimming pool, small lawn and hammock; suites are available.

Hotel Drisco
2901 Pacific Avenue; tel: 346-2880, toll-free: 800-634-7277; www.jdvhotels.com; bus: 3, 24; $$; map p.133 D2
An elegant, 100 year-old hotel tucked away in a beautiful, historical residential area of Pacific Heights. Great for those who have done the downtown thing and want a bit of peace and quiet among the City's upper crust. Complimentary town car service to Union Square and the Financial District is offered weekday mornings.

Hotel Majestic
1500 Sutter Street; tel: 441-1100, toll-free: 800-869-8966; www.thehotelmajestic.com; bus: 2, 3, 4, 38; $$; map p.134 A1
Constructed in 1902, the Majestic claims to be the oldest still-operating hotel in the city. Old-world atmosphere and good special rates.

Laurel Inn
444 Presidio Avenue; tel: 567-8467; toll-free: 800-552-8735; www.jdvhotels.com; bus: 1, 2, 4, 43; $$; map p.133 D1
Do not let the exterior fool you: this recently renovated inn has a lot to offer. A contemporary take on mid-century style, this hotel's rooms are each designed as if it were a modern studio apartment. It is a great option

Prices per night for a standard double room, exclusive of taxes (14 percent) in high-season. Prices do not include parking or breakfast unless noted and are liable to change, so always check before you book.

$$$$	over $350
$$$	$225–350
$$	$150–225
$	under $150

Above: the Hotel Del Sol *(see p.75)* is a great choice if you're traveling with children.

for returning tourists or extended-stay guests. Close to the semi-secret Sacramento Street shopping strip.

Marina Inn
3110 Octavia Street; tel: 928-1000, toll-free: 800-274-1420; www.marinainn.com; bus: 28, 30, 76; $; map p.134 A3
This is an inexpensive, gracious Victorian inn off Lombard Street, not far from the Golden Gate Bridge, the Presidio, and the upscale shopping on Union and Chestnut streets. The rooms are simply furnished; inside rooms are considerably quieter but do not have much natural light. A Continental breakfast is included in the price.

Metro Hotel
319 Divisadero Street; tel: 861-5364; www.metrohotelsf.com; bus: 6, 7, 21, 24; $; map p.137 E2
A comfortable and affordable hotel in the increasingly trendy NoPa (north of the Panhandle) location, just steps from Haight Street. Do

> While many boutique hotels do not have fitness centers, most have arrangements with offsite gyms where guests can work out for free or a reduced rate.

not look for amenities here. Rooms are small and sometimes noisy, but clean. The private garden is inviting. Lots of bars and inexpensive food options are nearby.

Haight-Ashbury and Golden Gate Park

Inn 1890
1890 Page Street; tel: 386-0486, toll-free: 888-466-1890; www.inn1890.com; bus: 7, 33, 37, 43, 71; $; map p.137 C2
This is a beautiful, 18-room corner Victorian bed-and-breakfast is in the heart of the Upper Haight neighborhood – one block from the fabulous Golden Gate Park – where the architecture survived the 1906 earthquake. Built in 1890, some rooms have their own fireplace. A great alternative to the towering hotels of downtown.

Red Victorian Bed and Breakfast Inn
1665 Haight Street; tel: 864-1978; www.redvic.com; bus: 7, 33, 37, 71; $; map p.137 D2
The Summer of Love is alive and well at this peace haven on Haight Street. Reasonably-priced 1960s-themed rooms have private baths, canopied beds, colorful quilts and tie-

dyed fabrics. No televisions but plenty of good vibes. The Red Victorian is perfect for the whimsical, budget traveler. Each room reflects a different theme, such as the Flower Child Room or the Playground, and the ambiance is friendly and casual. Book in and have fun.

Stanyan Park Hotel
750 Stanyan Street; tel: 751-1000; www.stanyanpark.com; bus: 7, 33, 43, 71; $$; map p.137 C2
This elegant, affordable early 20th-century boutique hotel located across the street from Golden Gate Park, steps from Haight Street and the infamous Hippie Hill. Large suites are ideal for families, and a continental breakfast is included.

Mission and Castro

24 Henry Guesthouse and Village House
24 Henry Street and 4080 18th Street; tel: 864-5686, toll-free: 800-900-5686; www.24henry.com; metro: F, K, L, M, T to Church; bus: 24, 33, 37; $; map p.137 E2
Two refurbished late-1800s Victorian houses have been turned into hotels. Each has a parlour and five bedrooms, right in the heart of the Castro.

Beck's Motor Lodge
2222 Market Street; tel: 621-8212, toll-free: 800-227-4360; www.becksmotorlodgesf.com; metro: F, K, L, M, T to Castro; bus: 37; $; map p.137 E1

> Prices per night for a standard double room, exclusive of taxes (14 percent) in high-season. Prices do not include parking or breakfast unless noted and are liable to change, so always check before you book.
> | | |
> |---|---|
> | $$$$ | over $350 |
> | $$$ | $225–350 |
> | $$ | $150–225 |
> | $ | under $150 |

> Some hotels view Internet access as a cash cow, with outrageous fees for online access in your room similar to direct-dialed long-distance. If you need to be constantly checking your email, try to find one with free Wi-Fi. If your hotel charges you, there is a good chance a local café will have free Wi-Fi.

Quintessential American motel, complete with garish furnishings (think pink walls and glasses sealed in plastic). You either think Beck's is kitsch fun, or you run away screaming. Prime location in the Castro, with a sundeck.

Noe's Nest
1257 Guerrero Street; tel: 821-0751; www.noesnest.com; metro: J to Church and 24th streets; bus: 48; $$

Tiny, five-room bed-and-breakfast inn with fireplaces, a Jacuzzi, WiFi, and a local neighborhood feel.

Parker Guesthouse
520 Church Street; tel: 621-3222, toll-free: 888-520-7275; www.parkerguestouse.com; metro: J to Church Street and 18th Street; bus: 33; $; map p.138 A1

A relaxed and welcoming guesthouse in the Castro with 21 rooms (only two with shared bathrooms) and terrycloth robes for every guest. The atmosphere is relaxed and welcoming, and a garden, steam room, library, lounge, piano, and sherry service complete the package.

Oakland, Berkeley and the Bay Area

Claremont Resort and Spa
41 Tunnel Road, Berkeley; tel: 510-843-3000; toll-free: 800-551-7266; www.claremont resort.com; $$$

Perched atop the Berkeley hills in the East Bay, the Claremont is modern in its services and amenities, but the architecture and grounds are a throwback to the golden age of Gatsby or Garbo. Truly an oasis of luxury, and with a fabulous restaurant to boot. The spa facilities are top-notch.
SEE ALSO PAMPERING, P.97

Inn Above Tide
30 El Portal, Sausalito; tel: 415-332-9535, toll-free: 800-893-8433; www.innabovetide.com; $$$$

Boasting that it is the only Bay Area hotel actually on the water, the Inn Above Tide is just that, perched over the Bay in Sausalito. Panoramic views include the San Francisco skyline, and you can watch the sailboats from your private deck, or as you soak in an oversized hot tub.

Wine Country

Ledson Hotel
480 First Street East, Sonoma; tel: 707-996-9779; www.ledson hotel.com; $$$$

The Ledson hotel, while less than a decade old, has become the ultimate lodging on the Sonoma Square. With only six rooms, guests truly feel indulged, and no detail is missed, from fireplaces and private whirlpool tubs to turn-down service. The downstairs lounge serves light fare and drinks.

MacArthur Place
29 East MacArthur Street, Sonoma; tel: 707-938-2929, toll free: 800-722-1866; www.macarthurplace.com; $$$$

The 7-acre (3-hectare) MacArthur Place is a sprawling, art-filled country inn and spa, perfect for a truly special occasion. There are 64 rooms and suites, the latter with fireplaces, hydroterapy tubs, and DVD players with six-speaker surround sound. Robe-clad guests stroll the impeccably landscaped gardens on their way to spa services such as Red Wine Grapeseed Baths and Chardonnay Sugar Scrubs. Bacchus would have approved.

Sonoma Hotel
110 West Spain Street, Sonoma; tel: 707-996-2996, toll-free: 800-468-6016; www.sonoma hotel.com; $$

A comfortable inn decorated in French-country style, in a good location within easy reach of Sonoma's wineries, shops, and restaurants. A continental breakfast and evening wine tasting are included in the rate. Rooms are simple and attractive, and all include a private bathroom.

Below: whether you prefer your surroundings to be classic *(left)* or eclectic *(right)*, San Francisco has hotel options to suit.

Literature

San Francisco has a remarkably rich and thriving literary tradition. From Mark Twain and Dashiell Hammett to Armistead Maupin and Amy Tan, writers of all sorts have scribbled in and about the City by the Bay, drawing inspiration from the spirited, swirling masses of colorful characters, diverse cultures, and unique cityscapes. Today, San Francisco still brims with established and would-be wordsmiths lured from all over the world, and hosts a bundle of bookstores, independent publishers, author readings, and writers' groups, often found linked to the lively café culture.

Literary History

San Francisco's star-studded literary history kicked off in the Gold Rush years, with **Mark Twain** penning *The Celebrated Jumping Frog of Calaveras County*. In 1879, **Robert Louis Stevenson** lived on Bush Street, writing in Portsmouth Square. On the Oakland waterfront, 'Prince of the Oyster Pirates' **Jack London** *(The Call of the Wild)* bought his first sloop at the still-standing First and Last Chance Saloon on what is now Jack London Square. Oakland remembers **Gertrude Stein** rather less fondly; she wrote of Oakland 'There is no there there'. Back across the Bay, **Dashiell Hammett** *(The Maltese Falcon)* spun hardboiled detective stories based on his Pinkerton Detective days.

In the mid-1950s North Beach became the epicentre of the Beat movement, attracting **Jack Kerouac** (author of Beat manifesto *On the Road*), **Lawrence Ferlinghetti**, **Philipp Whalen** and **Michael McClure**, among others. In 1955 **Allen Ginsberg** read his

Above: the Beats put the city's literary scene on the map.

incendiary poem *Howl*, which resulted in an obscenity trial for Ferlinghetti, his publisher; Kerouac memorialized the epic night in *Dharma Bums*. The Merry Pranksters, led by **Ken Kesey** *(One Flew Over the Cuckoo's Nest)*, and LSD-tinged exploits followed, described in **Tom Wolfe's** *The Electric Kool-Aid Acid Test*.

Armistead Maupin's 1976 *Tales of the City* chronicled the lives of young San Franciscans (Macondray Lane will look familiar), while writers **Maxine Hong Kingston** *(The Woman Warrior)* and **Amy Tan** *(The Joy Luck Club)* wrote

about the Chinese-American experience in San Francisco.

The Modern Lit Scene

San Francisco's literary scene is a busy affair. Readings, workshops, performances, and special events fill the calendar, and come October, the lively **LitQuake** festival (www.litquake.org) delivers several events. Periodicals include *Zyzzyva* (www.zyzzyva.org), *Juxtapoz* (www.juxtapoz.com), **Francis Ford Coppola's** *Zoetrope: All Story* (www.allstory.com), *The Believer* (www.believermag.com), and *McSweeny's* (www.mcsweenys.net). The latter two are produced by independent publisher McSweeny's, which was founded by **Dave Eggers** *(A Heartbreaking Work of Staggering Genius)*, who also set up 826 Valencia, a youth literary center.

Further Reading: Books about San Francisco

art-SITES San Francisco: the Guide to Contemporary Art-Architecture-Design, by Sidra Sitch, art-SITES Press (2003) *Footsteps in the Fog: Alfred Hitchcock's San Francisco*,

Left: browsing in the iconic City Lights Bookstore.

Spoiler alert! A sober plaque in Union Square's Burritt Alley honors Hammett's San Francisco-set *The Maltese Falcon*, but also gives away the thriller's end. Nearby, Dashiell Hammett Street is one of several honoring San Francisco literati. Another – Jack Kerouac Street – is near City Light Bookstore, the brains behind the plan.

by Jeff Kraft and Aaron Leventhal, Santa Monica Press (2002)

San Francisco Stories, edited by John Miller, Chronicle Books (1990)

Stairway Walks In San Francisco, by Adah Balalinsky, Wilderness Press, (2006)

Walking San Francisco on the Barbary Coast Trail, by Daniel Bacon, Quick Silver Press (1997)

A Writer's San Francisco: A Guided Journey for the Creative Soul, by Eric Maisel, New World Library (2006)

General Book Stores

Barnes & Noble
Fisherman's Wharf, 2550 Taylor Street; www.bn.com; tel: 292-6762; daily 9am–9pm; metro: F to Jefferson and Taylor streets; bus: 9X, 10, 30, 41; cable car: Powell-Mason; map p.134 B4
Major national chain booksellers in Fisherman's Wharf, with all the latest releases and an in-store café.

Borders Books and Music
400 Post Street; tel: 399-1633; www.borders.com; Mon–Thur 8am–11pm, Fri–Sat 8am–midnight, Sun 9am–11pm; BART and

metro: all lines to Powell; bus: 2, 3, 4, 38, 76; map p.135 C1
This Union Square store is one of the city's four outposts of the mega-chain; others are in the San Francisco Centre, the Stonestown Galleria, and in SoMa at 200 King Street.

City Lights Bookstore
261 Columbus Avenue; tel: 362-8193; www.citylights.com; daily 10am–midnight; bus: 12, 30, 41, 45; map p.135 C2
Left-leaning Lawrence Ferlinghetti founded this 'Beatnikdom' cornerstone, which hosts regular author readings and has strengths in

Below: quirky murals adorn Green Apple Books's facade.

poetry, world literature, the arts, and progressive politics.

Green Apple Books and Music
506 Clement Street; tel: 387-2272; www.greenapplebooks.com; Sun–Thur 10am–10.30pm, Fri 10am–11.30pm; bu`s: 1, 2, 4, 38; map p.136 B4
Well-loved Inner Richmond treasure trove, brimming with new and used titles.

Specialist Book Stores

Get Lost Travel Books
1825 Market Street; tel: 437-0529; www.getlostbooks.com; Mon–Fri 10am–7pm, Sat 10am–6pm, Sun 11am–5pm; metro: J, K, L, M, T to Church; bus: 26, 37; map p.138 A2
Equips voyagers with travel guides and tie-ins.

Modern Times
888 Valencia Street; tel: 282-9246; www.mtbs.com; Mon–Sat 10am–9pm, Sun 11am–6pm; bus: 14, 26, 49
Politically minded tomes, graphic novels, childrens books, and a Spanish language setion.

Willam Stout Architectural Books
804 Montgomery Street; tel: 391-6757; www.stoutbooks.com; Mon–Fri 10am–6.30pm, Sat 10am–5.30pm; bus: 9X, 12, 41; map p.135 C2
This store ends many a quest for coffee-table titles.

Movies

San Francisco is mad about movies and movies are mad about San Francisco. With its iconic views and backdrops, the city is no stranger to the silver screen; it cameos in everything from classics like Hitchcock's *Vertigo* to contemporary documentaries like *The Wild Parrots of Telegraph Hill*. A handful of local industry heavyweights also contribute to the general film frenzy. The calendar is crammed with first-rate film festivals, and the streets sparkle with neighborhood theater gems, among them rare single-screen movie theaters and utterly unique art-house theaters. In short, film-savvy San Franciscans are very well served.

On the Silver Screen

San Francisco's unique looks and recognized landmarks have long held an allure for movie-makers. In the 1930s, Howard Hawks' *Barbary Coast* relived the city's wild Gold Rush days and W.S. Van Dyke's *San Francisco* spectacularly recreated the 1906 earthquake. In 1941, Humphrey Bogart skulked Nob Hill backways in *The Maltese Falcon*, and a decade later, Kim Novak hurtled herself into the Bay in *Vertigo*.

In following years, the city streets saw serious wear and tear, with Steve McQueen tearing across the hills in *Bullitt* in 1968 (*The Rock* followed suit nearly 30 years later), and Barbra Streisand deftly dodg-

The Oakland Bay Bridge's cameo in *The Graduate* (1967) gave sharp locals a good laugh. One scene shows Benjamin supposedly driving east along the bridge on his way to Berkeley, but he was mistakenly placed on the scenic upper deck, which only carries traffic west into San Francisco.

ing cable cars in *What's Up Doc?* (1972). North Beach has seen the spotlight many times: Saints Peter and Paul Church hosted a *Dirty Harry* (1971) shoot-out, City Lights Bookstore starred in Beat-inspired *Heart Beat* (1980), and Tosca Café appeared in *Basic Instinct* (1992). More recently, San Francisco featured in the documentary *The Wild Parrots of Telegraph Hill* (2000), *The Princess Diaries* (2001), *Zodiac* (2007), and *Milk* (2008). Additionally, numerous films from all periods feature a myriad of landmark structures like the Golden Gate Bridge, Alcatraz, City Hall, and the Transamerica Pyramid.

Local Names

A number of familiar film faces have set up shop in the Bay Area. After leaving Hollywood in 1969, Francis Ford Coppola built up businesses here including the **American Zoetrope** movie studio, and recently George Lucas, of *Star Wars* fame, moved **Lucasfilm** into the Presidio. Across the Bay in Emeryville, **Pixar Animation Studios**

Above: the legendary car chase scene in *Bullitt*.

makes blockbuster animation, including *Toy Story* (1995), *Finding Nemo* (2003), *The Incredibles* (2004), *Ratatouille* (2007), and *Up* (2009).

Festivals

These festivals charge admission. Check websites for screening times and locations.
Noir City
www.noircity.com; Jan
Rare, classic film noir; think dark alleys and darker motives.
San Francisco International Asian American Film Festival
Tel: 863-0814; http://festival.

Left: classic San Francisco noir in *The Maltese Falcon*.

asianamericanmedia.org; Mar
The country's largest showcase of new Asian and Asian-American films.

San Francisco International Film Festival
Tel: 561-5000; www.sffs.org; Apr–May
Renowned showcase of nearly 200 new features, documentaries, and shorts.

San Francisco International LGBT Film Festival
Tel: 703-8650; www.frameline.org; June
The world's premier LGBT (Lesbian, Gay, Bisexual, Transgender) film festival.

San Francisco Jewish Film Festival
Tel: 621-0556; www.sfjff.org; July–Aug
The first and largest of its kind.

San Francisco Silent Film Festival
Tel: 777-4908; www.silentfiilm.org; July
Classic and rare silents accompanied by live music.

Spike and Mike's Festival of Animation
Tel: 858-459-8707; www.spikeandmike.com; Feb–Apr
Offbeat animated shorts.

Movie Theaters

4 Star
2200 Clement Street; tel: 666-3488; www.lntsf.com; bus: 1, 2, 28, 29, 38
Catch alternative world movies plus first-run Hong Kong flicks.

AMC Loews Metreon 16
101 4th Street; tel: 888-262-4386; www.westfiield.com/metreon; BART and metro: all lines to Powell; bus: 6, 9, 21, 66; map p.139 C4
Fifteen theaters covering recent releases and an IMAX screen.

Castro Theatre
429 Castro Street; tel: 621-6120; www.castrotheatre.com; metro: F, K, L, M, T to Castro; bus: 24, 33, 35, 37; map p.137 E1
One of the most beloved movie theaters in San Francisco, showing a repertory of the classic and avante-garde.

Landmark Clay
2261 Fillmore Street; tel: 267-4893; www.landmarktheatres.com; bus: 1, 3, 12, 22; map p.133 E1
One of five Landmark theaters in the city, this single-screen, comfy, former

nickelodeon now hosts independents and popular midnight movies.

Red Vic Movie House
1727 Haight Street; tel: 668-3994; www.redvicmoviehouse.com; metro: N to Carl and Cole streets; bus: 6, 7, 33, 37, 71; map p.137 C2
A Haight favorite supplying classics and unfamiliar fringe titles, from comfy couches.

Roxie
3117 16th Street; tel: 863-1087; www.roxie.com; BART: 16th Street; bus: 14, 22, 33, 49, 53; map p.138 A1
A popular Mission art-house theater with a risk-taking reputation and a documentary-heavy program.

Sundance Kabuki Cinema
1881 Post Street; tel: 346-3243; www.sundancecinemas.com/kabuki.html; bus: 1, 4, 22, 31, 38; map p.137 E4
Recently remodeled Japantown movie theater with giant seats shows independents and blockbusters.

Victoria Theatre
2961 16th Street; tel: 863-7576; www.victoriatheatre.org; movie days vary; BART: 16th Street; bus: 14, 22, 33, 49; map p.138 B1
The city's oldest operating theater is an ornate former vaudeville house dating from 1908.

Below: the Castro Theatre.

Museums and Galleries

S an Francisco is home to diverse art, history, and science museums. The majority are clustered downtown and in the SoMa district, but a number are also strewn about outlying neighborhoods. Prominent fine art collections are displayed at the San Francisco Museum of Modern Art and the M.H. de Young Memorial Museum among others, not to mention the world-class Asian Art Museum. Alongside these, a raft of museums celebrate San Francisco's history, as well as its ethnically diverse population.

Fisherman's Wharf

Hyde Street Pier Historic Ships Collection
Hyde Street on Jefferson Street; tel: 447-5000; www.nps.gov/safr; Aug 16–June 20 9.30am–5pm, June 21–Aug 15 9.30am–6pm; entrance charge, under 16 free, 1st Sun of month free; bus: 10, 19, 30, 49; cable car: Powell–Hyde; map p.134 B4
Moored here are six vintage vessels built in the late 19th and early 20th centuries. Tour below decks of the *Eureka* steam ferryboat, see how to set the topsail and staysail onboard the *Balclutha* square-rigger, or raise your voice to the tune of sailor songs at the monthly chantey sing-along (tel: 561-7171; 1st Saturday of month; reservations required). The other historic

ships onsite are two schooners, a steam tug, and a paddlewheel tug.

Ripley's Believe It or Not! Museum
175 Jefferson Street; tel: 771-6188; www.ripleysf.com; June–Sept Sun–Thur 9am–11pm, Fri–Sat 9am–midnight, Sept–May Sun–Thur 10am–10pm, Fri–Sat 10am–midnight; entrance charge; bus: 10, 47; map p.134 B4
This two-story museum's bizarre attractions and illusions – including a new mirror maze and candy factory added in 2010 – especially entertain younger visitors.

San Francisco National Maritime Museum
900 Beach Street; tel: 561-7100; www.nps.gov/safr; daily 10am–4pm; free; bus: 19, 31; cable car: Powell–Hyde; map p.134 A4
The historical Aquatic Park Bathhouse has been home to the San Francisco National Maritime museum since 1951. After three years of restoration work, the building reopened in 2009, with exhibits expected to return in 2010. The museum celebrates San Francisco's color-

ful maritime heritage with interactive exhibits, intricate models, oral history re-creations and scores of seafaring memorabilia. Until it reopens, visit the Maritime Park's Visitor Center (499 Jefferson Street at Hyde Street) for helpful information.

Chinatown

Chinese Historical Society of America Museum
965 Clay Street; tel: 391-1188; www.chsa.org; Tue–Fri noon–5pm; entrance charge,

On the first Thursday of each month, the San Francisco tradition of 'First Thursdays' turns typically calm galleries into lively, wine-sipping social events. This is when many galleries schedule their openings and then keep their doors open late.

Left: San Francisco's varied ethnic heritage is celebrated at the Pacific Heritage Museum.

under 6 free, 1st Thur of month free; bus: 1, 30; cable car: Powell-Hyde, Powell-Mason; map p.134 C2

Small displays in the historic Julia Morgan Chinatown YWCA explore Chinese history and culture in the US, including how Chinese contributions fueled the development of American West industries.

Union Square and Finacial District

Pacific Heritage Museum
608 Commercial Street; tel: 399-1124; www.ibankunited.com/ phm; Tue–Sat 10am–4pm; free; BART and metro: all lines to Montgomery; bus: 1, 10, 15, 41; map p.135 D2

This small museum housed in the historic US Subtreasury Building (on the site of the original US Branch Mint) focuses on Pacific Rim cultural, artistic, and economic achievements.

Wells Fargo Museum
420 Montgomery Street; tel:

396-2619; www.wellsfargo history.com; Mon–Fri 9am–5pm; free; BART and metro: all lines to Montgomery; bus: 1, 9X, 10, 30X, 41; cable car: California; map p.135 D2

An authentic, yellow-wheeled Concord Coach from the 1860s stands in this downtown lobby museum, on the site where Wells Fargo opened in 1852. Gold dust is displayed, and exhibits tell of dangerous stagecoach robbers and the 1906 earthquake.

Xanadu Gallery
140 Maiden Lane; tel: 392-9999; www.folkartintl.com; Tue–Sat 10am–6pm; free; BART and metro: all lines to Powell; bus: 5, 6, 7, 30, 38; map p.135 C1

Just off Union Square, San Francisco's only building designed by Frank Lloyd Wright (echoing his Guggenheim Museum in New York) houses a gallery of artwork, textiles, jewelry, and artifacts from around the world.

Right: Chinese sculpture of a tomb guardian, at the Asian Art Museum.

Left: striking design at the Contemporary Jewish Museum of San Francisco *(see p.85)*.

SoMa and Civic Center
Asian Art Museum
200 Larkin Street; tel: 581-3500; www.asianart.org; Tue–Sun 10am–5pm, Thur until 9pm; entrance charge, under 13 free, 1st Sun of month free; BART and metro: all lines to Civic Center; bus: 5, 19, 21, 47, 49; map p.138 B4

With 17,000 artworks spanning 6,000 years of history, this museum houses one of the world's most comprehensive collections of Asian art. After decades in Golden Gate Park, the museum moved in 2003 to new Civic Center quarters – formerly the city's main library building – which were redesigned by Gae Aulenti. Now, instead of books, the historic, beaux-arts building houses paintings, sculptures, ceramics, stoneware, basketry, puppets, weaponry, and textiles.

Special rotating exhibits are shown on the first floor, while the second and third floors showcase around 2,500 pieces from the permanent collection in regionally-grouped galleries

Above: the Museum of Modern Art has a eye-catching interior, exterior, and collection, including Jasper Johns' *Flag*.

covering China, Japan, Korea, India, Iran, the Himalayas, and Southeast Asia. Among the many treasures, look for a bronze Buddha on the third floor dated AD 388; it is the oldest dated Chinese Buddha known in the world. It is also one of some 7,700 objects donated by Avery Brundage, the Chicago industrialist whose endowment in the 1960s sparked the museum's creation.

Tea ceremony demonstrations (reservations recommended and extra charge required) are also held onsite.

The museum store supplies an array of unique, Asian-themed merchandise, and the cafeteria-style Café Asia provides Pan-Asian fare in a casual setting.

California Historical Society Museum
678 Mission Street; tel: 357-1848; www.californiahistorical society.org; Wed–Sat noon–4.30pm; entrance charge, under 6 free; BART and metro: all lines to Montgomery; bus: 7, 9X, 14, 30, 45; map p.135 D1
Early Californian history is chronicled by 5,000 oil paintings, drawings, costumes, lithographs, and

decorative arts. A fine collection of 500,000 photographs includes works by Eadweard Muybridge and Arnold Genthe.

Cartoon Art Museum
655 Mission Street; tel: 227-8666; www.cartoonart.org; Tue–Sun 11am–5pm; entrance charge, under 6 free, 1st Tue of month 'Pay What You Wish Day'; BART and metro: all lines to Montgomery; bus: 9, 14, 30, 45, 71; map p.135 D1
Original cartoons and animation art – of both underground and mainstream varieties – are showcased at this notable museum endowed by *Peanuts* creator Charles M. Schulz. Rotating exhibits draw from a 6,000-piece permanent collection that ranges from graphic novels and comic strips to political and advertising cartoons.

Catharine Clark Gallery
150 Minna Street; tel: 399-1439; www.cclarkgallery.com; Tue–Fri 10.30am–5.30pm, Sat 11am–5.30pm; free; BART and metro: all lines to Montgomery; bus: 9, 14, 15, 30, 45; map p.135 D1
A dedicated video project room is one of the draws of this top-notch gallery, which features sculpture, painting, and mixed-media works from

local, national, and international contemporary artists.

Contemporary Jewish Museum of San Francisco

736 Mission Street; tel: 655-7800; www.thecjm.org; Fri–Tue 11am–5pm, Thur 1–8pm; entrance charge, under 19 free; BART and metro: all lines to Montgomery; bus: 5, 9, 14, 30, 45; map p.139 C4

Contemporary perspectives on Jewish art, history, and culture are the focus here, explored through art, historical objects, music, film, and lectures. The new Daniel Libeskind-designed facility, opened in 2008, incorporates the historic Jessie Street Power Substation.

Crown Point Press

20 Hawthorne Street; tel: 974-6273; www.crownpoint.com; Mon–Sat 10am–6pm; free; BART and metro: all lines to Montgomery; bus: 6, 9, 10, 30, 45; map p.139 D4

Born as a print workshop in 1962, the press displays a range of etchings, engravings, aquatints, photogravure, and intaglio prints in its public gallery.

San Francisco Craft and Folk Art Museum

51 Yerba Buena Lane; tel: 227-4888; www.mocfa.org; Mon–Tue, Thur–Fri 11am–6pm, 1st Thur until 7.30pm; entrance charge, 18 and under free; BART and metro: all lines to Powell; bus: 5, 9, 14, 30, 45; map p.139 C4

On an appealing pedestrian lane of stores and cafés, this museum exhibits traditional and contemporary craft and folk art from all over the world.

San Francisco Museum of Modern Art

151 Third Street; tel: 357-4000; www.sfmoma.org; Mon–Tue 11am–5.45pm, Thur 11am–8.45pm, Fri–Sun 11am–5.45pm, from 10am Memorial Day–Labor Day; entrance charge, under 13

free, Thur 6–8.45pm half-price, 1st Tue of month free; BART and metro: all lines to Powell; bus: 5, 9, 30, 45, 71; map p.139 D4

The San Francisco Museum of Modern Art celebrated its 60th anniversary in 1995 by moving into a striking new SoMa location. The modernist building – marked by a truncated tower with black and white bands – was designed by internationally renowned Swiss architect Mario Botta.

Inside, natural light pours into an airy atrium and four floors of galleries. In them, a permanent collection strong in American Abstract Expressionism, Fauvism, and German Expressionism is displayed. Paintings and sculptures include Henri Matisse's seminal *Femme au Chapeau* (Woman with the Hat), painted in 1905, as well as works by Jackson Pollock, Paul Klee, Piet Mondrian, Pablo Picasso, Andy Warhol, Marcel Duchamp, Diego Rivera, and Georgia O'Keeffe. The museum also has a fine photography collection, including works by Alfred Stieglitz, Edward Weston, Ansel Adams, Dorthea Lange, Robert Frank, and William Klein. On the roof, a new sculpture garden is backdropped by lovely city views.

Look for cutting-edge design objects and contemporary art books at the museum store. Nearby, **Caffe Museo's** Italian-inspired menu is a popular bet for lunch breaks.

SEE ALSO BARS AND CAFÉS, P.37

San Francisco Museum of Modern Art Gallery

Fort Mason Building A; tel: 441-4777; www.sfmoma.org; Tue–Sat 11.30am–5.30pm; free; bus: 10, 19, 30, 47, 49; map p.133 E4

This lofty, light-filled space shows sculpture, paintings, photography, and mixed-

media work from Northern Californian artists. In addition, it offers an innovative art rental program.

The Shooting Gallery

839 Larkin Street; tel: 931-8035; www.shootinggallerysf.com; Tue–Sat noon–7pm; free; bus: 19, 38, 76; map p.134 B1

This un-intimidating gallery in the Tenderloin district specializes in exhibits of 'Low-Brow' artwork.

Society of California Pioneers Museum

300 4th Street; tel: 957-1849; www.californiapioneers.org; Wed–Fri and 1st Sat of month 10am–4pm; entrance charge; BART and metro: all lines to Powell; bus: 9X, 30, 45, 76; map p.139 D4

A sizeable collection of paintings, photographs, works on paper, silverware, and mining artifacts vividly chronicles California's history from the Gold Rush era to the 1940s.

Yerba Buena Center for the Arts

3rd Street between Mission and Howard; tel: 978-2700;

San Francisco has art galleries galore, showing and selling works from both emerging talent and internationally known names. For a handy guide containing maps, addresses, and details of specific shows and special events, pop into a gallery and pick up a copy of the **Art Now Gallery Guide – West Coast**, or the **San Francisco Bay Area Gallery Guide**. The crowd of established commercial dealers is densest near Union Square, but SoMa and the Mission also host a growing crop of galleries. A particularly popular address is 49 Geary Street: among others, the Stephen Wirtz, Jack Fisher, and photography-focused Robert Koch, Shapiro, and Fraenkel galleries share this high-rise.

de Young Museum

Upper Gallery level

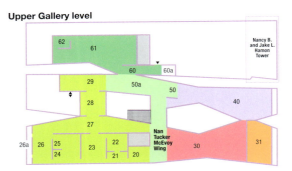

Concourse level

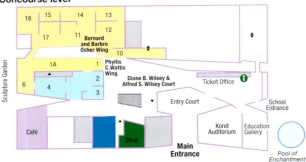

Exhibition level

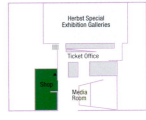

↕	Lift
	Art in America to the 20th Century
	Photography
	Textiles
	Africa
	New Guinea
	Oceania
	20th-Century and Contemporary Art
	Native American Art
	Piazzoni Murals Room
	Art of the Americas
	Koret Auditorium
	Herbst Special Exhibition Galleries
	Media Room
	Café
	Museum Store

www.ybca.org; gallery hours: Thur–Fri 2–8pm, Sat noon–8pm, Sun noon–6pm, 1st Tue of month noon–8pm; entrance charge, 1st Tue of month free; BART and metro: all lines to Montgomery; bus: 5, 7, 9, 30, 45; map p.139 D4

In a two-building complex, the YBCA exhibits contemporary art and community-based work, and presents contemporary dance, theater, and music performances.

Nob Hill

Cable Car Museum

1201 Mason Street; tel: 474-1887; www.cablecarmuseum.org; Apr–Sept daily 10am–6pm, Oct–Mar daily 10am–5pm; free; bus: 1, 12; cable car: Powell-Hyde, Powell-Mason; map p.134 C2

This historic cable car barn and powerhouse displays antique cable cars, engines, winding wheels, and other mechanical devices that help the beloved moving monuments run smoothly.

Central Neighborhoods

Exploratorium

3601 Lyon Street; tel: 561-0360; www.exploratorium.edu; Tue–Sun 10am–5pm; entrance charge, under 4 free, 1st Wed of month free; bus: 28, 30, 43; map p.133 D3

Hundreds of fascinating, hands-on exhibits are found at this museum of science, art, and human perception

To get in tune with the environment, head to the Exploratorium's Wave Organ – a wave-activated acoustic sculpture created by Peter Richards and George Gonzales in 1986. On a concrete and marble jetty, 25 organ pipes emit subtle tones (best heard at high-tide) as seawater swells in and out of them.

Above: looking down over the rainforest at the California Academy of Sciences.

conceived by Frank Oppenheimer. The varied topics explored include physics, computers, biology, visual perception, listening, language, and memory. In the bizarre Tactile Dome exhibit (extra charge; reservation recommended) visitors must crawl, climb, squeeze, and grope through a pitch-black maze of materials, honing in dramatically on their sense of touch.

See also Children, p.42

Haight-Asbhury and Golden Gate Park

California Academy of Sciences

55 Music Concourse Drive; tel: 379-8000; www.calacademy.org; Mon–Sat 9.30am–5pm, Thur also 6–10pm, Sun 11am–5pm; entrance charge, 3 and under free, third Wed of month free; metro: N to Irving Street and 9th Avenue; bus: 5, 21, 44; map p.136 B2

This eco-friendly interactive museum includes an aquarium, a planetarium, a natural history museum, a coral reef, a four-story rainforest, and a green living roof. See pen-

guins, parrots, sharks, and albino alligators; take a virtual safari in African Hall; or climb into the canopy of a living rainforest. On Thursday nights the museum throws a popular adults-only event – a chance to enjoy drinks, music, and the museum without youngsters underfoot.

M.H. de Young Memorial Museum

50 Hagiwara Tea Garden Drive; tel: 750-3600; www.famsf.org/deyoung; Tue–Sun 9.30am–5.15pm, Fri until 8.45pm, mid-Jan–Nov 9.30am–8.45pm;

Below: modern art at the M.H. de Young Memorial Museum.

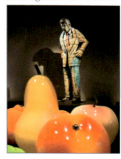

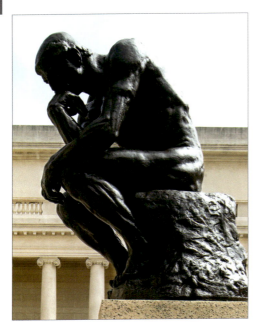

den, museum store, café, and panoramic views from its nine-story observation tower, which are particularly stunning on a clear day.

Mission and Castro

Galería de la Raza

2857 24th Street; tel: 826-8009; www.galeriadelaraza.org; Tue 1–7pm, Wed–Sat noon–6pm; free; BART: to 24th Street; bus: 14, 48, 49

This Mission gallery, founded in 1970, celebrates Chicano and Latino art and culture, and is a mixed space for art and activism.

Randall Museum

199 Museum Way; tel: 554-9600; www.randallmuseum.org; Tue–Sat 10am–5pm; donation suggested; metro: K, L, M to Castro; bus: 24; map p.137 E1

This hands-on, kid-friendly arts and science museum hosts a live animal exhibit as well as a woodshop, greenhouse, gardens, lapidary workshop, and arts and ceramic studios.

SEE ALSO CHILDREN, P.42

Around San Francisco

Palace of the Legion of Honor

34th Avenue and Clement Street; tel: 750-3600; www.famsf.org/legion; Tue–Sun 9.30am–5.15pm; entrance charge, under 13 free, 1st Tue of month free; bus: 1, 18, 38

Built to commemorate the California soldiers who died during World War I, the Legion of Honor reproduces an 18th-century Parisian palace on a three-quarter scale. Within the beautiful Beaux Arts building is a rich collection of ancient and European art that spans 4,000 years and includes more than 80 Rodin sculptures.

entrance charge, under 13 free, 1st Tue of month free; metro: N to Irving Street and 9th Avenue; bus: 5, 21, 44; map p.136 B2

In 2005, the M.H. de Young Memorial Museum *(see floorplan, left)* reopened in Golden Gate Park in a bold facility that replaced the one severely damaged by the 1989 Loma Prieta earthquake. The controversial design features a copper-clad exterior that will green to patina over time and a 144ft (44m) observation tower that stands out (literally and figuratively) in the natural park setting.

The spacious, light-filled interior hosts several fine collections: American art from the 17th through the 20th centuries; art from Africa, the Americas, and the Pacific; and a range of textiles. The concourse level hosts 20th-century and contemporary art (including works by Georgia O'Keeffe, Edward Hopper, and Grant Wood), art from the Americas, Native American art, and a room of murals. Upstairs, rare works from Africa, Oceania, and New Guinea are shown, as well as early American artworks and separate textile and photography exhibits.

The museum also mounts special exhibitions on the first floor and has a sculpture gar-

The Mission neighborhood is literally a colorful one: its streets (Balmy Alley for example) are decorated with over 200 murals. Guided tours of these artworks are given by the knowledgeable **Precita Eyes Mural Arts and Visitor Center** (tel: 285-2287; www.precitaeyes.org), founded in 1977. *(See also Walks and Views, p.129.)*

An original cast of Rodin's *The Thinker* poses in the outdoor Court of Honor. Inside, the sky-lit terrace level displays an array of antiquities from Greece, Rome, Egypt, Assyria, and Mesopotamia, including pottery, sculpture, and metalwork. The terrace level also displays European porcelain and works on paper.

European art from the 14th–20th centuries is shown on the upper level, including paintings, sculpture, tapestries, and decorative arts. Paintings include works from many European masters, such as Fra Angelico, El Greco, Rembrandt, Rubens, Watteau, Gainsborough, Cézanne, Renoir, Degas, Matisse, Monet, and Picasso. One highlight among the European decorative arts is the collection of French Baroque inlaid furniture. Three sculpture galleries include two devoted entirely to Rodin; look for famous Rodin works like *The Three Shades*, *Eve*, *The Kiss*, and *The Prodigal Son*.

After a tour of the galleries, recharge at the Legion Café and enjoy the breathtaking views of the ocean, Golden Gate Bridge, and Marin Headlands afforded by the museum's Lincoln Park perch.

Berkeley, Oakland, and the Bay Area

Chabot Space and Science Center
10000 Skyline Boulevard, Oakland; tel: 510-336-7300; www.chabotspace.org; Wed–Thur 10am–5pm, Fri–Sat 10am–10pm, Sun 11am–5pm, July 10–Sept 2 also Tue 10am–5pm; entrance charge, under 3 free

Right: sculpture at the Oakland Museum of California.

High in the Oakland hills both children and adults can have fun learning about the planet and universe at this center, which features interactive exhibits, an observatory, a planetarium, special stargazing events, and beautiful views of the Bay Area. Note that the center is pretty much only accessible by car.

Oakland Museum of California
1000 Oak Street, Oakland; tel: 510-238-2200; www.museumca.org; Wed, Sat–Sun 11am–5pm, Thur–Fri 11am–8pm; 2nd Fri of month until 9pm; entrance charge, under 9 free, 1st Sun of month free; BART: Lake Merritt
Reopened in 2010 after a major renovation and expansion, this dynamic museum provides dynamic chronological and theme-based exhibits (many of which are interactive) on the art, history, and environment of California. The Gallery of California Natural Sciences will reopen in 2012.

University of California, Berkeley Art Museum
2626 Bancroft Way; tel: 510-642-0808; www.bampfa.berkeley.edu; Wed–Sun 11am–5pm; entrance charge, under 13 free, 1st Thur of month free; BART: Downtown Berkeley; AC Transit bus: 7, 51
This collection of more than 16,000 artworks (one of the largest university art museums in the US) includes works by Mark Rothko, Jackson Pollock, and Albert Bierstadt. Across the street, the Pacific Film Archive offers daily screenings of movies pulled from a pool of 10,000 films that includes international classics, Soviet silents, rare animation, and the largest collection of Japanese films outside of Japan.

Music and Dance

San Francisco is vividly alive with music and dance, delivering rhythms sure to get shoes tapping and dance performance that showcase the fancy footwork of others. Operatic arias and symphonic melodies fill concert halls, chamber quintets perform in peaceful churches, jazz bands sizzle in intimate clubs, and hot rock, pop, and alternative bands jam on small stages and in spacious arenas alike, while in the San Francisco 1960s tradition, parks often become concert venues in the summer. Dance is not short on attention either, with varied traditional and experimental performances gracing the city's stages.

Classical

CLASSICAL COMPANIES
Chanticleer
Tel: 252-8589;
www.chanticleer.org
Donald Pippen's Pocket Opera
Tel: 972-8930; www.pocket opera.org
Kronos Quartet
www.kronosquartet.org
Philharmonic Baroque Orchestra
Tel: 252-1288; www.phil harmonia.org
San Francisco Contemporary Music Players
Tel: 278-9566; www.sfcmp.org
San Francisco Performances
Tel: 398-6449;
www.performances.org
Popular venues for hearing musical offerings from these companies include the **Yerba Buena Center for the Arts** *(see Museums and Galleries,*

p.85) and the **Florence Gould Theater** in the **California Palace of the Legion of Honor** *(see Museums and Galleries, p.88)*, in addition to the below venues.

VENUES
Herbst Theater
War Memorial Veterans Building, 401 Van Ness Avenue; tel: 621-6600; http://sfwmpac.org; BART: to Civic Center; metro: all lines to Van Ness; bus: 5, 21, 47, 49; map p.138 B3
An intimate venue, in an historic building with Beaux-Arts murals in the auditorium.

Below: performing at the War Memorial Opera House.

Aria-admirers turn out in droves to Golden Gate Park each fall for a relaxed, cultured afternoon of **Free Opera in the Park**.

Louise M. Davies Symphony Hall
201 Van Ness Avenue; tel: 864-6000; www.sfsymphony.org; BART and metro: all lines to Civic Center; bus: 5, 21, 47, 49; map p.138 B3
This elegant hall houses the acclaimed San Francisco Symphony Orchestra. Its main season runs September–July.
Old First Presbyterian Church
1751 Sacramento Street; tel: 474-1608; www.oldfiirstconcerts. org; bus: 1, 19, 47, 49; cable car: California; map p.134 B1
Old First Concerts often include chamber music.
St John's Presbyterian Church
2727 College Avenue, Berkeley; tel: 753-2792; www.chambermu sicsundaes.org; Sun 3pm; BART: Rockridge; bus: AC Transit 51
Chamber Music Sundaes feature the San Francisco Symphony.
War Memorial Opera House
301 Van Ness Avenue; tel: 864-3330; www.sfopera.com; BART and metro: all lines to Civic Center; bus: 5, 21, 47, 49; map p.138 B3

Left: live jazz is popular in San Francisco.

VENUES

Bimbo's 365 Club
1025 Columbus Avenue; tel: 474-0365; www.bimbos 365club.com; days and show times vary; bus: 30; cable car: Powell-Mason; map p.134 B3
Swank 1930s throwback nightclub with art deco detailing, showcasing acts ranging from rock to jazz.

Bottom of the Hill
1233 17th Street; tel: 621-4455; www.bottomofthehill.com; show times vary; bus: 19, 22; map p.139 D1
Great hard rockin' dive for punk, alternative, rockabilly, and more.

Café du Nord and the Swedish American Hall
2174 Market Street; tel: 861-5016; www.cafedunord.com; show times vary; metro: F, J, L, M, N to Church; bus: 22, 37; map p.137 E1
Rich red walls and dark woods set an intimate mood at this nightclub, restaurant, and live music venue. The crowd sips classic cocktails while enjoying ecletic music acts.

Elbo Room
647 Valencia Street; tel: 552-7788; www.elboroom.com; daily 9 or 10pm; BART: 16th Street; bus: 14, 22, 26, 33, 49; map p.138 B1

The glamorous beaux arts War Memorial Opera House is regularly filled with those keen to hear the San Francisco opera company perform. The fall season lasts September to November, and the summer season May to July.

Contemporary

San Francisco has a star-studded musical legacy and current culture. **The Grateful Dead**, **Jefferson Airplane** and **Janis Joplin** staged concerts in Golden Gate Park, and at the Fillmore and Avalon ballrooms. **Carlos Santana** grew up in the Mission, **Credence Clearwater Revival** came from the East Bay's El Cerrito, and **Green Day** and **Counting Crows** hail from Berkeley. Now, the Bay Area's eclectic music scene includes everything from hip hop to indie to electronica.

FESTIVALS
Hardly Strictly Bluegrass Festival
www.strictlybluegrass.com; Oct; free
Mission Creek Music and Arts Festival

www.mcmf.org; July; entrance charge
Noise Pop
www.noisepop.com; Feb; entrance charge
Outside Lands
www.sfoutsidelands.com; Aug; entrance charge
San Francisco Bluegrass and Old-Time Festival
www.sfbluegrass.org; Feb; entrance charge
Stern Grove Festival
www.sterngrove.org; June–Aug; free
Treasure Island Music Festival
www.treasureislandfestival.com; Oct; entrance charge

Below: San Francisco boasts a rich musical heritage.

Mission hipster destination, for the chill bar downstairs and the happening music scene upstairs: live and DJ-delivered jazz, hip-hop, funk, soul, indie-rock, and more.

Fillmore Auditorium
1805 Geary Boulevard; tel: 346-6000; www.thefiillmore.com; Mon–Sun show times vary; bus: 2, 3, 22, 38; map p.137 E4
Major headlining acts – from Snoop Dog to Norah Jones – in a historic 1960s venue.

Great American Music Hall
859 O'Farrell Street; tel: 885-0750; www.musichallsf.com; show times vary; bus: 2, 3, 27, 38; map p.138 B4

The intimate, legendary Fillmore Auditorium – where Bill Graham famously launched his empire in the 1960s – remains one of the city's best music venues. The venue's history lives on in photos, posters, and in one of Graham's classic, homey touches: a bowl of free apples for concert-goers to enjoy.

A former Barbary Coast bordello now lures international performers, playing rock, blues, folk, and more.

Hemlock Tavern
1131 Polk Street; tel: 923-0925; www.hemlocktavern.com; show times vary; bus: 2, 19, 38, 47, 49; map p.134 B1
Hipsters chill in the bar up front and open-air smoking room, and underground rock bands light up the intimate back.

Independent
628 Divisadero Street; tel: 771-1421; www.theindependent sf.com; show times vary; bus: 21, 24; map p.137 E3
Supplier of popular live rock, punk, folk, hip-hop, and more.

Masonic Center
1111 California Street; www.masonicauditorium.com; show times vary; bus: 1; cable car: California; map p.134 C1
Comfortable, sit-down auditorium with excellent acoustics hosts varied performances ranging from Van Morrison to jazz concerts to comedians.

Red Devil Lounge
1695 Polk Street; tel: 921-1695; www.reddevillounge.com; show times vary; bus: 1, 19, 27, 49, 76; map p.134 B2
A glowing neon red sign draws you into this intimate spot, low on attitude and showcasing local rock groups and 80s cover bands.

Slim's
333 11th Street; tel: 255-0333; www.slims-sf.com; show times vary; bus: 9, 12, 47; map p.138 B2
Jam-packed SoMa spot for live national touring acts, with a motley mix of rootsy music: blues, R&B, and alternative.

Thee Parkside
1600 17th Street; tel: 252-1330; www.theeparkside.com; show times vary; bus: 22; map p.139 D1
Potrero neighborhood rock 'n' roll joint, with special It's a Free Country Sunday concerts of rockabilly, country, and bluegrass (Sun 4pm; free).

Dance

COMPANIES

Alonzo King's Lines Ballet
Yerba Buena Center for the Arts, 700 Howard Street; tel: 863-3040 (info), 978-2787 (box offiice); www.linesballet.org; BART and metro: all lines to Montgomery; bus: 5, 7, 9, 30, 45; map p.139 D4
This top-notch contemporary ballet company performs at the Yerba Buena Center, and tours all over the world.

ODC Dance
3153 17th Street; tel: 863-6606; www.odcdance.org; show times vary; BART: 16th Street; map p.138 B1
This modern dance company, known nationally for its entrepreneurial savvy and artistic innovation, performs a variety of contemporary dance recitals, and puts on a well-

loved annual production of *The Velveteen Rabbit*.

San Francisco Ballet

War Memorial Opera House, 301 Van Ness Avenue; tel: 865-2000; www.sfballet.org; BART and metro: all lines to Civic Center; bus: 5, 21, 47, 49; map p.138 B3

The San Francisco Ballet takes the stage at the Opera House for its main season during February through April, presenting traditional full-length ballets and contemporary pieces. The annual *Nutcracker* production in December is very popular.

FESTIVALS

Ethnic Dance Festival

Tel: 474-3914; www.worldarts west.org/edf; June; entrance charge

Brings together soloists and companies, professionals and students, varied classical, sacred, social, and folk dance styles from all over the world.

Jazz

FESTIVALS

San Francisco buzzes with jazz events in summer and fall:

Fillmore Street Jazz Festival

www.fillmorejazzfestival.com; July; free

North Beach Jazz Festival

http://nbjazzfest.com; July; entrance charge varies

San Francisco Jazz Festival

www.sfjazz.org; Oct–Nov; entrance charge

SF Jazz Summerfest

www.sfjazz.org; June–Oct; free

VENUES

Biscuits and Blues

401 Mason Street; tel: 292-2583; www.biscuitsandblues. com; Tue–Thur 8pm, Fri–Sat 8pm and 10pm, Sun 8pm, some additional 10pm shows; BART and metro: all lines to Powell; bus: 38; cable car: Powell-Hyde, Powell-Mason; map p.134 C1

A Bay Area standard, this casual supper-club west of Union Square teams a Southern-style menu with soulful blues and blues-based rock.

Boom Boom Room

1601 Fillmore Street; tel: 673-8000; www.boomboom blues.com; show times vary; bus: 22, 38; map p.137 E4

Live blues – plus boogie, groove, and soul – keep this fun Fillmore joint hopping.

Saloon

1232 Grant Street; tel: 989-7666; www.sfblues.net/Saloon. html; Mon–Sun 9.30pm; bus: 12, 30, 41, 45; map p.135 C3

North Beach dive (the oldest bar in San Francisco) dishes out blues nightly.

Yoshi's

1330 Fillmore Street; tel: 655-5600; www.yoshis.com/sf; Mon–Sun 8pm and 10pm; bus: 22, 31; map p.137 E4

Opened in 2007, this outpost of the world-renowned Jack London Square jazz club (510 Embarcadero West, Oakland; tel: 510-238-9200), supplies big names and Japanese cuisine.

SEE ALSO RESTAURANTS, P.111

Music Stores

San Francisco is packed with gold mines for vinyl-lovers:

Amoeba Music

1855 Haight Street; tel: 831-1200; www.amoebamusic.com; Mon–Sat 10.30am–10pm; Sun 11am–9pm; bus: 7, 33, 43, 71; map p.137 C2

An independent institution in a converted-bowling alley.

Aquarius Records

1055 Valencia Street; tel: 647-2272; www.aquariusrecords. org; Mon–Wed 10am–9pm, Thur–Sun 10am–10pm; BART: 24th Street; bus: 14, 26, 49

Boutique-like independent.

Groove Merchant

687 Haight Street; tel: 252-5766; Tue–Sat noon–7pm, Sun noon–6pm; bus: 6, 22, 71; map p.137 E2

For an entertainingly alternative take on the classic *Nutcracker* ballet each winter, San Franciscans of all ages don their best sugar plum fairy tutus and pirouette over to the celebrated, offbeat, and fantastically-fun *Dance-Along Nutcracker*, presented by the **San Francisco Lesbian/Gay Freedom Band** (tel: 255-1355; www.dancealongnutcraker.org).

For the hippest of the hip.

Jack's Record Cellar

254 Scott Street; tel: 431-3047; call for hours; bus: 6, 7, 22, 71; map p.137 E2

The oldest record shop in the city, this historic place is a great stop-off for dusty 78s.

Rasputin Music

69 Powell Street; tel: 800-350-8700; www.rasputinmusic.com; Mon–Tue 10.30am–8pm, Wed–Sat 10.30am–9pm, Sun 11am–8pm; BART and metro: all lines to Powell; bus: 27, 31; map p.138 C4

A good choice for browsing the latest releases.

Rooky Ricardo's

448 Haight Street; tel: 864-7526; www.rookyricardos.com; daily noon–6pm; bus: 6, 7, 22; map p.138 A2

Boasts LPs and 45s from all genres and generations.

Below: dancers from the San Francisco Ballet Company.

Nightlife

San Francisco has nightlife options across the board, with international and local DJ's spinning for varied tastes, and live bands and comedy clubs spicing up the mix. Bear in mind, most dance clubs are 21 and over (ID required at the door) and entrance charges may be cash only. Slick venues have dress codes, but generally the diverse crowds are fittingly diversely attired. Many nightspots are hybrid affairs, blurring the lines between bars, lounges, and clubs, so for more suggestions see also *Bars and Cafés, p.34*, *Gay and Lesbian, p.58*, and *Music and Dance, p.90*.

Nightclubs

1015 Folsom

1015 Folsom Street; tel: 431-7444; www.1015.com; hours vary; bus: 12, 27; map p.139 C3
A mega-club delivering solid house and trance from top-notch DJ's to a young crowd.

111 Minna

111 Minna Street; tel: 974-1719; www.111minnagallery.com; Tue–Fri noon–5pm, nightly on a rotating schedule for special events (check online calendar); BART and metro: all lines to Montgomery; bus: 5, 14, 15, 45, 76; map p.135 D1
During the day, this space is an art gallery, but when the sun goes down, it slips on a nightclub vibe to host happy hours and an eclectic mix of artists, movie screenings, DJ's, and live performances.

222 Hyde

222 Hyde Street; tel: 440-0222; www.222hydesf.com; hours vary; bus: 19, 31; map p.138 B4
Hipsters brave the gritty Tenderloin streets for packed basement dancing at this DJ bar with a back-alley feel.

The Ambassador

673 Geary Street; tel: 563-8192; www.ambassador415.com;

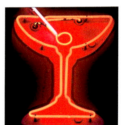

Above: always a welcome sign.

Tue–Fri 6pm–2am, Sat–Sun 8pm–2am; bus: 2, 3, 4, 27, 76; map p.134 B1
With exposed brick walls, giant chandeliers, and even rotary phones in booths to call the bartender, this lounge and DJ club exudes a suave vibe, which contasts starkly with its divey TenderNob neighbors.

DNA Lounge

375 11th Street; tel: 626-1409; www.dnalounge.com; hours vary; bus: 9, 12, 27, 47; map p.138 B2
Solid sound and lighting systems for an alternative crowd that comes to dance. There are also special DJ nights and live acts performing regularly.

End Up

401 6th Street; tel: 646-0999; www.theendup.com; Thur 10pm–4am, Fri 11pm–Sat 1pm, Sat 10pm–Mon 4am; bus: 12, 19, 27, 47; map p.139 C3
A diverse, hard-partying crowd – both gay and straight – carouses til dawn and beyond.

Harry Denton's Starlight Room

450 Powell Street; tel: 395-8595; www.harrydenton.com; Tue–Sat 6pm–2am, Sun noon–5pm; BART and metro: all lines to Powell; bus: 2, 9, 30, 38, 45; map p.134 C1
Live jazz, Big Band, and Motown hits performed high above Union Square in the Sir Francis Drake hotel.

Medjool

2522 Mission Street; tel: 550-9055; www.medjoolsf.com; bus: 14, 26, 49
This restaurant-nightclub offers something for everyone: dance to DJ tunes on the ground level, lounge and check out the crowd from the lofted level, or head up to the roof for cocktails with a view.

Mezzanine

444 Jessie Street; tel: 625-8880; www.mezzaninesf.com; hours vary; BART and metro: all lines to Powell; bus: 6, 7, 14, 21, 26; map p.139 C4

Left: hitting the dancefloor.

(www.melsdrive-in.com) are other good bets.

Bob's Donut and Pastry Shop
1621 Polk Street; tel: 776-3141; daily 24 hours; $; bus: 1, 19, 38, 47, 49; map p.134 B1
Old-fashioned satisfaction from mouthwatering glazeds and apple fritters.

Nopa
560 Divisadero Street; tel: 864-8643; www.nopasf.com; daily 5pm–1am; bus: 21, 24; map p.137 E3
Follow up Haight and Hayes Valley bar-hopping, or a concert at the Independent, with this airy, split-level space specializing in simple, organic, rustic food, like wood-grilled hangar steak, little fried fish, or flatbread with spicy sausage.

Osha Thai Noodle
696 Geary Street; tel: 673-2368; www.oshathai.com; Sun–Thur 11am–1am, Fri–Sat 11am–3am; $; bus: 2, 4, 27, 38; map p.134 B1
Debrief the night's adventures over Pad Thai in the TenderNob.

Transport Home

The Muni Owl Service runs from 1–5am on the Metro K, L, M, N, and T lines and the 5, 14, 22, 24, 38, 90, 91, and 108 bus lines (www.sfmta.com). BART runs until around midnight.

SEE ALSO TRANSPORTATION, P.123

Below: enjoying a cocktail.

For the latest bulletin on which buzz bands are playing and which DJ's are spinning, check out online guides like SFStation (www.sfstation.com) and Flavorpill (http://sf.flavorpill.net).

Dance to live and electronic sounds from both international and hot new talents.

Mighty
119 Utah Street; tel: 626-7001, info line: 762-0151; www.mighty119.com; hours vary; bus: 9, 22, 33, 53; map p.139 C2
An unpretentious crowd hikes out to this warehouse-type venue for good beats and breaks.

Ruby Skye
420 Mason Street; tel: 693-0777; www.rubyskye.com; Thur–Sat 8pm–4am; BART and metro: all lines to Powell; bus: 3, 27, 38, 76; map p.134 C1
Big DJ names draw big dancing crowds to this massive Union Square club.

Slide
430 Mason Street; tel: 421-1916; www.slidesf.com; Wed–Sat hours vary; BART and metro: all lines to Powell; bus: 2, 3, 27, 38, 76; map p.134 C1

Get dolled up to get in, then slide (watch those elbows and stilettos) into a slick downstairs nightclub.

Comedy Clubs

Cobb's Comedy Club
915 Columbus Avenue; tel: 928-4320; www.cobbscomedyclub.com; Thur–Sun show 8pm, Fri–Sat show 10.15pm too; bus: 30; map p.134 B3
Big name bookings include familiar faces from television.

The Punchline
444 Battery Street; tel: 397-7573; www.punchlinecomedyclub.com; daily show 8pm, Fri–Sat show 10pm too; BART and metro: all lines to Embarcadero; bus: 1, 10, 30X, 41; map p.135 D2
National and local talents crack up crowds every night of the week. Alumni include Robin Williams, Ellen DeGeneres and Chris Rock, so you never know when you might catch the next big thing.

Late-night Food

In addition to the post-club craving solutions below, Mexican taquerias in the Mission pizza in North Beach, and and Mel's Drive-In diners

Pampering

San Francisco has plush pampering solutions that will satisfy beauty product junkies, spa-addicts, and anyone simply craving a massage. A bevy of major international retailers, unique boutiques, and pharmacies supply the latest lotions and potions for skin, hair, and body, as well as high-end cosmetics and fragrances. Union Square in particular is happy hunting ground. Meanwhile, tranquil spas whisk stressed-out city-dwellers away from the noisy crowds and deliver facials, massages, and special signature treatments – many with an organic focus – to sooth and rejuvenate body, mind, and spirit.

Beauty Stores

Diptyque
171 Maiden Lane; tel: 402-0600; www.diptyqueparis.com; Mon–Sat 10am–6pm, Sun noon–5pm; BART and metro: all lines to Powell; bus: 2, 4, 38, 45, 76; cable car: Powell-Hyde, Powell-Mason; map p.135 C1

Ah-inducing aromas like the best-selling blackcurrant and Bulgarian rose Baies scent waft from this rare outpost of the elite Paris-based candle purveyor, which also concocts soaps and eaux de toilette.

Fresh
301 Sutter Street; tel: 248-0210; www.fresh.com; Mon–Wed 10am–7pm, Thur 10am–8pm, Fri–Sat 10am–7pm, Sun 11am–6pm; BART and metro: all lines to Powell; bus: 2, 3, 4, 30, 45; map p.135 C1

Product junkies rejoiced at the recent opening of this outpost Boston-based purveyor of posh cosmetics, skincare, and bodycare, which include a signature Sugar line.

MadKat Beauty
915 Cole Street; tel: 665-8448; Mon–Fri 10am–8pm, Sat 10am–

Above: a salesgirl tests the latest lip colour.

7pm, Sun 10am–6pm; metro: N to Carl and Cole streets; bus: 6, 33, 47; map p.137 D1

Finely edited selection of beauty products, including exclusive, international brands. Also at 1418 Grant Avenue (tel: 391-3841).

Pharmaca Integrative Pharmacy
925 Cole Street; tel: 661-1216; www.pharmaca.com; Mon–Fri 8am–8pm, Sat–Sun 9am–8pm; metro: N to Carl and Cole streets; bus: 6, 71; map p.137 D1

Homeopathic remedies, nutritional and botanical dietary supplements, aromatherapy, bath products, and conventional medications are found at this unique pharmacy.

SEE ALSO GAY AND LESBIAN, P.63

Spas

Barber Lounge
854 Folsom Street; tel: 934-0411; www.barberlounge.com; Tue–Fri 10am–8pm, Sat 9am–6pm, Sun 11am–5pm; bus: 5, 12, 27, 45, 76; map p.139 D4

Recently-opened modern salon-spa-barbershop hybrid caters to both genders with its full service menu, complete with hot-towel shaves and deep tissue massages.

Bliss San Francisco
181 3rd Street; tel: 281-0990; www.blissworld.com; Mon–Thur 10am–8pm, Fri–Sat 9am–9pm; BART and metro: all lines to Montgomery; bus: 9, 13, 30, 45, 76; map p.139 D4

Chic, spacious W Hotel day spa pampers with movie-while-you-manicure stations, men's and women's lounges, nine treatment rooms, and a brownie buffet.

Left: San Francisco's spas offer high-quality relaxation.

delivers deluxe pampering, an indoor infinity pool with stunning views, and spa cuisine.
SEE ALSO HOTELS, P.74

Therapeia Massage
1801 Bush Street; tel: 885-4450; www.therapeiaspa.com; Mon–Fri 10am–9pm, Sat–Sun 9am–8pm; bus: 1, 2, 3, 4; map p.134 A1
Day spa serves hot stone massage, endermologie, acupuncture, and more.

Tre Balm
3255 Sacramento Street; tel: 292-5129; www.trebalm.com; Mon–Fri 11am–7pm, Sat 9am–5pm, Sun noon–5pm; bus: 1, 2, 3, 4, 43; map p.133 D1
Elegant Laurel Heights beauty boutique and skin care studio, with coveted world-class products.

Tru Spa
750 Kearny Street; tel: 399-9700; www.truspa.com; Mon–Sat 9am–8pm; bus: 1, 41; map p.135 C2
Simple, fresh, treatment-focused day spa, offering facials with oxygen blasts and massages combined with aromatherapy or color therapy.

Below: laps and luxury at one of the Claremont's pools.

The **Westfield San Francisco Shopping Center** *(see Shopping, p.113)* hosts **Bare Escentuals** (www.bareescentuals. com), **Bath & Body Works** (www.bathandbodyworks.com), **The Body Shop** (www.bodyshop.com), **Kiehl's** (www.kiehls.com), and **Lush** (www.lush.com). Plus, **Sephora** (www.sephora.com) is found just across Market Street.

Burke Williams
845 Market Street; tel: 278-9740; www.burkewilliams spa.com; Mon–Sun 8am–10pm; BART and metro: all lines to Powell; bus: 3, 9, 14, 30, 38; cable car: Powell-Hyde, Powell-Mason; map p.138 C4
Lavish source of saunas, massages, facials, seaweed body wraps, and signature exfoliating and moisturizing treatments.

Claremont Resort and Spa
41 Tunnel Road, Berkeley; tel: 510-843-3000; www.claremont resort.com; BART: Downtown Berkeley, then AC Transit bus: 7
Pure luxury at this Berkeley landmark, where facilities

include a hydrotherapy circuit, two floatation tanks, an Aroma Spritz Bar, two swimming pools, and four saunas. A myriad of treatments are available.

International Orange
2044 Fillmore Street; tel: 888-894-8811; www.international orange.com; Mon–Fri 9am–9pm, Sat–Sun 9am–8pm; bus: 1, 2, 3, 4, 22; map p.133 E1
Fresh-feeling day spa and yoga studio (named for the Golden Gate Bridge's eye-popping paint color) supplies sumptuous treatments and yoga classes. There is also a relaxing redwood sundeck.

Kabuki Springs and Spa
1750 Geary Boulevard; tel: 922-6000; www.kabuki springs.com; daily 10am–9.45pm; bus: 2, 3, 4, 22, 38; map p.137 E4
Serene setting for facials, acupuncture, massages, and traditional communal baths.

Nob Hill Spa
1075 California Street; tel: 345-2888; www.huntingtonhotel. com; Mon–Sun 8am–8.30pm; bus: 1; cable car: California; map p.134 C1
Luxurious sanctuary hidden in the Huntington Hotel

97

Parks and Gardens

With sprawling parks, blooming botanical gardens, and neighborhood patches of green, San Francisco is full of open spaces perfect for whiling away time out of doors. Spend a day exploring the extensive grounds of Golden Gate Park, relax for a leisurely picnic in one of many sunlit squares, or pause for a few serene moments while enjoying a gorgeous view. Unless otherwise noted, these urban oases are open around the clock; however, though delightful by day, they are generally not safe places for star-gazing after dark.

North Beach, Telegraph Hill, and Russian Hill

Ina Coolbrith Park
Taylor and Vallejo Streets; bus: 41, 45; cable car: Powell-Mason; map p.134 B2
Dedicated to California's first Poet Laureate, this steep series of steps and terraces climbs high up Russian Hill to a small lookout with picturesque views of North Beach and the Bay Bridge.

Washington Square
Bordered by Union, Stockton, Filbert, and Powell streets; bus: 15, 39, 41, 45; map p.134 C3
Prime people-watching can be had at this park overlooked by Sts Peter and Paul Church (see Churches, p.44), where a rainbow of types (elderly Italians, Tai Chi devotees, sunbathers, Frisbee-tossers) escape from North Beach's congested streets.

Chinatown

Portsmouth Square
Bordered by Walter Lum Place and Clay, Washington, and Kearny streets; BART and metro: all lines to Montgomery; bus: 1, 9X, 30; map p.135 C2
Bordering the financial dis-

Above: a frisbee-player in Mission Dolores Park.

trict, this Chinatown square hosts morning Tai Chi sessions, Chinese chess tables and benches, neighborly chatting, and youngsters clambering on jungle gyms.

Union Square and Financial District

Justin Herman Plaza
End of Market Street at Embarcadero; BART and metro: all lines to Embarcadero; bus: 9, 12, 21, 41; map p.135 D2
Opposite the Ferry Building, this lively plaza space is shared by financial district

workers on lunch break, performers, skateboarders, and (in winter) ice-skaters.

SoMa and Civic Center

Yerba Buena Gardens
Bordered by Mission, Folsom, 3rd, and 4th streets; www.yerbabuena.org; Mon–Sun 6am–10pm; BART and metro: all lines to Powell; bus: 5, 6,14, 21; map p.139 D4
This urban oasis features grassy landscaping, fountains, cafés, public artwork, a waterfall memorial to Dr Martin Luther King, Jr, a carousel, an ice-skating rink, a bowling center, and the kid-friendly **Zeum** museum.
SEE ALSO CHILDREN, P.41

Nob Hill

Huntington Park
Bordered by California, Sacramento, Taylor and Cushman streets; bus: 1; cable car: California; map p.134 C2
Across the street from Grace Cathedral on Nob Hill, this well-maintained, bench-lined splash of green is a pleasant place to lounge and browse the occasional art show. The square's cen-

Left: the serene view from Alta Plaza Park.

avenues; metro: N to Duboce Street; bus: 6, 7, 71; map p.137 D2

This steeply sloped, wooded park (which, dating from 1867, is the city's oldest) delivers on the good views promised by its name, particularly with its northern prospects of the Golden Gate Bridge and Marin Headlands.

Golden Gate Park

Bordered by Fulton Street, Lincoln Way, Great Highway and Stanyan streets; tel: 831-2700; metro: N to Irving Street and 9th Avenue; bus: 7,18, 21, 44, 71; map p.136–7

Where rolling sand dunes once could be seen, Golden Gate Park's grassy hills now carpet more than 1,000 acres stretching from Haight-Ashbury to the Pacific Ocean. Inside the enormous park filled with copious gardens and groves, it is easy to forget about the city's hustle and bustle, especially on Sundays, when John F. Kennedy Drive is closed to car traffic. Scores of athletes are attracted by the many fields and miles of trails, not to mention the golf course,

In addition to her Poet Laureate claim to fame, Oakland librarian Ina Coolbrith is also remembered for mentoring a young Jack London and entertaining other literary greats at her home on Macondray Lane. Additionally, she was the niece of Mormon founder Joseph Smith Jr.

terpiece is a replica of the Roman Tartarughe Fountain.

Central Neighbourhoods

Alamo Square

Bordered by Steiner, Hayes, Fulton, and Scott streets; bus: 5, 21, 22, 24; map p.137 E3

Six brightly colored Victorian homes known as the Painted Ladies line this grassy square. Often called Postcard Row, the picturesque prospect is completed by a city skyline backdrop, and is one of San Francisco's most photographed sights.

Alta Plaza Park

Bordered by Clay, Steiner, Jackson, and Scott streets; bus: 1, 3, 12, 24; map p.133 E1

Designed by John McLaren, this Pacific Heights park

boasts grassy terraces, basketball and tennis courts, a playground, and sweeping views of the city.

Lafayette Park

Bordered by Laguna, Gough, Sacramento, and Washington streets; bus: 1, 12; map p.134 A1

In the midst of Pacific Heights mansions, this four-block park supplies tennis courts, excellent views, and a popular spot for local pups to play.

Haight-Ashbury

Buena Vista Park

Bordered by Haight Street and Buena Vista East and West

Below: the Presidio's beach is just one of the many attractions of this expansive park.

Above: a sunny day entices locals to hit Dolores Park.

polo field, tennis courts, horseshoe pits, archery field, pétanque courts, and fly-fishing pond. Others come to enjoy less strenuous diversions, making use of picnic tables and barbeque pits, or simply napping on the lawns. The park has plenty of character, housing prominent museums like the **de Young** and the **California Academy of Sciences**, as well as the historic Beach Chalet, a large Music Concourse, a hippie-beloved hill, a rose garden, and live bison.

SEE ALSO MUSEUMS AND GALLERIES, P.87

PARK HIGHLIGHTS
Conservatory of Flowers
John F. Kennedy Drive at Conservatory Drive; tel: 666-7001; www.conservatoryofflowers.org; Tue–Sun 9am–5pm, last entrance at 4.30pm; entrance charge, under 5 free, fiirst Tue of month free; bus: 5, 7, 21, 33, 71
Built in the late 1870s, this dramatic, glass-domed structure was modeled after the Palm House at the Royal Botanical Gardens in Kew,

England. Vibrantly colored tropical flowers are the main focus of nearly 2,000 plant species. Outside, the Dahlia Garden decorates the eastern side of the conservatory, while a little way west, 850 varieties of colorful rhododendron bloom every year in early summer in the McLaren Memorial Rhododendron Dell.

Dutch and Murphy Windmills
John F. Kennedy Drive; free; bus: 5, 18, 31, 38
Dating from the early 1900s, the windmills looming in the park's north-west corner once pumped water to the Strawberry Hill reservoir. Fittingly, a colorful spread of tulips blooms each spring near the Dutch Windmill.

Garden of Shakespeare's Flowers
Martin Luther King Jr Drive and Middle Drive East; free; bus: 44, 71
Visitors play name that flower in this lush garden where flowers and herbs mentioned in poems and plays penned by the famous bard decorate either side of a brick path.

Japanese Tea Garden
Tea Garden Drive; tel: 752-1171; www.japaneseteagardensf.com; daily, Mar–Oct 9am–6pm, Nov–Feb 9am–4.45pm; entrance charge, free under 5, free Mon, Wed and Fri before 10am; bus: 21, 44
This peaceful setting of cherry blossoms, bonsai conifers, carp ponds, and wooden bridges is the oldest public Japanese-style garden in the country. It tends to be a popular destination, so expect company while strolling and then snacking on tea and cookies.

Koret Children's Quarter
Kezar Drive; free; bus: 71
Formerly known as the Children's Playground, this public playground built in 1887 is the country's oldest. Nearby, youngsters ride on colorful, carved animals at the historic Herschell-Spillman carousel, which dates from 1912.

National AIDS Memorial Grove
Between Middle Drive East and Bowling Green Drive; tel: 750-8340; www.aidsmemorial.org; free; bus: 21, 33, 71
This peaceful grove is a living tribute to those whose lives have been affected by AIDS.

Portals of the Past
Between JFK Drive and Crossover Drive; free; bus: 5, 28, 29
At Lloyd Lake, six stately columns known as the Portals of the Past stand as the city's only public memorial

It is no accident that statues in Golden Gate Park are hidden by dense foliage. Uncle John McLaren, the park superintendent for a period of 53 years (1890–1943), notoriously detested statuary. Ironically, a prominent statue of the Scotsman himself now stands in the McLaren Memorial Rhododendron Dell.

to the 1906 earthquake and fire. Before the disaster, the white marble pillars formed the portico of the Towne mansion on Nob Hill.

San Francisco Botanical Garden, at Strybing Arboretum

9th Avenue and Lincoln Way; tel: 661-1316; www.sfbotanical garden.org; Mon–Fri 8am–4.30pm, Sat–Sun 10am–5pm; free; bus: 44, 71

Mediterranean, mild temperate, and tropical cloud-forest plants are among the 7,500 diverse species from all over the world found on these 55 acres of gardens. A 'Garden of Fragrance' is one of several specialty gardens.

Stow Lake

John F. Kennedy Drive; tel: 752-0347; charge for boat rentals; bus: 5, 28, 29

At this lake, the largest of the park's 11, rowboat and pedal boat rentals are offered, making for a leisurely afternoon gliding around with the turtles. At the lake's center, **Strawberry Hill** supplies the park's highest promontory.

SEE ALSO WALKS AND VIEWS, P.125

Mission and Castro

Mission Dolores Park

Bordered by Dolores, Church, 18th, and 20th streets; BART: to 16th Street; metro: J to Church Street & 18th Street; bus: 33; map p.138 A1

Frisky dogs and energetic ballplayers get their exercise in the lower part of this popular Mission park; higher up, picnickers enjoy the views and sun themselves.

SEE ALSO WALKS AND VIEWS, P.128

Around San Francisco

Lincoln Park

34th Avenue and Clement Street; bus: 1, 2, 18, 38

Wind-battered bluffs rim this 275-acre park, where a golf course, the grand **Palace of**

the **Legion of Honor**, and the Land's End lookout all reward visitors with great views.

SEE ALSO MUSEUMS AND GALLERIES, P.88

The Presidio

Bordered by Lyon Street and West Pacific Avenue; tel: 561-4323; www.nps.gov/prsf; bus: 28, 29, 43, 76, 82X; map p.132

A military post for more than 200 years, this 1,491-acre (603-hectare) shoreline park encompasses beaches, cliffs, woods, historical sites, a golf course, a lake, 14 miles (22.5km) of paved roads (making biking a popular way to explore), and 11 miles (18km) of hiking trails. A popular spot is Crissy Field, the restored tidal marshland along the Presidio's northern shore. Relaxing picnickers enjoy the great views, and walkers and bikers cruise the **Golden Gate Promenade** – a nice break from the city's typically hilly terrain.

For other sweeping vistas, head to the rocky, mile-long shore of **Baker Beach** (where swimming should be avoided) or the windswept bluffs above, along which abandoned defensive gun batteries are scattered. Other Presidio possibilities include relaxing at **Mountain Lake**, visiting the **San Francisco National Military Cemetery** (or the nearby pet cemetery), and checking out **Fort Point** (tours Fri–Sun 10am–5pm), a historical defense fortification below the Golden Gate Bridge.

Sigmund Stern Recreation Grove

Sloat Boulevard and 19th Avenue; metro: K, M to West Portal Avenue & Sloat Boulevard; bus: 23, 28

This peaceful, 33-acre park encompasses meadows, playgrounds, horseshoe pits, tennis courts, and the natural Pine Lake. However, Stern Grove is best known for the

free, outdoor summer concerts it has offered since 1938.

Sutro Heights Park

48th Avenue and Point Lobos Avenue; free; bus: 18, 38

When clear skies permit, this never-crowded former estate of one-time San Francisco mayor Adolph Sutro serves up a scenic view of the Cliff House, Ocean Beach, and the Pacific Ocean.

Below: some of Golden Gate Park's many highlights.

101

Restaurants

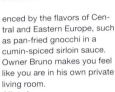

San Franciscans are serious about food. With thousands of restaurants to choose from, the best ones are not secret for long, and the boring, tasteless, or tacky are left to die on the vine. Not only is San Francisco an international hub of fine food, with groundbreaking Californian and exciting fusion cuisine, but the adventurous eater can seek out ethnic food from virtually every culture in the world. Diverse neighborhoods such as the Inner Richmond and Tenderloin offer a vast array from which to choose. Whether for brunch, lunch, or dinner, the options in San Francisco are both extensive and tasty.

Fisherman's Wharf

AMERICAN

Buena Vista
2765 Hyde Street; tel: 474-5044; www.thebuenavista.com; Mon–Fri 9am–2am, Sat–Sun 8am–2am; $$; bus: 10, 19, 30, 47; cable car: Powell–Hyde; map p.134 B4
A San Francisco institution and home of the legendary Irish Coffee, a delicious elixir made with Irish whiskey, frothed cream and coffee.

Eagle Café
Pier 39; tel: 433-3689; www.the tinfiish.net; Mon–Wed Sun–Thur 7.30am–9pm; $; metro: F to Embarcadero and Stockton Street; bus: 10, 39, 47; map p.134 C4
A great alternative to the many overpriced Wharf restaurants, the Eagle is a lively institution known for large portions, hearty breakfasts, stiff cocktails and stellar views.

CALIFORNIAN

McCormick and Kuleto's
900 North Point Street, Ghira-radelli Square; tel: 929-1730; www.mccormickandschmicks. com; daily 11.30am–10pm, Fri–Sat until 11pm; $$$; bus:

Above: grab some crab and a beer on Fisherman's Wharf.

10, 19, 30, 47; cable car: Powell–Hyde; map p.134 A4
Ghirardelli Square seafood spot popular for fabulous views and its huge variety of fresh, imaginative seafood dishes, as well as other tasty American fare.

ITALIAN

Albona
545 Francisco Street; tel: 441-1040; www.albonarestaurant. com; Tue–Sat 5–10pm; $$; bus: 30, 39; cable car: Powell–Mason; map p.134 B3
This Istrian restaurant serves Northern Italian dishes influ-

enced by the flavors of Central and Eastern Europe, such as pan-fried gnocchi in a cumin-spiced sirloin sauce. Owner Bruno makes you feel like you are in his own private living room.

Alioto's
8 Fisherman's Wharf; tel: 673-0183; www.aliotos.com; daily 11am–11pm; $$; metro: F to Jefferson Street and Taylor Street; bus: 10, 39, 47; map p.134 B4
The Alioto name stands for politics, feuds, family and fine food in San Francisco. For generations, this family-owned establishment has ruled the Wharf with fresh, local seafood dishes and Sicilian preparations.

Scoma's
Pier 47; tel: 771-4383; www.scomas.com; Mon–Thur noon–10pm, Fri–Sat 11.30am–10.30pm, Sun 11.30am–10pm; $$$; metro: F to Jefferson Street and Taylor Street; map p.134 B4
For a glimpse of the working man's Wharf, dine right on the pier at this old-school Italian spot that has been serving seafood, pasta and their acclaimed chowder for 45 years.

Left: San Francisco has many restaurants serving exquisite gourmet food.

endary atmosphere. Jazz and good times nightly.

CALIFORNIAN
Coi
373 Broadway; tel: 393-9000; www.coirestaurant.com; Tue–Sat 6–10pm; $$$$; bus: 12, 30, 45; map p.134 C2
Worthy of a very special occasion, the intimate and softly-lit Coi certainly lives up to its two Michelin stars. The 11-course menu from chef-owner and molecular-gastronomy wizard Daniel Patterson changes daily and features only the very best ingredients.

EAST ASIAN
Sushi on North Beach
745 Columbus Avenue; tel: 788-8050; www.northbeachsushi.com; Mon–Fri 11.30am–1.45pm, 5–9.30pm, Sat–Sun 5–9.30pm; $$; bus: 30, 41, 45; cable car: Powell-Mason; map p.134 C3
This family-run Asian establishment is a real find in the middle of Italian North Beach. Unique rolls, good-size pieces of fresh fish, and a fantastic miso soup set it apart from the rest.

Average price for a three-course meal and a half-bottle of house wine:	
$$$$	more than $100
$$$	$50–$100
$$	$25–$50
$	less than $25

SOUTHEAST ASIAN
Ana Mandara
891 Beach Street; tel: 771-6600; www.anamandara.com; Mon–Fri 11.30am–2pm, daily 5.30–9.30pm, Fri–Sat until 10.30pm; $$$; metro: F to Jones Street and Beach Street; cable car: Powell-Hyde; bus: 10, 19, 30, 47; map p.134 A4
French-Vietnamese-inspired fare at this place, maybe a little upscale for Fisherman's Wharf. Starters include crispy crab rolls, striped bass ceviche, and lobster with mango and coconut sauce.

North Beach, Telegraph Hill, and Russian Hill
AMERICAN
Mama's
1701 Stockton Street; tel: 362 6421; www.mamas-sf.com; Tue–Sun 8am–3pm; bus: 12, 39, 41, 45; map p.134 C3

This lively, crowded brunch staple just across from Washington Square draws long lines on the weekends with big egg dishes and pancakes.
Washington Square Bar and Grill
1707 Powell Street; tel: 433-1188; www.washingtonsquarebarandgrill.com; daily 5–10pm, Mon–Fri noon–3pm, Sun 11am–3pm; $$$; bus: 30, 41, 45; cable car: Powell-Mason; map p.134 C3
On Washington Square, and celebrated in countless *San Francisco Chronicle* columns, the 'Washbag' has had a culinary revival equal to its leg-

Below: very fresh seafood...

Tipping in the US is different from many other places in the world. Most waitstaff and bartenders make minimum wage and depend on tips for survival. Less than 15 percent means you were unsatisfied with the service. 18 percent is standard. 20 percent means you were happy with both service and food. Tipping nothing is very bad form. Percentages are calculated pre-tax. A quick way of calculating is to just double the tax (9.5 percent) and round up or down depending on level of satisfaction.

Above: from upmarket soul food to classic dim sum, San Franciscans have varied eating options.

EUROPEAN
O'Reilly's
622 Green Street; tel: 989-6222; www.oreillysirish.com; Mon–Fri 9am–2am, Sat–Sun 8am–2am; $; bus: 30, 41, 45; cable car: Powell-Mason; map p.134 C3

This Irish pub is a cozy place for a hearty brunch, eaten either in the cool, stone-worked interior, or on the pleasant sidewalk tables. Be sure to try the Guinness-battered fish and chips.

Zarzuela
2000 Hyde Street; tel: 346-0800; Tue–Sat 5.30–10pm; $$; bus: 41, 45; cable car: Powell-Hyde; map p.134 B3

A lively Spanish restaurant on the top of Russian Hill along the cable car route. This is a great place to drink sangria and share tapas or steaming plates of flavorful paella with a group of hungry friends.

ITALIAN
Firenze by Night
1429 Stockton Street; tel: 392-8485; Tue–Sat 5–11pm, Sun–Mon 5–10pm; $$; bus: 30, 41, 45; map p.134 C3

A traditional Northern Italian restaurant in North Beach on the edge of Chinatown. Famous for the outstanding pillowy-soft gnocci, the ten-der calamari, and the pappardelle pasta Toscana with rabbit. Treat yourself to a glass of housemade limoncello with dessert.

Franchino's
347 Columbus Avenue; tel: 982-2157; Tue–Sun 4–10pm; $$; bus: 30, 41, 45; map p.135 C2

Family-owned and -operated, friendly Franchino's serves classic Italian dishes at reasonable prices.

Golden Boy Pizza
542 Green Street; tel: 982-9738; www.goldenboypizza.com; Sun–Thur 11.30am–11.30pm, Fri–Sat 11.30am–2.30am; $; bus: 30, 41, 45; map p.134 C3

Golden Boy's Sicilian-style pan pizza is a favorite of North Beach bar-goers, and usually ordered by the slice. Look in the window and choose what whets the appetite.

L'Osteria del Forno
519 Columbus Avenue; tel: 982-1124; www.losteriadelforno.com; Sun–Thur 11.30am–10pm,

Average price for a three-course meal and a half-bottle of house wine:	
$$$$	more than $100
$$$	$50–$100
$$	$25–$50
$	less than $25

closed Tue, Fri–Sat 11.30am–10.30pm; $$; bus: 30, 41, 45; map p134 C3

For casual but satisfying Italian food, including marvelous antipasti, thin-crusted pizzas, a daily pasta dish, and a fine roast pork loin in a milky broth. This treasure is a kid pleaser as well. Cash only.

North Beach Restaurant
1512 Stockton Street; tel: 392-1700; www.northbeach restaurant.com; daily 11.30am–11.45pm; $$$; bus: 30, 41, 45; map p.134 C3

This venerable institution serves hearty Tuscan cuisine featuring homemade pastas, house-cured proscuitto and a dizzyingly comprehensive wine list.

LATIN AMERICAN
Pena Pacha Mama
1630 Powell Street; tel: 646-0018; www.pachamamacenter.org; Wed–Sun 5.30–10.30pm; $$; bus: 30, 41, 45; map p.134 C3

Experience the Bolivian hospitality of the Navia family and the robust organic flavors from their native country. Live traditional music most nights makes for an unforgettable experience. Cover charge on weekends.

Parking in San Francisco, especially downtown, can be brutal. If you do not want to pay the exorbitant lot rates, arrive at least 20 minutes early to find street parking, more in North Beach. Always read street signs and scan curbs for parking restrictions.

Chinatown

EAST ASIAN

Empress of China
838 Grant Avenue; tel: 434-1345; www.empressofchinasf.com; daily 11.30am–10pm; $; bus: 1, 30, 45; map p.135 C2
The only restaurant in Chinatown with a truly spectacular view gives diners a very good perspective on the neighborhood. The cocktail lounge overlooks Grant Avenue, while the dining room towers above Portsmouth Square. If you do not eat here, at least stop by for a drink and enjoy the ambience.

Far East Café
631 Grant Avenue; tel: 982-3245; www.fareastcafe.com; daily 11.30am–10pm; $; bus: 1, 30, 45; map p.135 C2
Food is good but not amazing, with all the standards of a Chinese restaurant. But the atmosphere is one of the best in Chinatown, with private booths, and century-old chandeliers.

House of Nanking
919 Kearny Street; tel: 421-1429; daily 11am–10pm; $; bus: 12, 41; map p.135 C2
Small and crowded, this popular spot draws long lines with its excellent, inexpensive Chinese food. Listen to the no-nonsense staff to find out what is good tonight.

Union Square and Financial District

AMERICAN

Michael Mina
335 Powell Street; tel: 397-9220;
Tue–Thur 5.30–9.30pm, Fri–Sat 5.30–10pm; $$$$; bus: 2, 3, 4, 30, 76; cable car: Powell-Hyde, Powell-Mason; map p.134 C1
Located in the Westin St Francis hotel, this warm, elegant spot has garnered two Michelin stars for its refined American cuisine (think ahi tuna tartare to start, lobster pot pie to follow, and huckleberry financier for dessert). The wine list is extensive, with a focus on Burgundy, Austria, and the Rhone.

Sam's Grill
374 Bush Street; tel: 421-0594; www.beldenplace.com/sams grill; Mon–Fri 11am–9pm; $$$; bus: 1, 45, 76; map p.135 C1
Although the three-martini business lunch may be a thing of the past, this old-school grill is still going strong after 125 years. Choose either the high-ceiling dining room or a private booth, and enjoy American cuisine free from pretension and impervious to change.

Tadich Grill
240 California Street; tel: 391-1849; www.tadichgrill.com; Mon–Fri 11am–9.30pm, Sat 11.30am–9.30pm; $$$; bus: 1, 10, 30X, 41; cable car: California; map p.135 D2
Tadich is a venerable institution that has been around in various incarnations since the Gold Rush, with wooden booths, white linen, and waiters as crusty as the sourdough. The menu of classics, includes lobster Newburg, crab Louis, and sand dabs. The cognoscenti order whatever fresh fish is available, grilled. Sidle up to the original mahogany bar, order a gin fizz and soak in old school San Francisco ambiance.

Taylor's Refresher
1 Ferry Building #6; tel: 318-3423; www.taylorsautomatic refresher.com; daily 10.30am–10pm; $; metro: F to the Embaracdero and Ferry Building; bus: 1, 12, 14, 31, 71; cable car: California; map p.135 E2
High-end diner fare with a gourmet flourish. Taylor's is famous for their burgers – patties are ¼lb Niman Ranch beef – as well as their decadent milkshakes, but you will also find grilled chicken sandwiches, über-fresh salads, sweet potato fries and other diner faves.

CALIFORNIAN

Aqua
252 California Street; tel: 956-9662; www.aqua-sf.com; Tue–Fri 11.30am–2.30pm, daily 5.30–10.30pm, Sun until 9.30pm; $$$$; bus: 1, 10, 12, 41; cable car: California; map p.135 D2

Below: the city's proximity to the ocean results in fantastic seafood.

Reservations are required at this sophisticated, fine-dining seafood restaurant that is consistently rated as the best in San Francisco. The presentation and service are top-notch and chefs from around the world vie to work here.

Bix

56 Gold Street; tel: 433-6300; www.bixrestaurant.com; daily from 5.30pm, also Fri 11.30am–2pm; $$$; bus: 10, 12, 41; map p.135 D2

A supperclub with a 1930s–40s ambiance, Bix supplies upscale munchables (mini lamb burgers, house-made mozzarella wrapped in prosciutto) along with heartier steaks and seafood dishes, all served up with classic cocktails and live jazz in swanky downtown digs.

EUROPEAN
Kokkari

200 Jackson Street; tel: 981-0983; www.kokkari.com; Mon–Fri 11.30am–2.30pm, 5.30–10pm, Fri until 11pm, Sat 5–11pm; $$$$; bus: 1, 12, 42; map p.135 D2

An Aristotle Onassis–sort of Greek taverna with beamed ceilings, a massive fireplace, Oriental carpets, and huge dishes of rich food. The crowd exudes a robust sense of well-being. Reservations advisable.

FRENCH
Fleur de Lys

777 Sutter Street; tel: 673-7779; www.flleurdelyssf.com; Tue–Thur 6–9.30pm, Fri 5.30–10.30pm, Sat 5–10.30pm; $$$$; bus: 2, 3, 27, 76; map p.134 C1

Average price for a three-course meal and a half-bottle of house wine:
$$$$	more than $100
$$$	$50–$100
$$	$25–$50
$	less than $25

Above: tucking in at a Japantown restaurant.

The premier French restaurant, with an elegant dining room and superior service.

Plouf

40 Belden Place; tel: 986-6491; www.ploufsf.com; Mon–Fri 11.30am–3pm, 5.30–10pm, Fri until 11pm, Sat 5.30–11pm; $$$; bus: 1, 2, 4, 30; map p.135 C1

There are a number of good café-restaurants with outdoor seating on Belden Place, a charming brick alley off Bush and Kearny streets. Plouf specializes in delicious seafood prepared with a French accent and the waiters also give the impression you have arrived in the Paris of the west.

INDIAN
Shalimar

532 Jones Street; tel: 928-0333; www.shalimarsf.com; daily noon–midnight; $; bus: 27, 38, 76; map p.134 B1

Consistently rated one of the best Indian restaurants in the city, this spot serves traditional and tasty Indian and Pakistani food. No alcohol. Cash only.

SOUTHEAST ASIAN
Slanted Door

1 Ferry Building #3; tel: 861-8032; www.slanteddoor.com; daily 11am–2.30pm, 5.30–10pm, Fri–Sat until 10.30pm; $$$; metro: F to the Embarcadero and Ferry Building; bus: 1, 2, 21, 31, 71; cable car: California; map p.135 E2

One of the premier restaurants in the city, serving wholesome, flavorful Vietnamese food. Make reservations far in advance.

SoMa and Civic Center
AMERICAN
Town Hall

342 Howard Street; tel: 908-3900; www.townhallsf.com; Mon–Fri 11.30am–2pm, daily 5.30–10pm, Fri–Sat until 11pm; $$$; bus: 12, 30, 45, 76; map p.135 D1

Below: vegetarian specialities are common too.

Regional American classics with a Southern accent (think buttermilk fried chicken and smoked andouille jambalaya) are served up nicely in this remodeled, historic building.

CALIFORNIAN
XYZ

181 3rd Street; tel: 817-7836; www.xyz-sf.com; Mon–Fri 6.30am–10.30am, 11.30am–2pm, 6–10pm, Sat 7am–2pm, 6–11pm, Sun 7am–2pm; $$$$; bus: 12, 30, 45, 76; map p.139 D4
In a handsome, chic space, XYZ offers modern-Cal fare, superb service, and an extensive, award-winning wine list, featuring over 500 different varieties.

EAST ASIAN
Yank Sing

101 Spear Street; tel: 957-9300; www.yanksing.com; Mon–Fri 11am–3pm, Sat–Sun 10am–4pm; $$; BART: to Montgomery; metro: all lines to Embarcadero; bus: 1, 2, 6, 7, 71; map p.135 E2
This sparkling-clean dim sum spot relies on fresh ingredients and serves up great dumplings. Perfect for dim sum first-timers.

EUROPEAN
Zuni Café

1658 Market Street; tel: 552-2522; www.zunicafe.com; Tue–Sun 11.30am–11pm, Fri–Sat until midnight; $$; BART and metro: all lines to Van Ness; bus: 6, 7, 47, 49, 71; map p.138 B3
Make reservations and elbow past the crowded copper bar for the best

> Some neighborhoods are known for a certain cuisine – burritos in the Mission, dim sum on Stockton Street and Broadway in Chinatown, Italian in North Beach, and Indian and Vietnamese in the Tenderloin.

roasted chicken and bread salad (for two) imaginable. The daily-changing menu is inspired by traditional Italian and French recipes.

FRENCH
Absinthe Brasserie and Bar

398 Hayes Street; tel: 551-1590; www.absinthe.com; Tue–Thur 11.30am–10pm, Fri 11.30am–11pm, Sat 11am–11pm, Sun 11am–10pm; $$; bus: 21, 47, 49; map p.138 A4
Upscale, American-influenced French and Northern Italian fare in a casually romantic atmosphere; specifically, that of a Belle Époque brasserie in the south of France – think rattan café chairs and period art up front, and leather banquettes and antique mirrors in the softly lit dining areas.

Le Charm

315 5th Street; tel: 546-6128; www.lecharm.com; Tue–Thur 11.30am–2pm, 5.30–9.30pm, Fri 11.30am–2pm, 5.30–10pm, Sat 5.30–10pm, Sun 5–8.30pm; $$; bus 12, 27, 30, 45, 76; map p.139 D3
French food's greatest hits, reasonably priced. Coq au vin, escargot, duck confit, crème brûlée, and classic French onion soup all share this comfortable, unpretentious stage.

VEGETARIAN
Ananda Fuara

1298 Market Street; tel: 621-1994; www.anandafuara.com; Mon–Sat 11am–8pm, Wed until 3pm; $; BART: to Civic Center metro: all lines to Civic Center; bus: 5, 7, 9, 71; map p.138 B3
Inexpensive and delicious, this is the perfect change of pace for vegetarians tired of veggie burritos and Caesar salads. There is much to order here, from meatless meatloaf to mushroom ravioli to vegan chocolate cake.

> Conventional wisdom says that in San Francisco there are more medical marijuana dispensaries than McDonald's restaurants.

Nob Hill
AMERICAN
Big 4

1075 California Street; tel: 771-1140; www.bissapbaobab.com; Sun–Wed 7am–10am, 5.30–10pm, Thur 7am–10am, 11.30am–3pm, 5.30–10pm, Fri 7am–3pm, 5.30–10pm, Sat 7am–11am, 5.30–10pm; $$$; bus: 1; cable car: California; map p.134 C1
The Big 4 is named after the four 'robber baron' railroad tycoons whose photos and memorabilia line the walls. Dark wood paneling adds to the men's-club ambiance and the hearty menu is suitably heavy on meat and game – from filet mignon and rack of lamb to wild boar chops.

CALIFORNIAN
1550 Hyde Café and Wine Bar

1550 Hyde Street; tel: 775-1550; www.1550hyde.com; Tue–Thur 6.30–9.30pm, Fri–Sat 6–10pm, Sun 5.30–9.30pm; bus: 12, 27; cable car: Powell-Hyde; map p.134 B2

Below: hard-at-work chefs prepare yet more tasty dishes.

Above: in the distinctive Haight tacqueria, Zona Rose.

Right on the cable-car route, this small, casually elegant gem in Nob Hill features a daily-changing menu of seasonal, organic Cal–Med fare as well as an eclectic, well-priced wine list.

ITALIAN
Nob Hill Café

1152 Taylor Street; tel: 776-6500; www.nobhillcafe.com; daily 11am–3pm, 5–10pm; $$; bus: 1; cable car: California; map p.134 C2

A cozy bistro, tucked in a quiet Nob Hill neighborhood, featuring delicious Tuscan cuisine. Loved by locals for great wine, ambience and the ethereal tiramisu. No reservations, so get there early.

Central Neighborhoods

AMERICAN
Elite Café

2049 Fillmore Street; tel: 673-5483; www.theelitecafe.com; Mon–Thur 5–10pm, Fri 5–10.30pm, Sat 10am–2.30pm, 5–10.30pm, Sun 10am–2.30pm, 5–9pm; $$; bus: 1, 3, 22; map p.133 E1

This locals' fave serves Cajun- and Creole-inspired dishes in an upscale, cheery atmosphere. An excellent raw bar beckons, as do the weekend brunch's biscuits, beignets, and Bloody Marys.

EAST ASIAN
Seoul Garden

1655 Post Street Miyake Mall, 2nd Floor; tel: 563-7664; www.seoulgardenbbq.com; daily 11am–midnight; $; bus: 2, 3, 22, 38; map p.138 A4

Savory meats cooked right at your table, with successful but unobtrusive flair. The meat is tender and succulent, but the spiciness is up to you. Never tried Korean? This is the place to start.

EUROPEAN
Suppenküche

601 Hayes Street; tel: 252-9289; www.suppenkuche.com; Mon–Sat 5–10pm, Sun 10am–2pm, 5–10pm; $; bus: 21; map p.138 A3

At one of the few German restaurants in the city, hearty portions of German classics – spætzle, schnitzel, potato pancakes – are served to a loud and lively crowd seated at long communal tables. Around 30 beers (mostly German) on tap.

Average price for a three-course meal and a half-bottle of house wine:

$$$$	more than $100
$$$	$50–$100
$$	$25–$50
$	less than $25

FUSION
Betelnut

2030 Union Street; tel: 929-8855; www.betelnutrestaurant.com; Sun–Thur 11.30am–11pm, Fri–Sat 11.30am–midnight; $$; bus: 22, 41, 45; map p.133 E2

A pan-Asian bar specializing in dumplings and noodle bowls with bold, exciting flavors.

VEGETARIAN
Greens

Building A, Fort Mason; tel: 771-6222; www.greensrestaurant.com; daily 5.30–9pm, Tue–Sat 11.45am–2.30pm, Sun 10.30am–2pm; $$; bus: 28; map p.133 E4

In a one-time army warehouse on the bay, an airy, upscale vegetarian restaurant that even non-veggies rave about. The Saturday evening prix-fixe menu is a relative bargain and comes with lovely bay views. Reservations are recommended. Its take-out counter, Greens to Go, is open all day.

Haight-Ashbury and Golden Gate Park

CARRIBEAN
Cha Cha Cha

1801 Haight Street; tel: 386-5758; www.cha3.com; daily 11.30am–4pm, 5–11pm, Fri–Sat until 11.30pm; $; bus: 7, 37, 43, 71; map p.137 C2

Smack dab in the middle of Haight-Ashbury, Cha Cha Cha is a fun place for tapas, Caribbean-inspired entrees and sangria. The crowd is young, hip and noisy.

INDIAN
Naan 'n' Curry

642 Irving Street; tel: 664-7225; www.naancurry.com; daily 11am–11pm; $; metro: N to Irving Street and 7th Avenue; bus: 6, 43; map p.136 B1

So much flavor for so little cash. This Inner Sunset location is one of several Indian/Pakistani eateries known for

> 'California Cuisine' is typified by seasonal, local produce, usually organic. Flavor combinations accentuate freshness, subtlety, and texture. Meat is not always the focal point.

its delicious food and low prices. Short on decor but long on spiciness, the chicken vindaloo, tikka masala and tandoori all hit the mark.

LATIN AMERICAN
Zona Rosa
1797 Haight Street; tel: 668-7717; daily 11am–9.30pm; $; bus: 7, 33, 37, 43, 71; map p.137 C2

Craving a burrito but don't want to go all the way over to the Mission? This groovy taqueria is good for a quick bite in a quirky setting. Vegetarian options are particularly popular.

MIDDLE EASTERN
Kan Zaman
1793 Haight Street; tel: 751-9656; www.kanzamansf.com; Mon–Thur 5pm–midnight, Fri 5pm–2am, Sat noon–2am, Sun noon–midnight; $; bus: 7, 33, 37, 43, 71; map p.137 C2

A perennial favorite with locals for dishes with Lebanese and Palestinian origins. Expect a loud, fun night

with belly dancers (Thur–Sat), spiced wine and hookah pipes with flavors like apple, pomegranate, and vanilla.

Mission and Castro

AFRICAN
Bissap Baobab
2323 Mission Street; tel: 826-9287; www.bissapbaobab.com; Tue–Sun 6–10.30pm; $$; bus: 14, 26, 33, 49

A funky, international spot with a diverse clientele, serving West African fare and refreshing, but potent, cocktails made from homemade juice. Standout dishes include the spinach pastele pastry, the tofu mafe with peanut sauce, and the oniony chicken dibi with couscous.

CALIFORNIAN
Foreign Cinema
2534 Mission Street; tel: 648-7600; www.foreigncinema.com; Mon–Thur 6–10pm, Fri 5.30–11pm, Sat 11am–3pm, 5.30–11pm, Sun 11am–3.30pm, 5.30–10pm; $$$; bus: 14, 26, 49

Dinner and a movie gets a new spin at this popular, industrial-chic eatery. Diners can choose to sit inside to enjoy the innovative California cuisine, or better yet, dine on the heated outdoor courtyard where films are screened nightly on a concrete wall.

Frances
3870 17th Street; tel: 621-3870; http://frances-sf.com; Tue–Sun 5–10pm, Fri–Sat until 10.30pm. metro: F, K, L, M, T to Castro; bus: 33, 35, 37; map p.137 E1

Opened in 2010, this relaxed Castro newcomer has become a fast favorite with local foodies. Chef-owner Melissa Perello's daily-changing menu of modern-Cal cuisine offers dishes like Sonoma duck breast with butter-bean ragout, and carmelized scallops with toasted farro and wild mushrooms.

EAST ASIAN
Blowfish Sushi To Die For
2170 Bryant Street; tel: 285-3848; www.blowfish.com; Mon–Fri 11.30am–2.30pm, Sun–Mon 5–10pm, Wed–Thur 5–10.30pm, Fri–Sat 5–11.30pm, Sun 5–11pm; $$$; bus: 27; map p.138 C1

An unconventional sushi restaurant catering to both fugu fans and a western palate, (sirloin rolls in addition to standard nigiri selections), Blowfish Sushi has a loud, fun, and swank atmosphere. The whimsical sake cocktails are tasty.

ITALIAN
Flour + Water
2401 Harrison Street; tel: 826-7000; http://flourandwater.com; daily 5.30pm–midnight; $$; bus: 12, 27

The small, focused menu changes daily at this all-the-rage Mission spot, which specializes in house-made, hand-rolled pastas; cured meats; and wood-fired, thin-crust Neopolitan pizzas.

LATIN AMERICAN
Espetus Churrascaria
1686 Market Street; tel: 552-8792; www.espetus.com; Mon–Fri 11.30am–2.30pm,

Below: healthy sushi is a local favorite.

R

Average price for a three-course meal and a half-bottle of house wine:	
$$$$	more than $100
$$$	$50–$100
$$	$25–$50
$	less than $25

Above: haute cuisine in the Wine Country.

5–10pm, Fri until 11pm, Sat noon–3pm, 5–11pm, Sun noon–3pm, 4–9pm; $$$; metro: all lines to Van Ness; bus: 6, 7, 37, 71; map p.138 B3
Leave the vegetarians out of this one. Espetus is a Brazilian steakhouse in the South American Rodizio style, in which various and copious skewered meats are carved at your table on the skewers they were cooked on. An all-you-can-eat, prix-fixe menu means you eat 'til you burst.

Panchita's 3
3112 22nd Street; tel: 821-6660; www.panchitas3.net; Tue–Sun 4–11pm; $$; bus: 12, 14, 49
Serving a mix of Mexican and Salvadorian fare, this is a great place for small groups or intimate, off-the-beaten path romantic dinners.

Pancho Villa
3071 16th Street; tel 864-8840; www.panchovillasf.com; daily 10am–midnight; $; BART: to 16th Street; bus: 14, 26, 33, 49; map p.138 B1

Here it is: the world renowned San Francisco burrito. Have a late lunch and you will not need dinner. As with most taquerias, pass on the refried beans and go with whole or black ones; you will appreciate the flavors and texture much better. Counter service only.

Puerto Alegre
546 Valencia Street; tel: 255-8201; Mon 11am–10pm, Tue 5–11pm, Wed–Sun 11am–11pm; $; BART: to 16th Street; bus: 14, 26, 33, 49; map p.138 B1
A great place for a group of friends to get well-fed, a bit loud, and a little loopy from the infamous Margaritas. Fine dining? No. Fun dining? Si.

VEGETARIAN
Café Gratitude
2400 Harrison Street; tel: 830-3014; www.cafegratitude.com; daily 10am–10pm; $; bus: 27
Vegan, vegetarian and raw food is served here, including soups, salads, pizzas, smoothies, and organic coffee, all made with the finest ingredients. The setting is comfortable and easy-going. Occasional live music and a friendly staff make this off-the-beaten-path gem a perfect spot any time of the day.

Below: the food at Sutro's, in the Cliff House, comes second to the great view over Ocean Beach.

Around San Francisco

CALIFORNIAN
Sutro's at the Cliff House
1090 Point Lobos, Ocean Beach; tel: 386-3330; www.cliffhouse.com: daily 11.30am–3.30pm, 5–9.30pm, Sun from 11am; $$$; metro: N to Ocean Beach; bus: 5, 18, 31
Incredible views of Ocean Beach, the Marin headlands and the Pacific Ocean make this well-designed, seasonal Cal-cuisine restaurant a truly desirable lunching location.

ITALIAN
Aziza
5800 Geary Boulevard, Richmond; tel: 752-2222; www.aziza-sf.com; Wed–Mon 5.30–10pm; $$$; bus: 2, 38
It takes a lot to get SF foodies to the outer Richmond, but Aziza delivers with its Moroccan-influenced cuisine.

MIDDLE EASTERN
Al-Masri
4031 Balboa Street, Richmond; tel: 876-2300; www.almasrisfca.com; Thur–Sun 5.30–10pm; $$; bus: 31, 38
Dinner at Al-Masri is an all-evening affair of unique Egyptian dishes and belly dancers, all in a fantasy courtyard atmosphere.

Oakland, Berkeley and the Bay Area

CALIFORNIAN
Bay Wolf Café
3853 Piedmont Avenue, Oakland; tel: 510-655-6004; www.baywolf.com; Tue–Fri 11.30am–2pm, Tue–Sun 5.30–10.30pm; $$$; AC Transit bus: 51, 57, 59
A monthly-changing Cal-Med menu maintains enviable quality, offsetting seasonal delights with a well-chosen wine list.

Chez Panisse
1517 Shattuck Avenue, Berkeley; tel: 510-548-5525; www.chezpanisse.com; restaurant: seatings Mon–Sat 6–6.45pm, 8.30–9.15pm, café: Mon–Thur 5–10.30pm, Fri–Sat 5–11.30pm; $$$; BART: to Downtown Berkeley
This is the birthplace of Californian cuisine, and founder Alice Waters is its mother, pioneering the use of local, seasonal produce. Courses are fixed by the chef, with two seatings a night. There is also a café. Reservations strongly advised.

EAST ASIAN
Yoshi's
510 Embarcadero West, Jack London Square, Oakland; tel: 510-238-9200; www.yoshis.com; Mon–Wed 5.30–9pm, Thur–Sat 5.30–10pm, Sun noon–2pm, 5–9pm; $$–$$$; BART: to Oakland 12th Street, then bus: 72, 58, 58X, 301
Modern Japanese cuisine at this renowned jazz club, considered one of the best in California. The food ranges from well-executed standards to more creative adventures in sashimi and nigiri. There is also a lively sushi bar. There is another Yoshi's in the Fillmore (1330 Fillmore Street; tel: 655-560).
SEE ALSO MUSIC AND DANCE, P.93

Wine Country

CALIFORNIAN
Martini House
1245 Spring Street, St Helena; tel: 707-963-2233; www.martinihouse.com; Mon–Thur 5.30–9pm, Sat 11.30am–3pm, 5.30–10pm, Sun 11.30am–3pm, 5.30–9pm; $$$
Adventurous Cal-cuisine served in beautifully

> The markup on wine by restaurants can be astronomical. Consider buying a bottle at a corner store or supermarket and paying 'corkage', a fee typically around $20 for the house to open your wine.

Above: enjoying a lunch out.

designed surrounds influenced by the region's Native American and wine-making history. The chef's tasting menu paired with wine is a particular treat, as is the special mushroom tasting menu.

FRENCH
Bistro Jeanty
6510 Washington Street, Yountville; tel: 707-944-0103; www.bistrojeanty.com; daily 11.30am–10.30pm; $$$
Excellent flagship restaurant from chef-owner Philippe Jeanty, with a seasonal menu of satisfying homey dishes such as Coq au Vin and cassoulet, served on the outdoor patio or in the attractive dining room.

French Laundry
6640 Washington Street, Yountville; tel: 707-944-2380; www.frenchlaundry.com; Mon–Thur 5.30–9pm, Fri–Sun 11am–1pm, 5.30–9pm; $$$$
Consistently voted the number one restaurant in the US, Chef Thomas Keller serves a masterful prix fixe menu (at $240 per head) to those lucky and smart enough to reserve a table months in advance. The nine-course dinner utilizes the finest ingredients with virtuoso preparation. Dress code.

111

Shopping

With San Francisco's colorful cosmopolitan array of stores, shopping in the city is a true joy. Large modern shopping centers and old-fashioned, boutique-lined neighborhoods enticingly display designer fashions, artwork and crafts, gorgeous antiques, gourmet foods, brimming bookstores, and utterly unique and offbeat gift shops, delighting throngs of window-shopping enthusiasts and deep-pocketed purchasers alike. See also *Children, p.43, Essentials, p.49, Fashion, p.52, Food and Drink, p.55, Literature, p.79, Music and Dance, p.93,* and *Pampering, p.96.*

Whirlwind Neighborhood Shopping Tour

To feel the city's shopping pulse beating most wildly, head to **Union Square**, where streets are stacked with elegant emporiums and retail chains, and lanes are lined with high-end designer stores.

Close by is another bustling bazaar, **Chinatown**. **Grant Avenue** especially is awash with porcelain, paper parasols, and tea-selling apothecaries. If souvenir-hunting here somehow manages to be unsuccessful, turn to **Fisherman's Wharf** and Ghirardelli Square for more truckloads of trinkets. For hippie-inspired paraphernalia though, head to **Haight Street**, a jumble of independent music, secondhand clothing, and head shops.

Hip **Mission** boutiques also serve offbeat fare, from ethnic threads to mod furniture to pirate supplies, while **Hayes Valley** delivers a cool composition of art galleries, and contemporary boutiques. Slightly edgy style is also found on **Polk Street** as it leaves posh Russian Hill for the gritty Tenderloin, with vintage and new wares for varied budgets.

More solely sophisticated clusters of beauty outlets, boutiques, and restaurants stretch along **Union** and **Chestnut streets**. **Fillmore** and **Sacramento streets** also present a stroll-worthy menu of deluxe delicacies ranging from Florentine soaps and vintage French furnishings to high-end European shoes.

San Francisco's sport shop team includes **Niketown** (278 Post Street; tel: 392-6453; www.nike.com; Mon–Sat 10am–8pm, Sun 11am–7pm; BART and metro: all lines to Powell; bus: 4, 30, 38, 45, 76; map p.135 C1) for swooshes; **Sports Basement** (610 Mason Street; tel: 437-0100; www. sportsbasement.com; Mon–Fri 9am–9pm, Sat–Sun 8am–8pm; bus: 28, 29, 76; map p.132 C3) for gigantic bargains; and **Lululemon** (327 Grant Avenue; tel: 402-0914; www.lululemon. com; Mon–Fri 10am–7pm, Sat 10am–8pm, Sun 11am–6.30pm; bus: 30, 45; map p.135 C1) for cool apparel.

European flavor is also found in **North Beach**, where contemporary clothing shops cozy up to dens of quaint curios and antique maps.

Shopping Centers

The Cannery
2801 Leavenworth Street; tel: 771-3112; www.thecannery. com; Mon–Sat 10am–6pm, Sun 11am–6pm; metro: F to Jones and Beach streets; bus: 10, 19, 30, 47; cable car: Powell-Hyde; map p.134 B4
The former Del Monte fruit cannery now attracts tourists with collectibles and live courtyard entertainment.

Crocker Galleria
50 Post Street; tel: 393-1505; www.shopatgalleria.com; Mon–Fri 10am–6pm, Sat 10am–5pm; BART and metro: all lines to Montgomery; bus: 3, 10, 30, 76; map p.135 D1
This airy glass-arched pavilion is lined with galleries and specialty boutiques.

Embarcadero Center
Sacramento between Battery and Drumm streets; tel: 772-0700; www.embarcadero center.com; daily 10am–5pm; BART and metro: all lines to

Left: retail heaven, near Union Square.

Embarcadero; bus: 1, 10; map p.135 D2

Four Financial District towers supply flower-potted patios, wide walkways, eateries, and familiar retail faces of the Banana Republic flavor.

Japantown Center

Post Street, between Fillmore and Laguna Streets; www.sf japantown.org; bus: 2, 3, 22, 38; map p.137 E4

This cluster of Japanese restaurants and boutiques, including elegant clothing and home decor, vintage silk kimonos and trendy apparel.

Westfiield San Francisco Shopping Center

865 Market Street; tel: 512-6776; http://westfiield.com; Mon–Sat 9.30am–9pm, Sun 10am–7pm; BART and metro: all lines to Powell; bus: 6, 30, 45; cable car: Powell-Hyde, Powell-Mason; map p.138 C4

Escalators spiral up a nine-story atrium past mall regulars, with Nordstrom's departments on the top five levels. A lateral expansion leads to Blooming-dale's, affordable imports such as Zara and H&M, and a dash of designer outposts, including Furla and Juicy Couture.

Department Stores

Barney's New York

77 O'Farrell Street; tel: 268-3500; www.barneys.com; Mon–Sat 10am–7pm, Thur until 8pm, Sun 11am–6pm; BART and metro: all lines to Powell; bus: 4, 14, 27, 38; cable car: Powell-Hyde, Powell-Mason; map p.134 C1

An outpost of the Big Apple-based emporium, Barney's oozes with fashionable, decadent designs.

Bloomingdale's

845 Market Street; tel: 856-5300; www.bloomingdales.com; Mon–Sat 10am–9pm, Sun 11am–7pm; BART and metro: all lines to Powell; bus: 4, 30, 38, 45, 76; cable car: Powell-Hyde, Powell-Mason; map p.139 C4

A recent addition to the Westfield Centre, this upscale department store is well-stocked with gleaming designer displays.

Gump's

135 Post Street; tel: 982-1616; www.gumps.com; Mon–Sat 10am–6pm, Sun noon–5pm; BART and metro: all lines to Powell; bus: 4, 30, 38, 45, 76; cable car: Powell-Hyde, Powell-Mason; map p.134 C1

A sumptuous San Francisco institution, Gump's reels in well-heeled gift-givers with refined jewelry and home adornments.

Macy's

170 O'Farrell Street; tel: 397-3333; www.macys.com; Mon–Fri 10am–9pm, Sat 9am–9pm, Sun 11am–7pm; BART and metro: all lines to Powell; bus: 4, 30, 38, 45, 76; cable car: Powell-Hyde, Powell-Mason; map p.134 C1

Abiding, affordable department store standard, Macy's is capped with the Cheese-cake Factory and Burger Bar restaurants, both offering views of Union Square. Cross Stockton Street for the men's store.

Below: Asian design from Gump's *(left)* and Chinatown *(right)*.

Neiman Marcus
150 Stockton Street; tel: 362-3900; www.neimanmarcus.com; Mon–Wed and Fri–Sat 10am–7pm, Thur 10am–8pm, Sun noon–6pm; BART and metro: all lines to Powell; bus: 4, 30, 38, 45, 76; cable car: Powell-Hyde, Powell-Mason; map p.134 C1

A puffed-up purveyor (nicknamed 'Needless Markup'), Neiman Marcus has a well-edited selection of glam and luxe labels.

Nordstrom
Westfiield San Francisco Centre, 865 Market Street; tel: 243-8500; www.nordstrom.com; Mon–Sat 10am–8.30pm, Sun 10am–7pm; BART and metro: all lines to Powell; bus: 4, 30, 38, 45, 76; cable car: Powell-Hyde, Powell-Mason; map p.134 C1

Five classy tiers offer varying affordability, with a notable shoe selection and unbeatable return policy.

Saks Fifth Avenue
384 Post Street; tel: 986-4300; www.saksfiifthavenue.com; Mon–Wed 10am–6pm, Thur–Sat 10am–7pm, Sun 11am–6pm; BART and metro: all lines to Powell; bus: 30, 38, 45, 76; cable car: Powell-Hyde, Powell-Mason; map p.134 C1

Saks is a reliable source of fashionable trendy labels and trusty designer standbys. The men's store is just down the block.

Stores

ANTIQUES AND CURIOS
African Outlet
524 Octavia Street; tel: 864-3576; http://theafricaoutlet.net; daily 10am–7.30pm; bus: 5, 21; map p.138 A3

Bright fabrics, sculptures, instruments, and jewelry.

Aria
1522 Grant Avenue; tel: 433-0219; Tue–Sat 11am–6pm, Sun noon–5pm; bus: 30, 39, 41, 45; map p.135 C3

Fantastical French flea market flair, from photographs and letters to anatomical drawings.

Jackson Square
Tel: 398-8155; www.jacksonsquaresf.com; hours vary by store; bus: 1, 10, 30X, 41; map p.135 D2

The most concentrated source for old objects of desire is undoubtedly this historic square, where a variety of traders have outlets, selling fine and decorative arts, from period textiles and silver to antique maps and French impressionist paintings from the 17th and 18th centuries.

Past Perfect
2224 Union Street; tel: 929-7651; daily 11.30–7pm; bus: 22, 41, 45; map p.133 E2

Intriguing spread of mid-20th century vintage furniture, lighting, home accessories, clothes, and artwork.

Schein & Schein
1435 Grant Avenue; tel: 399-8882; www.scheinandschein.com; Tue–Sat 11am–7pm; bus: 12, 30, 41, 45; map p.135 C3

Thousands of compelling antique maps and prints from the 14th to 19th centuries.

Timeless Treasures
2176 Sutter Street; tel: 775-8366; www.timelesstreasuressf.com; Mon–Sat 11am–6pm, Sun 1–5pm; bus: 2, 3, 38; map p.137 E4

Union Square cooks up several trusty recipes for happy homemakers. Gourmet cookware and gadgets are served by ever-charming **Sur la Table** (77 Maiden Lane; tel: 732-7900; wwww.surlatable.com; Mon–Fri 10am–6pm, Sat 10am–7pm, Sun 11am–6pm; bus: 4, 30, 38, 45, 76; map p.134 C1) and luxurious linens by San Francisco institution **Scheuer Linens** (340 Sutter Street; tel: 800-762-3950; www.scheuerlinens.com; Mon–Sat 9.30am–5.30pm; bus: 30, 45, 76; map p.135 C1).

Aiming to satisfy an attractive, personal, and utilitarian aesthetic, this friendly vintage home furnishings store in Pacific Heights offers everything from antique mirrors to rewired French chandeliers to jewelery, not to mention the exceptional collection of vintage letters.

ARTS AND CRAFTS
Adolph Gasser
181 2nd Street; tel: 495-3852; www.gassers.com; Mon–Fri 9am–6pm, Sat 10am–5pm; BART and metro: all lines to Montgomery; bus: 10, 76; map p.135 D1
Photo nirvana for professionals and hobbyists alike.

Britex Fabrics
146 Geary Street; tel: 392-2910; www.britexfabrics.com; Mon–Sat 10am–6pm; BART and metro: all lines to Powell; bus: 2, 30, 38, 76; cable car: Powell-Hyde, Powell-Mason; map p.135 C1
Relied on by serious sewers and dabblers alike, these four floors teem with brocades and silks, 30,000 button styles, lace trims, ribbons, and bargain remnants.

Noe Knit
3957 24th Street; tel: 970-9750; www.noeknit.com; Mon–Thur 11am–8pm, Fri–Sun 11am–6pm; metro: J to Church and 24th streets; bus: 48

Knitters rejoice at this great stash of fine yarns, needles, and books.

Paper Source
2061 Chestnut Street; tel: 614-1585; www.papersource.com; Mon–Fri 10am–7pm, Sat 10am–6pm, Sun 11am–5pm; bus: 22, 28, 30, 43; map p.133 E3
Stock up here for bookbinding, fancy invitations, giftwrapping, and other crafty projects. Also at 1925 Fillmore Street; tel: 409-7710.

HOMEWARES
Candelier
33 Maiden Lane; tel: 989-8600; Mon–Sat 10am–6pm; BART and metro: all lines to Powell; bus: 2, 30, 38, 76; cable car: Powell-Hyde, Powell-Mason; map p.135 C1
Tucked away on a quiet side street, this small shop is brimming with luxury brand candles and home accessories – candlesticks, votives, soaps, scented stationery, and decor.

The Gardener
1 Ferry Building; tel: 981-8181; www.thegardener.com; Mon–Fri 10am–7pm, Sat 8am–6pm, Sun 10am–5pm; BART and metro: all lines to Embarcadero; bus: 1, 12; map p.135 E2
Looking for great gardening gloves, handsome rosewood bowls, and other charmingly

rustic home tools and accessories? This is the place.

Nest
2300 Fillmore Street; tel: 292-6199; www.nestsf.com; Mon–Fri 10.30am–6.30pm, Sat 10.30am–6pm, Sun 11am–6pm; bus: 1, 3, 22, 24; map p.137 E3
Specializing in artsy home goods, Nest offers whimsical, Parisian-flavored baubles, books, and more.

TOYS AND TREASURES
Chinatown Kite Shop
717 Grant Avenue; tel: 989-5182; www.chinatownkite.com; bus: 1, 9X, 30, 45; cable car: California, Powell-Hyde, Powell-Mason; map p.135 C2
Choose from a rainbow of kite kinds – appliqués, airplanes, deltas, dragons – along with parafoils and windhelows.

Kidrobot
1512 Haight Street; tel: 487-9000; www.kidrobot.com; Sun–Thur 11am–7pm, Fri–Sat 11am–8pm; bus 6, 33, 37, 71; map p.137 D2
For imited edition urban art toys (plastic, plush, and vinyl) and bold, artist-designed apparel, look no further.

Paxton Gate
824 Valencia Street; tel: 824-1872; www.paxton-gate.com; daily 11am–7pm; bus: 14, 26, 49; map p.138 B1
Unconventional collection of items inspired by the garden and natural sciences, including tools, taxidermy, and tea.

OTHER
Flight 001
525 Hayes Street; tel: 487-1001; www.fllight001.com; Mon–Sat 11am–7pm, Sun 11am–6pm; bus: 6, 7, 47, 49; map p.138 A3
This purveyor of cool jet-setting gear sells everything from silk eye-masks and mod clocks, to bags, passport holders, guidebooks, and electronics.

Below: fine writing materials at Paper Source.

Sport

San Francisco teems with wide-ranging athletic opportunities, from hang-gliding to hiking, and from bicycling to boating. Runners, joggers, and walkers patrol flat stretches like the Golden Gate Promenade and ambitiously climb terrifically steep hills. Only swimming can be problematic: beaches present stunning vistas, but also host treacherous tides, cold water, and frequent fog. The mild climate encourages athletes to keep moving year round, but spectators also have many choices in rooting for professional sports teams, both in San Francisco and across the Bay.

Participant Sports

The Recreation and Park Department (tel: 831-2700; www.parks.sfgov.org) oversees over 200 parks, playgrounds, and open spaces, including a vast array of free facilities. Also, consider a trip north: Napa and Sonoma counties offer horseback riding, and whale-watching is popular in Monterey and Mendocino.

BOATING/WATER SPORTS

As far as water sports go, whatever floats your boat is possible. Note that the Bay's currents and winds challenge even experienced sailors.

Blue and Gold Fleet
Tel: 705-8200; www.blueand goldflleet.com

Hornblower Dining Cruises and Events
Tel: 438-8300; www.horn blower.com

These charter firms supply bay boating, including trips to Alcatraz and Angel Island.

Kite Wind Surf

Tel: 877-521-9463; www.kitewindsurf.com
Equipment rentals and lessons are available for

Above: windsurfing in the Bay.

sailboats and power boats, and windsurfing novices can take lessons.

CYCLING

San Francisco has a thriving bike culture, and cycling is a popular way to explore the city. For rules of the road, city bike lanes, maps and routes, see http://bicycling.511.org or www.sfbike.org (the latter also outlines how avoid the steepest hills).
SEE ALSO TRANSPORTATION, P.122

FISHING

Sport-fishing charter boats set out from Fisherman's Wharf (www.sfsportfiishing.com). If sea-

sickness is a problem, consider casting a line from Municipal Pier in Aquatic Park.

Lake Merced Boating and Fishing Company

1 Harding Road; tel: 831-2700
Freshwater trout fishing is found south of the city. This company supplies boats, licenses, bait, and tackle.

Miss Farallones

Tel: 346-2399; www.miss farallones.tripod.com
Among the most popular fishing trips, these go to the Bay and Pacific Ocean to catch halibut, bass, salmon, and various bottom fish.

GOLF

San Francisco boasts beautiful municipal golf courses. Reservations recommended.

68 Lincoln Park
34th Avenue and Clement Street;

With its penchant for holistic living, it is no surprise that San Francisco overflows with yoga schools of all kinds. With four locations, **Yoga Tree** (www.yoga treesf.com) is a common choice, offering classes in many styles, plus workshops and retreats.

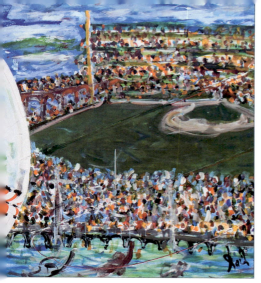

Left: passion takes on mural form at AT&T Park.

Golden Gate Park Skate and Bike
3038 Fulton Street; tel: 668-1117; www.goldengatepark skateandbike.com
Skates on Haight
1818 Haight Street; tel: 752-8375; www.skatesonhaight.com

Spectator sports
Check the websites for game schedules and ticket availability; note that tickets can be hard to come by for the Giants' and '49ers' games.

BASEBALL
The San Francisco Giants
AT&T Park, 24 Willie Mays Plaza; tel: 972-2000; www.sfgiants. com; metro: N, T to 2nd and King; bus: 10, 30, 45, 47; map p.139 E3
The city's beloved local team take the field at a new stadium with an old-time feel.
Oakland A's
Oakland-Alameda County Coliseum, 7000 Coliseum Way, Oakland; www.oaklandathletics. com; BART: Coliseum
Oakland's premier team.

BASKETBALL
The Golden State Warriors
Oracle Arena, 7000 Coliseum Way, Oakland; tel: 888-479-4667; www.nba.com/warriors; BART: Coliseum
This complex is home to the NBA's local great hopes.

FOOTBALL
'49ers
Monster Park, 602 Jamestown Avenue; tel: 656-4900; www.sf 49ers.com; bus: 9X, 28X, 47X
From August to December, the home team play here.
Oakland Raiders
Oakland-Alameda County Coliseum, 7000 Coliseum Way, Oakland; tel: 800-724-3377; www. raiders.com; BART: Coliseum
A better bet for tickets.

---

tel: 221-9911; www.lincolnpark gc.com; bus: 1, 2, 18, 38
An 18-hole, 5,149yd/m beauty.
Presidio Golf Course
300 Finley Road; tel: 561-4661; www.presidiogolf.com; bus: 1, 2, 3, 4, 33; map p.132 B1
Historic, scenic spot to tee up.

HANG GLIDING
Consistently good coastal winds delight hang-gliders. Up-to-the-minute wind info for Fort Funston is available (www.flyfunston.org).
The San Francisco Hang Gliding Center
Tel: 510-528-2300; www.sfhanggliding.com
Specializes in tandem hang-

Below: jogging in the Presidio.

gliding, launching from Marin's Mt Tamalpais.

HIKING
To the North, Mt Tamalpais provides beautiful hiking trails. Within city limits, the challenging Coastal Trail from Fort Point to the Cliff House affords spectacular views (but be sure to avoid the unstable cliffs).
SEE ALSO WALKS AND VIEWS, P.124

JOGGING/RUNNING
The annual **Bay to Breakers 12K** (www.baytobreakers.com) in May attracts outrageously-costumed joggers; the **San Francisco Marathon** (www.run sfm.com) draws serious runners in July. Trails wrap through Golden Gate Park, the Marina Green, and Crissy Field.

INLINE SKATING
The vehicle-free roads of Golden Gate Park on Sundays are very skate-friendly. The **Friday Night Skate** (Midnight Rollers) attracts hundreds of social skaters, who set off from Bryant Street and Embarcadero at 9pm for a 12½-mile (30km) run (www.sfskaters.org). Rent skates at:

117

Theater and Cabaret

San Franciscans have a brilliant spectrum of theatrical flavors to enjoy. Performances range from classical to contemporary, traditional to cutting-edge, and just about everything in between. Major commercial theaters stage Broadway hits, while non-profit theaters push new pieces and playwrights. The theater district's heartbeat thumps most vigorously on Geary Street, just west of Union Square, but stages are sprinkled about other districts as well, and avid theater-goers fill neighborhoods all over town.

Theater Information

For the city's current theatrical menu, peruse the Sunday *Datebook* section of the *San Francisco Chronicle*, or free alternative weeklies including the *SF Weekly* or *Bay Guardian*, found in cafés, bookstores, and newspaper boxes. Their websites (www.sfgate.com/eguide, www.sfweekly.com, and www.sfbg.com) and online city guides such as www.sfstation.com are also useful.

Where to Buy Tickets

TIX Bay Area

Union Square; tel: 433-7827; www.tixbayarea.com; Tue–Fri 11am–6pm, Sat 10am–6pm, Sun 10am–3pm; BART and metro: all lines to Powell; bus: 30, 45, 76; map p.135 C1
Sells half-price performance-day tickets beginning at 11am.

THIRD-PARTY TICKET AGENTS
These agencies will add a booking fee.
City Box Offiice
Tel: 392-4400;
www.cityboxoffiice.com
Tickco.com

Tel: 800-279-4444;
www.tickco.com
Ticketmaster
Tel: 800-745-3000;
www.ticketmaster.com

History

San Francisco's early theater tradition started with a proliferation of melodeons (theater-bar-music halls) but more 'serious' theater picked up at the turn of the 20th century. In 1967, the **American Conservatory Theater**, led by Bill Ball, had its San Francisco premiere, soon becoming a nationally reputed regional theater. The **Magic Theater** has premiered early works by major playwrights such as Sam Shepard (playwright-in-residence during 1975–83) and the **Asian-American**

Free **Shakespeare in the Park** (tel: 800-978-7529; www.sfshakes.org) spotlights the Bard each summer, and the **San Francisco Fringe Festival** (www.sffringe.org) serves up untraditional and uncensored fare come fall.

Theater Company (tel: 543-5738; www.asianamericantheater.org) has worked with David Henry Hwang (author of *M. Butterfly*) and Philip Kan Gotanda.

Major Theaters

American Conservatory Theater
415 Geary Street; tel: 749-2228; www.act-sf.org; show times vary; bus: 2, 4, 9, 27, 38; cable car: Powell-Hyde, Powell-Mason; map p.136 B4
A highly reputable, Tony Award-winning regional theater that consistently delivers solid classical and contemporary fare.

Berkeley Repertory Theatre
2025 Addison Street, Berkeley; tel: 510-647-2900, 510-647-2949; www.berkeleyrep.org; generally Tue 8pm, Wed 7pm, Thur–Fri 8pm, Sat 2pm and 8pm, Sun 2pm and 7pm; BART: Downtown Berkeley
A renowned Berkeley theater that delivers an adventurous, diverse program.

Curran Theater
445 Geary Boulevard; tel: 551-2000; www.shnsf.com; show

Left: San Francisco is a popular launchpad for big plays.

Silent spectacle is not the goal of the Tony Award-winning **San Francisco Mime Troupe** (tel: 285-1717; www.sfmt.org; free). Instead, they use 'mime' in the ancient sense of mimic and mockery, offering satirical, very left-wing performances in San Francisco and other Bay Area parks.

times vary; BART and metro: all lines to Powell; bus: 3, 27, 38, 76; cable car: Powell-Hyde, Powell-Mason; map p.136 B4
An elegant, historic theater staging Broadway tryouts and favorites including *Wicked* and *Jersey Boys*.

Magic Theatre
204 Bay Street; tel: 441-8822; www.magictheatre.org; show times vary; bus: 10, 22, 28, 30; map p.134 C4
A dedication to new works makes for an impressive list of plays premiered here.

Orpheum Theatre
1192 Market Street; tel: 551-2000; www.shnsf.com; show times vary; BART and metro: all lines to Powell; bus: 3, 27, 38; cable car: Powell-Hyde, Powell-Mason; map p.138 B3
A grand San Francisco Historical Landmark presents large-scale Broadway productions.

Fringe Theaters

New, quirky and experimental works can be found here:
Exit Theatre
Tel: 931-1094; www.sffringe.org

Intersection for the Arts
Tel: 626-2787; www.theintersection.org
The Marsh
Tel: 800-838-3006; www.themarsh.org
New Conservatory Theatre Center
Tel: 861-8972; www.nctcsf.org

Cabaret
Asia SF
201 9th Street; tel: 255-2742; www.asiasf.com; Wed–Sun 5–9.45pm; BART and metro: all lines to Civic Center; bus: 12, 14, 19, 26; map p.138 B3
'Gender illusionists' serve up Cal-Asian cuisine and lots of saucy entertainment.

Reservations required.
Beach Blanket Babylon
Club Fugazi, 678 Green Street; tel: 421-4222; www.beachblanketbablyon.com; Wed–Thur 8pm, Fri 6.30pm, Sat 6.30pm and 9.30pm, Sun 2pm and 5pm; bus: 12, 30, 41, 45; map p.134 C3
A legendary experience, this is a gloriously campy and continually updated pop-culture spoof. Buy tickets in advance and arrive early. Adults-only except for Sunday matinees.

Teatro ZinZanni
Pier 29; tel: 438-2668; www.zinzanni.org; Thur–Sat and some Wed 6.55pm, Sun 5.55pm; metro: F to Embarcadero and Sansome Street; bus: 10; map p.135 D4
Cabaret, cirque, and spectacle make for over-the-top diversion, delivered over a fine, five-course dinner.

Right: Beach Blanket Babylon.

Transportation

A major hub for flights from all over the world, San Francisco is easily reached by air, while visitors from other parts of the United States can opt to travel by rail or bus. Once here, the city and its outlying areas are comfortably navigable by public transportation. In San Francisco, a car is not generally necessary to see the sights, and can prove to be something of a hassle, especially when you can get such great views while riding a cable car to the tops of the city's hills. Efficient, affordable and comprehensive, San Francisco's public transportation network makes it easy to be green.

Getting to San Francisco

BY AIR

San Francisco International Airport (SFO)
1 McDonnell Road, San Francisco; tel: 650-821-8211, toll-free: 800-435-9736; www.fllysfo.com
SFO is the major international airport for northern California. From Europe, all the major airlines offer non-stop flights or connections via New York, Chicago, or Los Angeles. It also receives non-stop, or one-stop, flights from all the principal Pacific airports. For foreign travelers, many of the US airlines

Everyday, airplanes dump millions of pounds of carbon-dioxide and other noxious greenhouse gasses into the atmosphere. To 'offset' this big carbon footprint, travelers can purchase carbon credits that, based on the distance traveled, invest money into renewable energy and energy efficiency programs. For more information visit www.sustainabletravel international.org, or www. jpmorganclimatecare.org.

offer deals for visiting several American cities.

Despite being 13 miles away, downtown San Francisco is easy to get to. Taxis and shuttles line the inner circle of the transportation zones of the Arrivals/Baggage Claim Level, while BART (Bay Area Rapid Transit), located at the Departures/Ticketing Level at the International Terminal and accessible from the Domestic Terminal by the Airtrain, takes passengers to downtown San Francisco and across the bay to various cities, for minimal cost. SFO is blanketed by Wi-Fi and can be used for a fee.

Oakland International Airport (OAK)
1 Airport Drive, Oakland; tel: 510-563-3300; www.fllyoak land.com
The Oakland airport is located 4 miles (6.5km) south of the city's downtown, and is accessible by BART. A hub for low-cost carriers, OAK is a more economical alternative to the bigger and busier SFO.

San Jose International Airport (SJC)
1732 North 1st Street, San Jose;

tel: 408-277-4759; www.sjc.org
The smallest of the three airports, Mineta San Jose International Airport is nearly 50 miles from downtown San Francisco.

BY BUS

Greyhound
San Francisco Transbay Terminal, 425 Mission Street; tel: 495-1569; www.greyhound.com; map p.135 D1
Downtown, just east of Market Street, the Transbay Terminal is a major hub for the transcontinental Greyhound bus service.

BY TRAIN

Amtrak
Emeryville depot, 5885 Horton Street, Emeryville; information line: 800-USA-RAIL; www.am trak.com
While Amtrak, the cross-continental passenger rail line, does not connect directly to San Francisco, it has a free shuttle to deliver passengers to and from the depot in Emeryville, located in the East Bay. For longer trips, Amtrak can be frustrating as passenger trains share

Left: San Francisco's most iconic mode of transportation.

infinitely simpler. They are $3 and available at the Muni kiosks at the Powell and Market and Powell and Beach Cable Car terminals, and in most stores where general maps are sold. They are also posted at many Muni metro and bus stops.

For all Muni metro and bus lines, adult fare is $2. Exact change is necessary, but transfer slips are given, allowing you to transfer twice to different Muni metro or bus lines within a 90-minute time frame. 1, 3, or 7-day visitor passports provide unlimited rides on Muni-operated transport, including the cable cars. They are available at information booths in the baggage claim area at San Francisco International Airport, at the San Visitors Visitors Center at Market and Powell streets (go down the stairs towards the BART entrance by the cable car turnaround), and at Hyde and Beach streets, near Ghirardelli Square. For route planning and general information, see **www.sfmta.com**.

Cable Cars
Cable Cars are also operated by Muni, but are the exception to most of the Muni

---

For help navigating the entire Bay Area public transit system, including Muni buses and metro streetcars, and BART, call 511, or look online at **www.511.org**. 511 offers assistance with planning trips using public transportation, traffic and drive time information, tips for traveling with bikes, and links to various municipal transit agencies.

---

the rail lines with, and must defer to, the freight lines, causing significant delays. Nonetheless, it still remains a green alternative to air travel and some routes are quite picturesque.

BY CAR
Despite congestion, hills, and the problem of what to do with your vehicle upon arriving, San Francisco is easy to reach by car. Interstates 101 and 80 pass through the city, while Interstates 5 and 99 are not too far away in the Central Valley. State Highway 1 runs along the coast of California and the western part of San Francisco.

Getting Around San Francisco
MUNI
Buses and Metro
Muni, the San Francisco Municipal Transit Agency, encompasses the city's diesel and electric buses, streetcars which run on lightrail lines underground through downtown, the historic F-line streetcars (comprising a collection of vintage trams from all over the world), and of course, the cable cars.

Purchasing a map is highly recommended and will make a stay in San Francisco

---

Below: the sleek BART system in action.

rules. Fares can be purchased at the kiosk at each terminal, or when you board. Drivers do give exact change, but no transfers. They are also considerably more expensive at $5 per trip. Often crowded with tourists, they ride over San Francisco's famous hills.

BART (BAY AREA RAPID TRANSIT)
www.bart.gov

Fast, quiet, and efficient, BART allows passengers to get around the Bay Area in comfort. All BART lines travel through San Francisco, extending to San Francisco International Airport, and under the bay to Oakland, Berkeley, and beyond.

Its stations provide maps that clearly explain routes and fares, and nearby ticketing machines allow passengers to purchase tickets. For buying a ticket without exact change, passengers may carry a balance on their ticket for future use, or utilize one of the change machines also located in the stations.

Four BART lines run through downtown and provide the quickest way to reach the Mission district, or Oakland and Berkeley. BART trains are referred to by their final destination; to get to Berkeley, take the Richmond train; to reach the Coliseum,

Taking a cable car ride is one of the classic San Francisco experiences. However, waits to board at the cable car turnaround at Fifth and Mission can be long. A better bet for speed and a seat may be to board the California line at Van Ness or the Ferry Building; the hills are steeper, so the views on this route of Nob Hill, Chinatown and the Financial District are extra-spectacular.

Above: ferries from the Hyde Street Pier are a great way to see more of the Bay Area.

board either a Freemont or Dublin-Pleasonton train.

TAXIS
Taxis are a great, though expensive, way to get about when the majority of San Francisco's public transit shuts down, around 12.30am. They hover around popular tourist or nightlife spots, but in out-of-the-way locations it is advisable to call a radio-dispatched taxi.

DeSoto Cab Company
Tel: 970-1370

Green Cab
Tel: 626-4733

Luxor Cab Company
Tel: 282-4141

Yellow Cab
Tel: 333-3333

CYCLING
Around San Francisco, there are plenty of places to ride that are reasonably flat and far from exhaust fumes. Cycling through Golden Gate Park is a favorite, especially on Sundays, when many of the roads are automobile-free. Riding along the Golden Gate Promenade and crossing Golden Gate Bridge is a

stunning ride, although difficult if the wind is up. In Sausalito, visitors can catch the ferry back to San Francisco. Bikes can be rented hourly or for the day, with rates varying by type of bike, but it is usually $20–60 per day, and $7–10 per hour.

SEE ALSO SPORT, P.116

Bay City Bike
2661 Taylor Street and 1325 Columbus Avenue; tel: 346-BIKE; www.baycitybike.com; daily from 8am; bus: 10, 30, 47; map p.138 C4 and map p.134 B4

Blazing Saddles
1095 Columbus Avenue, including a number of locations on

Below: legs of steel are required for riding up the hills.

Fisherman's Wharf; tel: 202-8888; www.blazingsaddles.com; daily from 8am; metro: F to Fisherman's Wharf; bus: 10, 19, 30; map p.134 B3

Golden Gate Park Bike and Skate
3038 Fulton Street; tel: 668-1117; www.goldengatepark bikeandskate.com; Mon–Fri 10am–5pm, Sat–Sun 10am–6pm; bus: 5, 21, 31, 33; map p.136 B3

WALKING
The best way to see San Francisco is by walking. Only 7 by 7 miles (11 by 11km), it is easy to cover great distances while seeing many different neighbor-hoods and glimpsing how residents live. Walking the hills provides spectacular views of the city and the rest of the Bay Area. Bring a map, comfortable shoes, and an extra layer of clothing in case the famous San Francisco fog rolls in. Always be alert while crossing intersections. Taxis can be particularly aggressive.

DRIVING
San Francisco is a difficult city to drive and park in, often taxing the most experienced local drivers. It is crisscrossed with one-way streets, and the fast paced driving culture can easily unnerve any visitor. If it is necessary to rent a car, all the major car rental companies have outlets at San Francisco International Airport and around the city. Or if you only need a car for a few hours, rent from Zipcar (www.zipcar.com).

Avis Rental Car
675 Post Street; tel: 929-2555 or 800-331-1212; www.avis.com; map p.134 C1

Enterprise
350 Beach Street; tel: 474-9600 or 800-261-7331; www.enterprise.com; map p.134 B4

Hertz Rent A Car
55 4th Street; tel: 957-9425 or 800-654-3131; www.hertz.com; map p.134 C1

Getting Around the Bay Area

FERRIES
Many locals use ferries to get to and from work, but for visitors, they provide a great scenic and environmental alternative to driving. Departing from Fisherman's Wharf or the Ferry Building, they travel to Angel Island, and throughout the North and East Bay areas. Tickets can be purchased at the ticket windows next to the ferry terminals.

Blue and Gold Fleet
Pier 39 Marine Terminal, The Embarcadero at Beach Street; tel: 705-8200; www.blueand goldflleet.com; map p.134 C4

Golden Gate Ferry
Ferry Building, The Embarcadero at Market Street; tel: 455-2000; www.goldengateferry.org; map p.135 E2

CALTRAIN
Main San Francisco depot, 700 4th Street; information line: 800-660-4287; www.caltrain.org; map p.139 D3

Caltrain runs alongside Highway 101 to San Jose, with limited extensions all the way to Gilroy. It is largely a commuter train, but for visitors headed to the Peninsula or the South Bay, it is an enjoyable ride, complete with comfortable seating, an upper deck with tables, and a car to accommodate passengers with bikes. Caltrain's terminus is near the AT&T Park and many San Francisco Muni bus and metro lines, helpful for geting passengers around the city. Every Caltrain stop has an electronic ticket machine at which passengers can purchase tickets.

INTERCITY BUSES
Neighboring transit systems also connect San Francisco with other Bay Area cities. These buses can be caught at various stops downtown, or at the Transby Terminal, located at 1st and Mission streets.

Alameda Contra-Costa County Transit District
Information line: 510-891-4700; www.actransit.org

Golden Gate Transit
Information line: 455-2000; www.goldengate.org

San Mateo County Transit District
Information line: 510-817-1717; www.samtrans.org

Below: Muni buses remain one of the most efficient ways of getting around town.

Walks and Views

W hile strenuous, San Francisco is a pedestrian's paradise. Its many peaks offer sweeping vistas of the city, its parklands make walkers feel like hikers, and its condensed topography makes it easy to jump from one neighborhood to the next. There are hiking trails, strolls through residential areas, and even guided walking tours where knowledgeable locals offer insight into the depths of Chinatown, the highs of Haight-Ashbury, and the city's Victorian past. Below are a few suggestions to get the most out of your footwear, and a few places to find inspirational views without the perspiration.

Bird's Eye Views

Coit Tower
1 Telegraph Hill Boulevard; tel: 362-0808; daily 10am–5pm; entrance fee for the elevator; bus: 39; map p.135 C3
The crown of the landmark Coit Tower adds another 210ft (64m) to the 275ft (84m) Telegraph Hill, making it a pinnacle of the northern part of the city. Views extend all the way to the Golden Gate, North Bay, and Mount Diablo, and to the south, downtown and Mount Sutro.

Tower at M.H. de Young Memorial Museum
50 Hagiwara Tea Garden Drive; tel: 750-3600; www.famsf.org/deyoung; Tue–Sun 9.30am–5.15pm, Fri until 8.45pm mid-Jan–Nov; entrance charge, under 13 free, 1st Tue of month free; metro: N to Irving Street and 9th Avenue; bus: 5, 21, 44; map p.136 B2
From the top of the de Young's twisting 144ft (44m) copper tower, the amazing panorama of San Francisco's cityscape is a work of art. The 360 degrees of floor-to-ceiling windows reveal with postcard-like clarity the city's central highs and lows, its range of greenery and architectural styles, and the distant landmarks that make the skyline famous.
SEE ALSO MUSEUMS AND GALLERIES, P.87

Into the Wild
While remaining a tight urban metropolis, San Francisco has managed to keep part of itself a little wild. Hiking boots can indeed be necessary within city limits, what with the bare hills in the south and the vast Presidio covering the northwest coast. Unusually for a metropolitan center, San Francisco offers the opportunity to get some mud on your feet while admiring its breath-taking skyline.

Below: the striking tower at the de Young Museum offers spectacular views.

Left: the Coit Tower and the tip of the Transamerica Pyramid stand out dramatically in North Beach's skyline.

Pacific Ocean. Keep an eye out for the remnants of shipwrecks on the rocks below.

The trail is an easy 3½-mile (5.6km) round trip, with spectacular views of the Marin Headlands and the Golden Gate Bridge. It also passes the **Palace of the Legion of Honor** and ends in the fashionable Lincoln Heights neighborhood.
SEE ALSO MUSEUMS AND GALLERIES, P.88

Mt Davidson Park
Start: Dalewood Way and Myra Way; daily 6am–10pm; bus: 36
Covered in eucalyptus and anointed with a 103ft (31m) cross commemorating the Armenian Genocide, Mt Davidson is San Francisco's highest peak. Fortunately, it is not necessary to climb its entire 927ft (282m) to reach the top. From the park entrance, it is an easy, moderate walk to the summit, less than a half mile. The south-eastern side is bare

Below: admiring the view of Ocean Beach.

Lover's Lane is the oldest foot trail in the Presidio. As early as 1776, soldiers began walking the 3-mile trail to Mission Dolores, the only other Spanish settlement on the San Francisco peninsula.

For all hikes, be sure to wear layers, including a windbreaker if available. Comfortable shoes with good, sturdy traction are a must. Throughout the various parks, paved trails frequently give way to rough terrain demanding attention and surefootedness.

San Francisco is known for its wildlife, including rare bird species. Coyotes have also been seen in Golden Gate Park and the Presidio. If one is sighted, give it enough space and do not try to approach it. They are not known to bother humans and will usually run away once spotted.

GOLDEN GATE PARK
Strawberry Hill
Start/End: Stow Lake Road; metro: N to Irving Street and 9th Avenue; bus: 5, 21, 33, 44; map p.136 A2

Crossing Stow Lake are two stone bridges off Stow Lake Drive, making it is easy to access this island peak. It is a leisurely walk on a network of unpaved paths to the top of Golden Gate Park's highest hill. The elegant Chinese pavilion and beautiful waterfall may provide easy distractions, as do the early morning congregation of waterfowl on the lake. The wooded summit of Strawberry Hill overlooks the Japanese Tea Gardens and Stow Lake, and on clear days, is blessed with views of the Golden Gate Bridge and Mount Diablo.

AROUND SAN FRANCISCO
Land's End Trail
Start: Merrie Way and Point Lobos Avenue; bus: 18, 38
End: El Camino del Mar and 32nd Avenue; bus: 1, 2, 18
Many consider Land's End to be the wildest part of San Francisco. At the far end of the Merrie Way parking lot, the trail begins under a canopy of cypress trees and quickly rises high above the sharp cliffs plunging into the

Above: the coast around San Francisco is an area of great natural beauty.

and has commanding views of the Financial District, Hunter's Point, and San Bruno Mountain. The western side, thick in foliage, descends to the foggy Sunset District and the Pacific Ocean. The park's 40 acres (16 hectares) are criss-crossed with walking trails.

The Presidio: Ecology Trail-Lovers' Lane
Start: Presidio Boulevard Gate at Pacifiic Avenue; bus: 3, 43; map p.133 D1
End: Arguello Boulevard Gate; bus: 1, 4, 33; map p.132 C1

The Presidio's nearly 1,500 acres (607 hectares) is as diverse at it gets in any urban park. With views of the Golden Gate Bridge and San Francisco Bay, and historic buildings, woods, grasslands, and coastal walks, complete with old gun batteries from the turn of the 20th century, it is easy to spend an entire day here. The 1.8-mile (2.9km) Ecology Trail-Lover's Lane is a good start, however.

From the Presidio Gate, head straight down Lovers' Lane, which runs parallel to Presidio Boulevard into the residential Tennessee Hollow. Continue on, crossing Liggett and MacArthur streets and eventually making a left on Presidio Boulevard. Make another left on Funston Avenue, and continue, passing Officers' Row. After crossing Moraga Avenue, the Ecology Trail begins.

On the trail, head straight up the hill, but keep right when it intersects with other unmarked trails. Here it begins to pass through groves of cypress trees and fields of native plants. To the left will be a large trail leading to Inspiration Point, a popular lookout. Going straight, the Ecology Trail will continue and terminate at the Arguello Boulevard Gate. For more details, and a map of the Presidio with its other hiking trails, visit www.bahiker.com/sfhikes/inspoint.html.

Twin Peaks
Start: Twin Peaks Boulevard and Crestline Drive; bus: 37

The Crestline stop on the 37 bus brings passengers to the trailhead between the peaks. From here, hikers can walk the rocky ridgeline north or south, and summit each peak. Celebrated as the best panoramic view of the city, it is also home to redtail hawks, cottontail rabbits, and the endangered Mission Blue Butterfly. A guided map of the park can be downloaded from: www.parks.sfgov.org.

Neighborhood Walks
TELEGRAPH HILL
Filbert and Greenwich Steps
Start: Coit Tower; bus: 39; map p.135 C3
End: Sansome Street; bus: 10; map p.135 D3

Through gardens and quaint stairways, this steep descent down to the waterfront is one the most picturesque walks in the city. Both steps begin at the south-east corner of the Coit Tower lookout and parking lot. For the Filbert Steps, turn right down the paved path that runs next to and slightly below Telegraph Hill Boulevard. Where the road bends to the right at Filbert Street, a street in name only, turn left down the steps. Cross Montgomery Street, and descend the staircase on the other side. Beginning on either side of a

> Overgrown and lined in paths of uneven brick and stone, Macondray Lane inspires the romantic in everyone. Armistead Maupin used it as inspiration for his Barbary Lane in *Tales of the City*, a series of books chronicling life in San Francisco from the mid 1970's to the mid 1980's.

row of parking spaces are the Filbert Steps. Continue down to Sansome Street at the bottom of the hill.

For the Greenwich Steps, descend the narrow brick steps beginning at the southeast corner of Coit Tower parking lot. It will end at the cul-de-sac at Montgomery Street. Take the lower road to the left-hand side. After about 200yds, there is a wide walkway angling down on the left. This will become the Greenwich Steps, which is largely a long cement walkway until it sharply descends to Sansome Street.

RUSSIAN HILL
Hyde Street and Macondray Lane
Start: Lombard and Hyde streets; bus: 30, 41, 45; cable car: Hyde-Powell; map p.134 B3
End: Taylor and Union streets; bus: 30, 41, 45; cable car: Hyde-Powell; map p.134 B3
At the crest of the city's most famous curvy street, head south on Hyde Street. Across the street is George Sterling Park, which offers tennis and great views of the Golden Gate Bridge and Marina District. Continue down the leafy Hyde Street until Green Street. Turn left, which will be a bit of a climb, but lasts only one block. At Jones Street turn left again, and continue for half a block. On the right, the lush Macondray Lane looks like a private walkway with an imposing 'Private Property' sign. Do not worry, it is there to discourage illegal parking.

Turn right down the pedestrian alleyway, and continue down the narrow

path and rickety stairs to Taylor Street. Turn left and continue to Union Street. If wishing to go on to North Beach, head down the hill for two more blocks.

THE WESTERN ADDITION
Lower Haight– Alamo Square
Start: Haight and Pierce streets; bus: 6, 7, 71; map p.137 E2
End: Fulton and Divisadero streets; bus: 5, 21, 24; map p.137 E3
Surrounded by large 1920s era apartment buildings, sprawling Queen Anne's, ornate single home Victorians (notably the 'Painted Ladies' on the eastern side), and high enough to capture the splendor of City Hall, Alamo Square is the crown jewel of the Western Addition and Lower Haight districts. To get there, follow Pierce Street north, up the hill. It is a steep climb, but worth the exertion.

After crossing Fell and Oak streets, Pierce narrows, eventually colliding with Alamo Square. Cross Hayes Street and take the stone steps into the park, keeping to the left. Alamo Square is a favorite neighborhood spot where locals love to unleash their dogs. Take the cement path across the park, and at the corner of Fulton and Scott streets, turn left on Fulton Street, heading away from the dome of City Hall. On the corner of Divisadero and Fulton streets sits Café Abir, a nice place to grab a relaxed cup of coffee or a beer.

HAIGHT ASHBURY– CASTRO DISTRICT
Buena Vista Park and Castro Street
Start: Haight Street and Central Avenue; bus: 6, 37, 43, 71; map p.137 D2

Below: (from top) ascending the Filbert steps; 'Victorians' in North Beach and the Haight.

Above: Mission Dolores Park is a great place to finish a walk.

End: Castro and Market streets; bus: 24, 33, 37; map p.137 E1
In addition to great city views and the lush beauty of Buena Vista Park, this walk also journeys past grand and beautifully restored Victorians, including the Spreckels Mansion, built in 1897. Beginning at the foot of Buena Vista Park, head up the steep sidewalk clinging to the edge of the park. This is Buena Vista Avenue West, which soon becomes Buena Vista Avenue East when it, and the park, turn sharply to the north-east.

At this point, a path into the park leads to a breathtaking view of downtown. Continue circling the park on Buena Vista Avenue East until Buena Vista Terrace. Turn right. At 14th Street turn left. Continue until Castro

When the city converted its many cemeteries into parks, workers were ordered to use the unclaimed headstones for the new trails and gutters. Out of respect for the dead, many decided to leave the pieces facing up, where they can still be seen today in Buena Vista Park.

Street and turn right. Here Castro descends toward Market Street, where the rainbow-flagged neighborhood begins.

THE MISSION
Around Mission Dolores Park
Start: Market and Dolores streets; bus: 22, 37; metro: F, J, K, L, M, T to Church; map p.138 A2
End: Mission and 18th streets; bus: 14, 22, 33, 49, 53; BART: to 16th Street; map p.138 B1
Beginning at the base of the California Volunteers' Monument and across from the US Mint, follow the wide palm tree-lined Dolores Street. At 16th Street, the historic **Mission Dolores** sits next to the ornate Basilica. Both are open for visitors; a small donation is requested. Continue on until 18th Street. Here Dolores Park begins, sloping up to the beautiful Liberty Heights district with spectacular views of the city. At 18th Street, turn right. After a block or so, the Mission begins in earnest. Continue until Mission

Street, where stores, bars, cafés, and restaurants lure in any visitor.
SEE ALSO CHURCHES, P.45

MARINA DISTRICT–THE PRESIDIO
Golden Gate Promenade
Start: Aquatic Park at Van Ness Avenue and Beach Street; bus: 30, 47, 49; map p.134 A4
End: Fort Point; bus: 28; map p.132 A4
Beginning at the 1930s Aquatic Park, the Golden Gate Promenade follows the edge of the city to Fort Point, under the Golden Gate Bridge. Begin by heading west away from Fisherman's Wharf. Soon the wide cement walkway rises to the top of Fort Mason and offers views of the Marina District and the Golden Gate Bridge. Continue on the path down to Laguna Street, and stay to the right. Follow the sidewalk as the street turns and becomes Marina Boulevard. From here, it passes through the Marina Green, alongside the Saint Francis Yacht Club, and into the newly restored Crissy Field.

Below: colorful murals adorn the Women's Building in the Mission; the Precita Eyes tour takes you all over the district.

Above: evening falls on Russian Hill *(see p.127)*.

You can either stay to the left, or cut through the orderly row of cypress trees to the water. The nearby Crissy Field Center and Warming Hut Café, located at the end of the promenade, offer coffee and other delicious rewards. Early morning at the lagoon is a great time for bird watching.

Guided Walks

There are countless walking tours available throughout San Francisco, focusing on different cultural and historical aspects of the city. Most are about 2 hours with prices ranging from $15 to $30.

A free alternative is **City Guides**, sponsored by the San Francisco Public Library. It offers tours daily on a variety of subjects around the city. For details, visit www.sfcityguides.org.

Barbary Coast Trail
Tel: 454-2355; www.barbary coasttrail.org
This self-guiding tour travels through San Francisco's bawdy past. Starting at the old Mint near Market and Mission streets, and lead by a series of bronze sidewalk markers, it tours North Beach, Chinatown, and Fisherman's Wharf. Additional books, maps, and audio tours are available.

FOOT! Tours
Tel: 793-5378; www.foottours.com
Laugh your way through San Francisco on the only walking tour lead by comedians. Offering a wide range of tours, the guides are not only funny, but also experts at San Francisco culture and history.

Precita Eyes Mural Arts
Tel: 285-2287; www.precitaeyes.org
Head to the Visitor Center and Art Store at 2981 24th Street for this distinctive and fascinating tour. Beginning in the lush Balmy Alley between 24th and 25th, the non-profit Precita Eyes Mural Arts tours the colorful and distinctive murals adorning the fences and building faces throughout the Mission. The guided walks, Saturdays and Sundays 11am and 1.30pm, explore the cultural, political, and artistic influences of the city's most accessible public art.

Victorian Walking Tours
Tel: 252-9485; www.victorian walk.com
Starting every day at Union Square at 11am, this 2½ hour tour travels Pacific Heights and other grandiose neighborhoods, and includes an inside tour of a Victorian house in the Queen Anne style.

Wok Wiz Walking Tours
Tel: 650-355-9657; www.wok wiz.com
To get a taste of Chinatown, sign up for Shirley Fong-Torres' tour. While including the history and architecture of the area, Fong-Torres' focus is on food. Daily tours include an optional dim sum lunch, so come with an empty stomach.

Atlas

The following streetplan of
San Francisco makes it easy to find
the attractions listed in the A–Z
section. A selective index to streets
and sights will help you find other
locations throughout the city.

Map Legend

Symbol	Description	Symbol	Description
	Freeway	Ⓜ	Metro
	Divided highway	●	Cable car
	Main roads	🚌	Bus station
	Minor roads	– – –	Ferry
	Footpath	❶	Tourist information
	Railroad	★	Sight of interest
	Pedestrian area	⚲ ☥	Temple
	Notable building	✚	Cathedral / church
	Park	☾	Mosque
	Hotel	✡	Synagogue
	Urban area	⚱	Statue / monument
	Non urban area	✉	Post Office
† †	Cemetery	✚	Hospital
		❋	Viewpoint

p132 p133 p134 p135

p136 p137 p138 p139

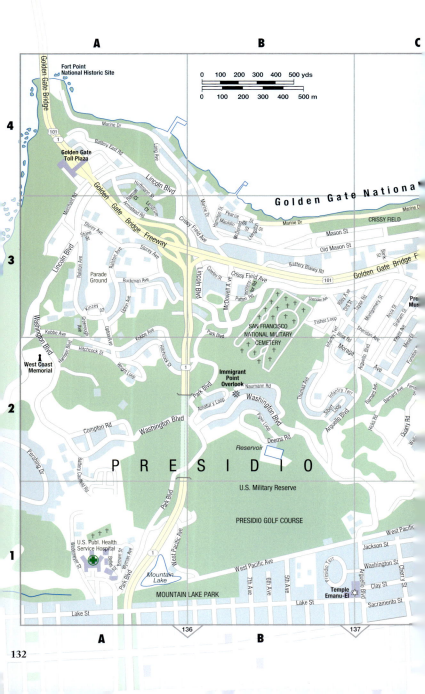

Fort Point
National Historic Site

4

Golden Gate Bridge

Marine Dr

101
1

**Golden Gate
Toll Plaza**

Battery East Rd

Long Ave

Golden Gate Bridge Freeway

Hoffman St
Lendrum Ct
Barnard Ct
Armistead Rd

Lincoln Blvd

Crissy Field Ave

Marine Dr

Golden Gate National

CRISSY FIELD

Marine Dr

Halleck St
Pearce St
Mauldin St
McDonald St
Liggett St
Lundeen St

Mason St

Old Mason St

Battery Blaney Rd

101

Golden Gate Bridge F

3

Mendell Rd

Lincoln Blvd

Stone Ct
Stone St

Storey Ave

Ralston Ave

Storey Ave

Kinzey St

Union Ave

Greenough Ave
Kobbe Ave

Liggett Ave

Parade
Ground

Ruckman Ave

Cowles St

McDowell Ave

Crissy Field Ave

Patten Rd

Sheridan Ave

Fisher Loop

SAN FRANCISCO
NATIONAL MILITARY
CEMETERY

Riley Ave
Byrd St
Taylor Rd
Montgomery St

Sheridan Ave

Moraga

Arguello Blvd

Graham St
Keyes Ave
Aura St
Mesa St
Funston

**Pre
Mus**

2

Washington Blvd

West Coast
Memorial

Hanson Rd
Hitchcock St

Wright Loop

Hitchcock St

Kobbe Ave

Park Blvd

Park Blvd

1

**Immigrant
Point
Overlook**

Naumann Rd

Amatury Loop

Washington Blvd

Thomas Ave

Infantry Terr

Barnard Ave

Infantry Terr

Stilwell Loop

Arguello Blvd

Barnard Ave

Hicks Rd

Quarry Rd

Ferre

Wal

Compton Rd

Washington Blvd

Piper Loop

Deems Rd

Reservoir

P R E S I D I O

Pershing Dr

Battery Caulfield Rd

Park Blvd

U.S. Military Reserve

PRESIDIO GOLF COURSE

West Pacific

Jackson St

West Pacific Ave

Washington St

Clay St

Cherry St

1

U.S. Publ. Health
Service Hospital

Wedemeyer St
Brown St
Bliss St
Wyman Ave

Park Blvd

West Pacific Ave

1

*Mountain
Lake*

West Pacific Ave

7th Ave
6th Ave
5th Ave

Presidio Terr

**Temple
Emanu-El**

Arguello Blvd

Sacramento St

MOUNTAIN LAKE PARK

Lake St

Lake St

Lake St

p132   p133   p134   p135

p136   p137   p138   p139

4

Marina Small Craft Harbor

East Harbor

Fort Mason Center

creation Area

Yacht Rd

Marina Dr

Marine Dr

Marina Green Dr

MARINA GREEN

Jefferson St

Marina Blvd

West Harbor

Marina St

Jauss St

Allen St

Mason Street

Marina Blvd

Doyle Drive

Jefferson St

Beach St

Casa Way

Avila

Rico Way

Retiro Way

Cervantes Blvd

Pierce St

Mallorca

Beach St

North Point St

Buchanan St

Laguna St

3

Exploratorium

Lagoon

Palace of Fine Arts

101

Bay St

Baker St

Broderick St

Beach St

North Point St

Bay St

Capra Way

MARINA

Avila St

Alhambra St

Toledo Way

Way

Bay Street

FUNSTON PLAYGROUND

Chestnut St

Magnolia St

Francisco St

Gorgas Ave

Birmingham Rd

Thornburg Rd

Edgle Rd

Letterman Army Institute of Research

n Blvd

Kennedy Rd

Letterman Digital Arts Center

Richardson Ave

Chestnut St

Francisco St

Lombard St

Hotel Del Sol

Moulton St

Fillmore St

Greenwich St

134

Presidio Blvd

Summer Ave

Letterman Dr

Dewitt Rd

Lombard St

Lyon St

Baker St

Broderick St

Divisadero St

Lombard St

Scott St

Pierce St

Steiner St

Pixley

Filbert St

Buchanan St

Vedanta Temple Ψ

Ave

Morton St

Pershing Dr

Sanches St

Simonds Loop

Sherman Rd

Simonds Loop

Shafter Rd

COW HOLLOW PLGD

Greenwich St

Filbert St

Union St

Union St

Green St

PACIFIC HEIGHTS

Green St

2

Clark Ave

Sibley Rd

West Broadway

Baker St

Green St

Vallejo St

Scott St

Marianne Terr

Convent of the Sacred Heart ✝

Vallejo St

Broadway

Broadway

Pierce St

Pacific Ave

Bromley Pl

Jackson St

S KAHN ROUND

Pacific Ave

Hotel Drisco

Rayclff Terr

Webster St–Historic District

PRESIDIO HEIGHTS

Presidio Ave

Jackson St

Washington St

Baker St

Lyon St

Broderick St

Divisadero St

Scott St

ALTA PLAZA PARK

Steiner St

Fillmore St

Washington St

Clay St

Pacific Medical Center ✚

1

Locust St

Laurel St

Walnut St

Clay St

PRESIDIO HEIGHTS PLGD

Laurel Inn

Sacramento St

Sacramento St

Perine Pl

California St

FILLMORE

Webster St

Orben Pl

LAUREL HEIGHTS

California St

California St

Pine St

Pine St

Pierce St

California St

Pine St

Wilmot St

St Dominic's Catholic Church ✝

Bush St

A

B

C

4

Fort Mason Center

Golden Gate National Recreation Area

Municipal Pier

Hyde Street Pier

Historic Ships
Balclutha
Eppleton Hall
C.A. Thayer
Alma
Eureka

S.F. Maritime National Historic Park

AQUATIC PARK

Beach

VICTORIAN PARK

Maritime Museum

Argonaut

Ghirardelli Square

S.S. Jeremiah O'Brien

↑ **Alcatraz**

Pier 45

U.S.S. Pampanito

Pier 43

Pier 47

Fisherman's Wharf

Musée Mécanique

Jefferson St

Wharf Inn

Taylor St

Mason St

Powell St

The Cannery

Anchorage

Jones St

Leavenworth St

Pier 39

Aquarium of the B

The Embarcader

Beach St

Stockton St

North Point Street

Bay St

Tuscan Inn

VanBewater

Museo Italo Americano

FORT MASON

Polk St

Larkin St

Columbus Ave

North Point Street

Francisco St

Chestnut St

Fielding St

Venard Alley

Pfeil

Moss

Golden Gate National Recreation Area

3

The Marina Inn

Bay St

Francisco St

Chestnut St

Octavia St

Gough St

Franklin St

Van Ness Ave

North Piebra Terr

RUSSIAN Reservoir HILL PARK

San Francisco Art Institute

Houston St

Water St

San Remo

R U S S I A N

NORTH BEACH PLAYGROUND

Tuscany Alley

Francisco St

NORTH

Sts & Pa

Washi Squa

Lombard St

Chestnut St

Lombard St

Greenwich St

Germania Terr

Lurmont Terr

Lombard St

Val-

paraiso St

Russell

Rickel

MICHELANGELO PLGD

Washington Square

Powell-Mason-Line

BEACH

Beach Blanket Babylon

Nort Beac Museu

Laguna St

Harris Pl

Filbert St

Greenwich St

Filbert St

Union St

Atten St

Havens St

Macondray Ln

H I L L

Taylor St

COOLBRITH PARK

Jones St

Florence

Fallon St

Powell St

133

Octagon House

Union St

Green St

101

Holy Trinity Russian Orthodox Cathedral

Bonita St

Vallejo St

Green St

White St

Larkin St

Hyde St

Rockland

Waldo Alley

Lynch St

Glover St

R. Levy Tunnel

Bernard St

Macon St

Autumn

John St

Cable Car Museum

Pratt Alley

2

Whittier Mansion

Broadway

Vallejo St

Haas-Lilienthal House

HELEN WILLS PLGD

Pacific Ave

Broadway

McCor-

mick St

Morrell

Suzome St

Wall St

Reed St

Priest St

Jones St

NOB HILL

Leavenworth St

Pleasant St

Miller Pl

Ewer Pl

Mason St

Frelman St

Powell St

Wetmore St

Spreckels Mansion

Jackson St

Washington St

Jackson St

Washington St

Clay St

Sacramento St

Troy Alley

Acme Alley

Golden Ct

Helena

Grace Cathedral

HUNTINGTON PARK

Fairmo

InterContinental Mark Hopkins

Huntington

Renais Star Co

1

Pacific Medical Center

LAFAYETTE PARK

Clay St

Washington St

California Street-Line

California St

Pine St

Masonic Center

Joan Pl

St Francis Memorial Hospital

White Swan Inn

Petite Auberge

Golden Gate

Hotel Rex

Inn at L

Buchanan St

Jackson St

Laguna St

Gough St

Franklin St

Van Ness Ave

Sacramento St

California St

Pine St

Bush St

Austin St

Fern St

Bush St

Sutter St

Hemlock St

Hotel Vertigo

Austin St

Fern St

Cosmo Pl

Mike-

chaom Pl

Andrews

Agadio

Monaco

Westin St

Warwick

Nii

Fra

Cliff

Pine St

Buchanan St

Octavia St

Gough St

Daniel Burnham Ct

Hotel Majestic

Sutter St

Post St

Cedar St

Post St

Geary St

Jones St

Shannon St

Taylor St

Mason St

The Serrano

CURRAN Theatre

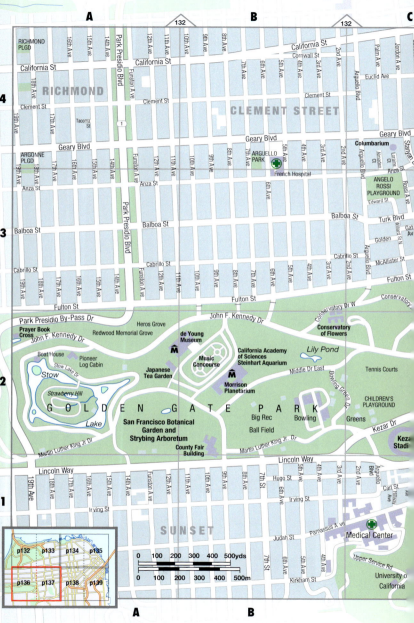

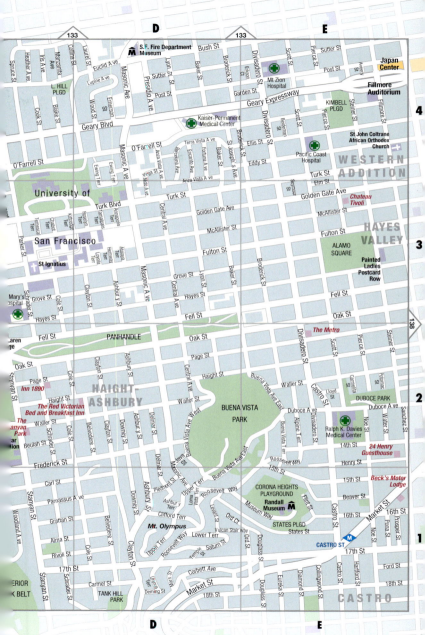

D   133   133   E

S.F. Fire Department Museum

Bush St

Sutter St

Japan Center

Mt Zion Hospital

Fillmore Auditorium

Euclid Ave

Masonic Ave

Presidio Ave

Lyon St

Baker St

Broderick St

Divisadero St

Scott St

Pierce St

Post St

Post St

Lupine Ave

Avery St

Sutter St

L. HILL PLGD

Heather Ave

Iris Ave

Manzanita Ave

Collins St

Laurel St

Wood St

Emerson St

Garden St

Geary Expressway

KIMBELL PLGD

Steiner St

Fillmore St

4

Spruce St

Cook St

Blake St

Geary Blvd

Kaiser-Permanent Medical Center

O'Farrell St

Terra Vista Ave

St Joseph's Ave

Ellis St

Broderick St

Scott St

Pierce St

Beideman St

St John Coltrane African Orthodox Church

O'Farrell St

Ewing Terr

Anza Vista Ave

Barcelona Ave

Encelia Ave

Fortuna Ave

Baker St

Eddy St

Pacific Coast Hospital

Turk St

Elm St

WESTERN ADDITION

Vega St

Anza Vista Ave

Nido Ave

University of

Turk Blvd

Turk St

Golden Gate Ave

Golden Gate Ave

Central Ave

McAllister St

Chateau Tivoli

Tamalpais Terr

Annapolis Terr

McAllister St

Fulton St

HAYES VALLEY

Parker Ave

Chabot Terr

Kittredge Terr

Roselyn Terr

Tamalpais Terr

San Francisco

Fulton St

ALAMO SQUARE

3

Hemlock Terr

Hemway Terr

Loyola Terr

Anderson Terr

St Ignatius

Grove St

Lyon St

Baker St

Broderick St

Painted Ladies Postcard Row

Mary's Hospital

Grove St

Cole St

Masonic Ave

Ashbury St

Central Ave

Grove St

Hayes St

Fell St

Hayes St

Fell St

Oak St

PANHANDLE

Oak St

Divisadero St

Scott St

Pierce St

Steiner St

The Metro

138

Laren ge

Fell St

Oak St

Page St

2

Oak St

Stanyan St

Page St

Inn 1890

Cole St

Clayton St

Ashbury St

Central Ave

Haight St

Page St

Waller St

Buena Vista Ave East

Castro St

DUBOCE PARK

Duboce Ave

Sanchez St

The Red Victorian Bed and Breakfast Inn

Haight St

Belvedere St

Clayton St

Downey St

Ashbury St

Delmar St

Waller St

Waller St

BUENA VISTA PARK

Buena Vista Terr

Lloyd St

Carmelita St

Potomac St

anyan Park ar tion

Waller St

Beulah St

Schrader St

Cole St

Alpine Terr

Duboce Ave

Noe St

Water St

Ralph K. Davies Medical Center

24 Henry Guesthouse

Frederick St

Delmar St

Masonic Ave

Buena Vista Ave West

Roosevelt Way

14th St

Henry St

Beck's Motor Lodge

Carl St

Piedmont St

Upper Terr

Buena Vista Ave West

15th St

15th St

Beaver St

Market St

16th St

1

ERIOR K BELT

Parnassus Ave

Ashbury St

Ashbury Terr

Roosevelt Way

CORONA HEIGHTS PLAYGROUND

Museum Way

Flint St

Castro St

Noe St

Prosper St

Pond St

Woodland Ave

Stanyan St

Grattan St

Belvedere St

Clifford Terr

Levant St

Randall Museum

Ord Ct

States St

16th St

Alma St

Cole St

Clayton St

Roosevelt Way

Lower Terr

Saturn St

Ord St

STATES PLGD

Douglass St

CASTRO ST

17th St

Eureka St

Diamond St

Hartford St

Ford St

Rivoli St

Mt. Olympus

Upper Terr

Tremble St

Vulcan Stair Way

18th St

17th St

Schrader St

Cole St

Clayton St

Upper Terr

Vienna Terr

Deming St

Corbett Ave

Market St

Douglass St

Collingwood St

Castro St

18th St

TANK HILL PARK

Carmel St

18th St

CASTRO

D   E

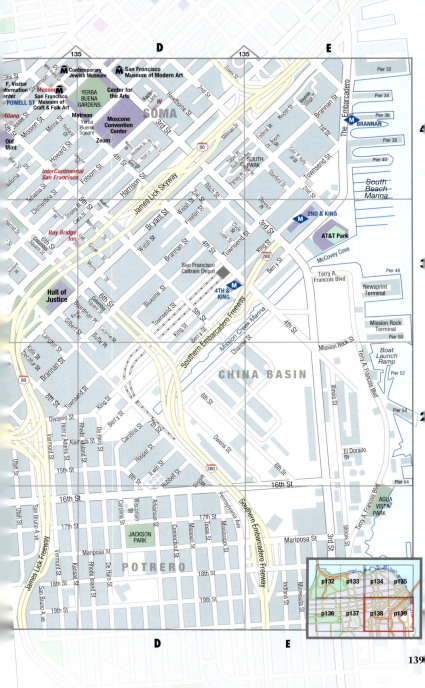

D | 135 | 135 | **D** | **E**

Ellis St
F. Visitor
formation
enter
POWELL ST
Milano
Old
Mint
Natoma

Stevenson St
Mossen
San Francisco
Museum of
Craft & Folk Art
Mission St
Minna St
Howard St
Tehama St
Clementina St
InterContinental
San Francisco
Bay Bridge
Inn
Clara St

Contemporary
Jewish Museum
YERBA
BUENA
GARDENS
Metreon
Yerba
Buena
Square
Zeum

San Francisco
Museum of Modern Art
Center for
the Arts
SOMA
Moscone
Convention
Center

W

2nd St
Hawthorne St
Rincon St
Essex St

The Embarcadero
Pier 32
Pier 34
Pier 36
BRANNAN M

Folsom St
Harrison St
James Lick Skyway

Bryant St
Welsh St
Ritch St
Welsh St
Branan St
Morris St
Langdon St
Gilbert St
Butte Pl
Bluxome St

Hall of
Justice

San Francisco
Caltrain Depot
**4TH &
KING** M

SOUTH
PARK

Pier 38
Pier 40

*South
Beach
Marina*

2ND & KING M

AT&T Park
McCovey Cove

Southern Embarcadero Freeway
Mission Creek Marina
Channel St
4th St

Terry A.
Francois Blvd
Pier 48
Newsprint
Terminal

Mission Rock
Terminal
Pier 50

Boat
Launch
Ramp
Pier 52

CHINA BASIN

Mission Rock St
Illinois St
Terry A. Francois Blvd
Pier 54

Division St
Henry Adams St
Alameda St
Rhode Island St
De Haro St
Carolina St
Hooper St
Irwin St
Hubbell St
Berry St
King St
6th St
Owens St
El Dorado
St
Pier 64

15th St
16th St
16th St
Vermont St
Utah St
San Bruno Ave
Carolina St
Wisconsin St
Arkansas St
Connecticut St
Missouri St
Texas St
Mississippi St
Pennsylvania Ave
Southern Embarcadero Freeway
Mariposa St
3rd St
Illinois St
Terry A. Francois Blvd

AGUA
VISTA
PARK

17th St
**JACKSON
PARK**
Mariposa St
Kansas St
Rhode Island St
De Haro St
17th St
18th St
19th St
Missouri St
Texas St
Connecticut St
18th St

POTRERO

James Lick Freeway
San Bruno Ave
Vermont St
18th St
19th St
Utah St
San Bruno Ave

Indiana St
Minnesota St
19th St

p132 | p133 | p134 | p135
p136 | p137 | p138 | p139

D | **E**

139

Selective Index for Street Atlas

Index

Insight Smart Guide: San Francisco
Updated by: Barbara Rockwell
1st edition compiled by:
Lisa Crovo Dion; Dan Dion;
Elizabeth Linhart Money;
Barbara Rockwell
Proofread and indexed by: Penny Phenix
Edited by: Sarah Sweeney

Photography by: APA/Abe Nowitz,
Richard Nowitz, and Daniella
Nowitz except: Alamy 65tl;
Bancroft Library 64tl, 64cl;
Corbis 46b, 55b, 65bl, 66cr, 67tl,
67br, 78, 93; APA/David Dunai 127t;
Getty 62t, 94/95; Rex 80/81; Eyevine
94/95, 118/119; Istockphoto 64tr;
Lee Foster 67bl; Ronald Grant
Archive 80l; Catherine Karnow
54c,119; Robert A. Minkin 67tl;
Heider Ribeiro 82/83; Photolibrary
87; Taj Hotels 68/69
Picture Manager: Steven Lawrence

Maps: Tom Coulson (Encompass
Graphics Ltd); James Macdonald;
Neal Jordan-Caws
Series concept: Maria Lord
Series Editor: Jason Mitchell

Second Edition 2010
First Edition 2008
© 2010 Apa Publications GmbH & Co.
Verlag KG Singapore Branch, Singapore.
Printed by CTPS-China

Worldwide distribution enquiries:
Apa Publications GmbH & Co. Verlag KG
(Singapore Branch) 38 Joo Koon Road,
Singapore 628990; tel: (65) 6865 1600;
e-mail: apasin@signet.com.sg
Distributed in the UK and Ireland by:
GeoCenter International Ltd
Meridian House, Churchill Way West,
Basingstoke, Hampshire RG21 6YR;
tel: (44 1256) 817 987;
e-mail: sales@geocenter.co.uk

Distributed in the United States by:
Langenscheidt Publishers, Inc.
36–36 33rd Street 4th Floor, Long Island
City, New York 11106; tel: (1 718) 784
0055; e-mail: orders@langenscheidt.com
Contacting the Editors
We would appreciate it if readers would alert
us to outdated information by writing to:
Apa Publications, PO Box 7910, London
SE1 1WE, UK; fax: (44 20) 7403 0290;
e-mail: insight@apaguide.co.uk
No part of this book may be reproduced,
stored in a retrieval system or transmitted
in any form or by any means (electronic,
mechanical, photocopying, recording or
otherwise), without prior written permission
of Apa Publications. Brief text quotations
with use of photographs are exempted for
book review purposes only. Information has
been obtained from sources believed to be
reliable, but its accuracy and completeness,
and the opinions based thereon, are
not guaranteed.

144

WINE COUNTRY
pages 28–29

AROUND
SAN FRANCISCO
pages 24–25

Woodland
Sacramento
Lodi
Stockton
Escalon
Woodland
Vacaville
Napa
Santa Rosa
St Helena
Sonoma
Healdsburg
Jenner
Bodega Bay
Inverness
Sebastopol
Point Reyes Lighthouse
San Rafael
San Francisco
Vallejo
Berkeley
Oakland
Hayward

10 miles
10 km

Oakley
Antioch
Pittsburg
West Pittsburg
Round Valley Park
Morgan Territory Regional Park

Black Hills

Oyster Point
2106
Mt Diablo State Park
Eagle Peak 2368
Mt Diablo 3849
Alamo Oaks
Danville

Clayton
Concord
Walnut Creek
Moraga
Lafayette
Alamo
San Ramon Cr
Redwood Regional Park

Sacramento
Luther E. Gibson Fwy
Benicia
Benicia Capitol State Hist Site
Martinez
Briones Regional Park
Orinda Village
Orinda
Mormon Temple
Tilden Reg. Park
Univrsty of California at Berkeley

Napa
Napa Co. Airport
American Canyon
Napa River

Suisun Bay

Six Flags Marine World
Vallejo
Carquinez Strait
Crockett
Pinole
Rodeo
Hercules
San Pablo Res
El Sobrante
Kensington
El Cerrito
Berkeley
Albany
Oakland
Wildcat Canyon Regional Park

Sonoma
Wildcat Mtn 682
Sears Point
Black Point
Petaluma River
Ignacio
Marshwood
Novato
Marin County Airport
Olompali State Historic Park
Mt Burdell Open Space Preserve
Novato Cr.
Santa Rosa

San Pablo Bay

San Pablo
North Richmond
Richmond
San Pablo Strait
San Rafael
China Camp State Park
San Quentin
Santa Venetia
San Anselmo
Fairfax
Ross
Kentfield
Larkspur
Corte Madera
Mill Valley
Muir Woods National Monument
Mt Tamalpais State Park
Tiburon
Sausalito
Bay Area Discovery Museum
Angel Island State Park
Alcatraz Island
Golden Gate
Angel Island

Redwood Fwy
San Rafael